Madison's Metronome

American Political Thought
Wilson Carey McWilliams and Lance Banning
Founding Editors

Madison's Metronome

The Constitution, Majority Rule, and the Tempo of American Politics

Greg Weiner

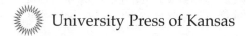 University Press of Kansas

Published by the University Press of Kansas (Lawrence, Kansas 66045), which was organized by the Kansas Board of Regents and is operated and funded by Emporia State University, Fort Hays State University, Kansas State University, Pittsburg State University, the University of Kansas, and Wichita State University

Library of Congress Cataloging-in-Publication Data

Weiner, Gregory.
 Madison's metronome : the Constitution, majority rule, and the tempo of American politics / Gregory Weiner.
    p. cm. — (American political thought)
 Includes bibliographical references and index.
ISBN 978-0-7006-1840-8 (cloth : alk. paper)
ISBN 978-0-7006-2895-7 (pbk. : alk. paper)
1. Madison, James, 1751–1836—Political and social views. 2. United States—Politics and government—Philosophy. 3. Majorities. 4. Republicanism—United States—History—18th century. 5. Federal government—United States—History—18th century. I. Title.
 E342.W44 2012
 973.5'1092—dc23
          2011042402

British Library Cataloguing-in-Publication Data is available.

Printed in the United States of America

10 9 8 7 6 5 4 3 2 1

For Rebecca

Contents

Preface

The political thought of James Madison is heavily trod territory, especially as it pertains to the extent of his commitment to republicanism, a question that has preoccupied scholars of the founding for more than a century. The present study arose from this long debate's failure, or so it seemed to me, to account for a fundamental fact: Madison himself would have regarded the question of whether he believed in majority rule as absurd. Asking Madison whether he supported majority rule would have been like asking Sir Isaac Newton whether he was normatively committed to the law of gravity. In both cases, the normative preferences of theorists are irrelevant to the underlying empirical facts: apples fall from trees, and majorities in republican societies sooner or later get what they want.

Yet Madison's writings are indeed replete with the expressions of concern about majority rule that have impelled a diverse and rich tradition of commentary. Hence, I explore how, on Madison's account, to ensure majorities rule reasonably in a political culture in which majorities rule inevitably. Madison's answer is time: majorities that must cohere for an interval before prevailing are likelier to behave reasonably because the passions that motivate unreasonable behavior are inherently short-lived. I call this implicit doctrine "temporal republicanism." I use this phrase to emphasize both its compatibility with and its contrast to other interpretations of the Founders' thought, such as civic republicanism. The basic idea is that temporal republicanism, like civic republicanism, embodies a set of values—including public-spiritedness and respect for the rights of others—broader than purely the technical device of majority rule. In Madison's case, however, the most reliable means of achieving those values is relying on the natural power of time to defuse passions.

This study is hardly the first to observe the importance of delay and deliberation in Madison's thought. I have endeavored, however, to pursue this theme across a broad span of public and private writings—an approach that involves a host of methodological challenges, several of which bear commentary before proceeding.

First, the study of American political thought occupies an often constructive but occasionally contested zone between the disciplines of political theory and history. Many eminent studies of the founding have struck a balance between the two by focusing on writings that occupy a single historical period, such as George W. Carey's analyses of *The Federalist* or Colleen Sheehan's assessments of Madison's writings during the 1790s. Because the present study assesses a theme in Madison's thought that I assert did not substantially change over the course of his life, because I aim to show its operation across the entirety of his career, and because I do so by drawing together strands dispersed across his writings, this project presents evidence in a manner that may occasionally seem jarring, especially to historians who are accustomed to a more chronological approach. I have organized the work according to themes: the particular functions that time serves, Madison's analysis of the passions, and so forth. Within these themes, I draw on writings as they illustrate the claims under consideration, not always as they occur in an unfolding chronological narrative. I have attempted to minimize the extent to which I oscillate in time, but it is often the case that the best illustration of a given theme involves, for example, pairing a quotation from a late-in-life letter with an observation from *The Federalist* or an episode from Madison's political career.

This method would be less defensible if Madison's views on time had changed over time. But they did not. Nor is this especially surprising. Madison's views about time and the passions arose from psychological assumptions that were commonly held in his day and that one would not necessarily expect to change in response to events. Madison maintained a largely unchanging concern about impulsivity in politics. The changes we see in Madison's views of majority rule arise largely from his evolving beliefs about who, exactly, was behaving impulsively: abusive and transient majorities in the 1780s, the Adams regime in the 1790s, the nullifiers in the 1820s. But I am unaware of any evidence that Madison's underlying beliefs about the distorting and transient nature of passions changed. I do not, however, mean to present a portrait of a static Madison who exhibits either a heroic consistency or a lack of dynamic thought. I would merely observe, with Drew McCoy, that Madison was born a subject of George II and died a citizen of Andrew Jackson's republic. It would be extraordinary, and not altogether admirable, if he never changed his mind during that period. This study simply presents one issue on which he did not do so. Nor do I mean to claim that time is in any sense the key to unlocking Madison's thought. I mean merely to present one significant and consistent dimension of his writings that, I believe, merits careful analysis.

There is another claim, or set of them, I do not intend to make. Scholarship on Madison has tended to alternate between excoriation and hagiography. I hope to have avoided both. Majority rule is neither the end-all nor the be-all of politics, so to say Madison's commitment to that principle was complete is not to say his political thought is beyond reproach. On the contrary, he may have trusted majorities too much; he may have appreciated the restless character of American politics too little. Supporters of both majority rule and individual rights will find reasonable fault with the Madison portrayed in the interpretation that follows. I seek merely to understand him on his own terms, whatever flaws or strengths that exploration may reveal.

In coming to a more accurate understanding of Madison's thought, it is important not to equate his democratic theory with the Constitution itself. Madison is miscast as the father of the Constitution. He lost several foundational battles at the Philadelphia Convention. By Forrest McDonald's count, "of seventy-one specific proposals that Madison moved, seconded, or spoke unequivocally in regard to, he was on the losing side forty times."[1] More important than that quantity is the quality of some of the battles he lost. Madison saw an unqualified national negative on state laws as so crucial that he feared his failure to achieve it would consign the constitutional system to failure. Similarly, the convention's rejection of his proposal for a council of revision that would review legislative bills deeply disappointed him. Rather than the father of the Constitution, Madison is better understood as the attending physician at its birth—and, later, as its tutor. No one did more to bring the Constitution into existence; only Washington did more to shape its early life. The sheer tenure of Madison's public career—he was one of the younger delegates to the convention and its last survivor, and he was present at or a respected commentator on virtually every major political event in between—placed him in a position of undeniably profound influence over the formative years of the new regime. But Madison, as he insisted himself, was not the Constitution embodied.

Finally, at various places I have invoked illustrations from either contemporary or, in historical terms, relatively recent politics. These include the New Deal regime, the ongoing health care controversy, and disputes over various assertions of rights. Generally speaking, I have tried to minimize the use of controversial illustrations so as not to distract from the underlying interpretive intent of this study. However, I wish to emphasize, first, that it is never my intention to impute any conclusions as to contemporary events to Madison himself; and second, that in identifying tensions between the Madisonian order and certain aspects of the contemporary regime, I do not mean necessarily to say I disagree with the programs or principles in question. To say, for example, that the New Deal regime is incompatible in considerable respects with the constitutional order as Madison envisioned it is not the same as opposing the programs in question. It is to say, however, that it matters whence we began. One could do worse for a guiding philosophy than deviating from that beginning only with a measure of self-awareness, humility, and intellectual respect.

I have accrued several intellectual debts in the preparation of this book. Alan Gibson believed in the project. Fred Woodward and his colleagues at the University Press of Kansas stewarded it with patience, encouragement, and skill, and their review process made this a much stronger book. Isaac Schlecht provided editorial assistance. James H. Read's comments on the manuscript were invaluable. John Tomasi and the Political Theory Project of Brown University provided support that made completion of this book possible, as have my colleagues at Assumption College, B. J. Dobski, Daniel J. Mahoney, and Geoffrey Vaughan. Patrick Deneen's reflections on citizenship, participation, and localism were a profound influence. Richard Boyd provided both substantive and professional guidance. Gerald Mara and R. Bruce Douglass were gifted teachers to me, as they continue to be to many others. As for George W. Carey (TME), the last of the gentleman scholars, I can only express the hope that this work is worthy of his example, the influence of which is evident on every page.

My personal debts are no less profound. I am grateful to Arnold and Marcia Kaplin for their insight, encouragement, and much more, as well as to Jason Brennan, Justin Litke, Jack Moline, Mo Steinbruner, Todd Stubbendieck, and Matt Townley. Words cannot discharge my profound debt to Martin and Phyllis Weiner, exemplars of learning and pillars of unremitting support and disproportionate pride. Hannah, Jacob, and Theodore Weiner have inspired, amused, encouraged, tolerated, and provided a general example of eager and innocent curiosity that I hope I can emulate and they can sustain. Were there an academic convention for footnoting sources of inspiration, moral support, constructive needling, and constant kindness, Rebecca Weiner's name would appear on every page—in which case it would still be necessary for me to say that there are no words.

Introduction

"The Sovereign Physician of our Passions"

Twelve-year-olds do not read Michel de Montaigne anymore, much less take notes. James Madison did both, and a circa 1763 entry in his childhood commonplace book indicates that one of the French essayist's observations made a particular impression: "Time," Montaigne wrote and Madison transcribed, "is the Sovereign Physician of our Passions, & gains its End chiefly by supplying our imaginations with other & new Affairs, wearing out the Old by new impressions." To this, Madison added an observation of his own: "Our passions are like Torrents which may be diverted, but not obstructed."[1]

History provides no direct support for a dramatic link between the boy's reading that day and the statesman's political theory decades later. Madison did not quote Montaigne in writing again. But the sentiment he formulated in his own hand bears a striking resemblance to his lifelong assumption about popular majorities—that they were bound to get their way sooner or later, and hence could be diverted but not obstructed—while the quotation he recorded from Montaigne presaged his view of time as central to the proper operation of republicanism: Because time defuses the passions, majorities should prevail only after cohering for an interval sufficient to ensure that reason rather than impulse guides their will. This study argues that these elements of Madison's thought—the centrality of time and the inevitability of majority rule—converge to form an implicit doctrine that may be called "temporal republicanism."

Both elements have received substantial attention in the extensive literature on Madison. Madison's commitment to majority rule has been carefully documented in a redemptive strain of late twentieth-century scholarship, epitomized by the work of Lance Banning, that reasserts his republicanism against decades of interpretation that cast the Founder as a reactionary aristocrat who sought to shield the propertied few from the landless masses.[2] Martin Diamond, George W. Carey, Alan Gibson, James Read, Gary Rosen, and many others have also highlighted the importance of deliberation, and hence of delay, in Madison's thought, while Colleen Sheehan has emphasized his belief in a sort of civic education that instilled the habits of tolerance and reasonableness necessary for republican life. Michael Zuckert's scholarship casts Madison as a "natural rights republican," although of a "less strenuously republican" bent than Jefferson. The study that follows aspires to refine these interpretations by establishing the following features of Madison's democratic theory.

First, at no time did Madison contemplate either the possibility or desirability of any mode of government other than majority rule. He criticized the decisions of majorities with which he disagreed; he believed certain kinds of majorities under certain kinds of conditions were prone to error or abuse; he denied that a decision was just merely because a majority had reached it. But he never questioned the majority's rightful authority to make decisions, and his criticism of certain majorities in certain situations does not impeach his majoritarian credentials any more than a critic of the Congress or the president today could be accused of opposing Articles I or II of the Constitution.[3] On the contrary, I hope to show that many of the passages in which Madison criticizes majorities most harshly also affirm their ultimate right to bind the community.

This normative commitment to popular government must be understood in the context of Madison's empirical belief that majority rule was inevitable, something like a law of nature, in republican societies. Perhaps the most consistent assumption behind his political thought was the futility of what he dismissed as "parchment barriers" that attempted to impose rules without regard for the political and sociological realities in which they would operate. This fact is overlooked if Madison's political thought is evaluated as though it were an abstract philosophical enterprise whose object was identifying the ideal regime. His intent, rather, was to overlay political mechanisms onto existing sociological forces he accepted as unalterable in their essential characteristics. Institutions, rules, and compacts worked within the boundaries set by political reality; their chief purpose was to channel rather than dam the energies of popular majorities; and if they were to succeed, they had to establish a more or less self-regulating and self-perpetuating mechanism that drew its power from the inherent conditions of republican society. This self-regulating character of the constitutional order is crucial to an accurate understanding of Madison's thought. He never understood himself to be engaged in a debate about the advisability of majority rule per se; the question was always under what circumstances majorities would prevail.

Hence, and second, Madison maintained a lifelong concern about impulsivity in politics. The majorities he criticized were almost always those that formed, spread, and prevailed quickly, a point underscored by his frequent portrayal of them with metaphors like fire and contagious epidemics that connoted sudden eruptions of sentiment sweeping across populations or political institutions before there was time for thoughtful consideration. Political decisions, institutions, or majorities that concerned Madison were "impetuous,"[4] "hasty,"[5] "precipitate,"[6] "overheated,"[7] and contaminated by "contagious passion."[8] A majority acting under such circumstances was prone to error because it was unlikely to perceive its long-term interest in treating minority groups justly—what Tocqueville called the American doctrine of "self-interest well understood."[9] Moreover, impulsive majorities were apt to change their minds quickly and repeatedly, so enshrining their views as policy at any one moment during such turmoil would be arbitrary.

Third, Madison's solution to the problem of impulsivity was to harness what he saw as the inherent power of time to dissipate passions. One purpose of delay was to facilitate deliberation, but in another and perhaps broader sense, its usefulness lay not in what occurred in the interval between impulse and decision. The interval itself was the point. Time would ensure that passion subsided, reason resumed its throne, and transient appetites yielded to long-term interests. My intent in identifying this feature of Madison's thought is not to deny the importance of either deliberation or civic education. This study does argue, however, that this cooling process was necessary for both, and that Madison regarded it often to be sufficient for reasonable behavior. Moreover, a majority that cohered for a sufficient duration was probably settled and thus unlikely to change its mind, barring changed circumstances. As a result, institutions or majorities that Madison saw as seasoned with time and ripe to prevail were "cool,"[10] "deliberate,"[11] "settled,"[12] and focused on "permanent" needs rather than immediate desires.[13] He wrote in Federalist 63: "As the cool and deliberate sense of the community ought, in all governments, and actually will, in all free governments, ultimately prevail over the views of its rulers: so there are particular moments in public affairs, when the people, stimulated by some ir-regular passion . . . may call for measures which they themselves will afterwards be the most ready to lament and condemn."[14]

Madison can be cast as antimajoritarian only by excising the first half of the passage. Taken as a whole, it provides a synopsis of his democratic thought. To begin with, the normative and the empir-ical intersect: the people's "cool and deliberate" sense both should and will prevail. Impulsive measures are apt to arise at "particular" moments brought about by "irregular" passions, formulations that suggest such will not be the normal course of events, and that it is therefore a mistake to interpret the entire Constitution as a project to thwart popular majorities. But such moments will arise; such majori-ties will be likeliest to be unjust or unsettled if they impose their will in a hectic rush; and, conversely, they will be liable to reflect liberal values if they persist long enough to survive the series of constitu-tional processes necessary to prevail.

Consequently, one function of the Constitution was to serve as a metronome setting the proper tempo for republican politics. The natural and sometimes appropriate pace was allegro; often, though, Madison utilized constitutional mechanisms to slow the pace of pol-itics to a leisurely andante. Thus the idea of temporal republicanism: majorities should prevail when they have cohered for a duration ap-propriate to a given set of circumstances. From this perspective, pro-gressive commentators like James Allen Smith, Charles Beard, and James MacGregor Burns misplace their criticism in describing as an-tidemocratic institutional arrangements that require supermajorities or seemingly redundant consensuses from multiple branches of gov-ernment. Madison's perspective is lateral rather than vertical: rather than asking how many people agree with a given view at one dis-crete point in time, the decisive question is how long a majority has cohered. The relevant measure is a time-lapse photograph, not a snapshot.

This dynamic rather than static perspective helps to illustrate why many otherwise persuasive analyses that portray Madison as concerned with what kind of majorities prevailed risk confusing the issue. Such a framework more accurately captures his perspective than does the claim that he was antirepublican, but simply asking which majorities prevail might reasonably be understood to place

Madison in the hardly republican position of endorsing majority rule so long as the majorities in question were ones with which he agreed. Madison did not look out at the overlapping majorities—those that Federalist 10 suggests exist in an extended republic and that David Truman[15] depicts as a defining feature of a pluralistic society—and, at one static moment in time, select those that ought to prevail and dismiss those he viewed as unjust. Such a position might be liberal, an adherent of liberalism might describe it as preferable to majority rule, but it would be difficult to call it majoritarian. A dynamic rather than static perspective—one that projects each individual majority across time—more accurately characterizes Madison's beliefs: any majority was to prevail if it cohered for a sufficient interval.

Crucially, any majority that cohered for a sufficient interval was to prevail even if Madison believed it to be unjust. He could comfortably espouse this view because he remained confident that the most virulently unjust majorities—such as those bent on violating religious liberty—would never cohere, so that to the extent unjust majorities would prevail, they would likely pertain to ordinary questions of policy. Indeed, Madison thought it highly unlikely that unjust majorities would persist, so much so that their persistence itself might be taken as strong evidence of their justice. But here as in other cases we shall encounter, the decisive question is not whether Madison would have endorsed any given majority, but rather whether he would have endorsed some other principle for making decisions.

This question helps to illustrate why the prevailing liberal–republican paradigm in Madison scholarship substantially muddies the inescapably majoritarian character of his thought.[16] The redemptive strain of literature, for example, has largely concluded that Madison sought to balance his liberal and republican commitments. Lance Banning's view is typical: "Convinced that neither [popular control nor individual rights] could be secure without the other, temperamentally unable to decide between his 'liberal' and his 'republican' convictions, Madison set out to rescue *both* of the ideals enunciated in the Declaration at a time when growing numbers of Americans believed that they might have to choose."[17]

Banning is clearly correct that Madison cherished liberalism and republicanism and that he was aware of the tension between the two.[18] Still, his claim that Madison was reluctant to choose between liberalism and republicanism is accurate history but unsatisfying democratic theory. The entire point of the tension between majority rule and individual rights is that sooner or later, situations will arise—and, in Madison's life, more than once did—in which majorities behave unreasonably despite all institutional or cultural precautions. In these situations, one must choose, and to see the issue from Madison's perspective, it is vital to focus on the actual alternatives among which the choice must be made. These are not, on his view, majority rule or liberalism. The alternatives are majority rule or some other decision-making mechanism.

This choice is obscured if we pit liberalism against republicanism as if both were two points on the same axis. To understand Madison's democratic theory, we must recognize that liberalism and republicanism are, instead, different vectors altogether. Majority rule is a mechanism for making decisions, while liberalism is a criterion for evaluating them. Joseph Schumpeter makes the distinction: "Democracy is a political *method*, that is to say, a certain type of institutional arrangement for arriving at political—hence legislative and administrative—decisions and hence incapable of being an end in itself, irrespective of what decisions it will produce under any given historical conditions. And this must be the starting point of any attempt at defining it."[19]

Isolating majority rule as a decision-making mechanism clarifies the essential question: did Madison ever endorse any other means of making decisions? The emphatic answer is that he did not—not even the present-day conception of judicial review, which Beard wrongly imputes to him,[20] and not even in those cases in which he criticized the particular decisions majorities made. To be sure, Madison endorsed the right of revolution in the very worst circumstances, but this extremity constituted a departure from political society, not a legitimate act within it. The fact that majority rule and liberalism operate on different vectors enables Madison to say without contradiction that the former is the only just means of making decisions, while the latter indicates the value to which he hopes those decisions conform. His "Memorial and Remonstrance," directed, significantly, against a violation of the right he held to be most sacred—that of conscience—states: "True it is, that no other rule exists, by which any question which may divide a Society, can be ultimately determined, but the will of the majority; but it is also true, that the majority may trespass on the rights of the minority."[21] This statement deals with two separate issues. The first was how decisions were made; the second, the character of those decisions. There is no instance in which Madison claimed that unjust majority decisions altered his views on how decisions should be made. Because there was no alternative to majority rule—indeed, it is safe to assume Madison would have feared that any other decision-making mechanism, such as variations on monarchy or aristocracy, would have yielded even less liberal ones—the challenge was to make it likelier that majorities would behave justly.

This was hardly an unusual view; on the contrary, Madison's contemporaries would have been surprised to hear that criticism of the outcomes of majority rule was in any sense incompatible with the belief that majority rule was nevertheless the only just mechanism for decision making. Consider a famous statement of Jefferson, who surely was a more ardent adherent of individual rights than almost any other founder, Madison included: "Although the will of the majority *is in all cases to prevail,* that will to be rightful must be reasonable."[22] By this, Jefferson meant no more than the hardly surprising fact that majorities sometimes made unjust decisions. That did not mean there was any more just method of decision making.

Rather than Banning's formulation—that Madison was unwilling to choose between his liberal and republican commitments—it is therefore more precise to say he sought to reduce the number of occasions in which such a choice would be necessary. This was the power of time. Madison never articulated this doctrine of temporal republicanism systematically, nor does it explain the totality of his thought. This study does contend, however, that temporal republicanism is one important feature of Madison's thought and that it is latent in views to which he adhered more or less consistently over the course of his career.

The chapters that follow explore how temporal republicanism operates in several core areas of Madison's political thought: the extended republic theory of Federalist 10, the Bill of Rights, and constitutional interpretation, among others. In varying ways, critics have held up each of these areas as evidence of Madison's closet aristocratism. The perspective of temporal republicanism instead shows that in each case, Madison's objective was not to thwart majorities but rather to season them with time. Having set forth the basic features of this theory and its operation in Madison's thought, I shall explore the implications of temporal republicanism for contemporary politics, with this chief among them: to the extent Madison's democratic theory depends on time, the virtue on which it hinges is patience. If so, fundamental features of Madison's democratic thought stand in tension with a twenty-first-century ethos of instant gratification and communication—what William E. Scheuerman has called "the social experience of speed."[23]

We begin with Madison's views on majority rule, an unfolding drama in three acts—creation, participation, and reflection—during each of which we shall encounter features of Madison's thought that affirmed his unchanging commitment to majority rule even as his views on other subjects evolved. The intent of this discussion is not to provide a complete narrative of Madison's views on majority rule. Rather, it is to highlight important and sometimes overlooked features of his thought that illustrate his majoritarianism across three periods of otherwise considerable change: the founding crucible of the 1780s, Madison's long tenure as a participant in the regime he helped create, and finally his theoretically fruitful retirement.

Chapter One

Madison on Majorities

The 1780s—in many ways the formative period of Madison's political life—witnessed a profound crisis of self-government, but the malady itself has been frequently misdiagnosed. Although Madison clearly witnessed and raised repeated concerns about abusive majorities within the states, his primary concern was the impotence of national majorities. There is no question that majorities within the states committed repeated abuses—Madison went so far as to say "injustices," a word he did not lightly employ—but the fundamental political fact of the period was a crisis of authority at the center, and the defining feature of that crisis was the inability of national majorities to decide national issues. The abuses of local majorities were only symptoms of that illness. The Articles of Confederation empowered as few as four states to block action—and any state to block revision of the governing framework itself—which repeatedly enabled majorities within a state or states to inhibit national majorities. Moreover, the Articles Congress could requisition revenue from the states but had no means of enforcing collection, rendering it effectively impotent.

The results were evident in virtually every sphere of policy. Commerce was hampered by internecine trade disputes between states, which in turn made it impossible for Congress to enact meaningful trade agreements with foreign nations. Public finance stood at the perpetual brink of collapse. In 1782, for example, Congress requisitioned $8 million from the states and received only $430,031; the cost of operating the army alone stood at $5.7 million.[1] All told, requisitions accounted for scarcely 6 percent of national revenue during the Revolution. Congress consequently piled debt atop debt, but the same political dynamics that required the borrowing impeded repayment. New debts were taken out to pay interest on old ones. The only available recourse was paper money, and reams of it. "The result," economic historian Sidney Ratner writes, "was predictable—severe inflation accompanied by depreciation of bills of credit."[2] In 1777, a dollar of paper currency nominally equaled the same amount in gold; by 1781 a purchaser needed more than $160 of paper to obtain a single dollar of specie.[3] Meanwhile, as Congress paid troops with promissory notes, unrest mounted. Attempts to remedy the situation by empowering Congress to levy imposts failed because such a measure would have required the unanimous assent of the states. Tasked with drafting a notice imploring states to comply with requisitions, Madison cast the situation starkly. If Congress was unable to establish public finance on sustainable footing, "the great cause which we have engaged to vindicate, will be dishonored & betrayed; the last & fairest experiment in favor of the rights of human nature will be turned against them; and their patrons & friends exposed to be insulted & silenced by the votaries of Tyranny and Usurpation."[4]

Significantly, Madison repeatedly cast this problem as one of abusive minorities that were permitted to thwart the principle of majority rule. His most consistent critique of the Articles was that they allowed a minority of states to block major decisions: "Could any thing in theory, be more perniciously improvident and injudicious," he asked in the Virginia ratifying convention, "than this submission of the will of the majority to the most trifling minority?"[5]

The situation within the states was hardly better.[6] Seven states printed paper money; when the New Hampshire legislature refused to do so, it found itself face to face with an armed mob—an extreme but hardly isolated example of what was, in many states, the literal rule of mobs demanding everything from paper money to abolitions of debts. Absent a uniform currency, "every dealing across a state line [was] a small exercise in financial wizardry."[7] Shay's Rebellion deeply troubled the nation's political leadership, especially the inability of the national government to respond to it, a concern that would ultimately lead to the constitutional provision guaranteeing every state a republican form of government. "The trouble with almost every state," Clinton Rossiter reflects, "was that it was governed weakly or erratically; the trouble with the United States is that it was governed hardly at all."[8]

None of this is to say society itself was plunged into turmoil. On the contrary, historians have long debated the extent of the crisis.

John Fiske's celebrated *The Critical Period of American History* characterized the nation as "drifting toward anarchy" during the 1780s, while Gordon Wood has more recently emphasized positive social trends such as population and economic growth.[9] What seems beyond dispute, however, is that the United States had become ungovernable at the national level and nearly so within the states. The crisis, in short, was political.

It was in this milieu that James Madison wrote one of his most celebrated statements of concern about majorities run amok: his 1787 memorandum "Vices of the Political System of the United States"—which was in fact an emphatic endorsement of majority rule at the national level. Commentaries on the memorandum, a numbered list of 12 critiques of the political order, have typically focused on its most theoretically intensive sections, numbers 9, 10, and 11. Taken in isolation, one can readily see how they might fuel an antimajoritarian reading of Madison. These sections are in fact replete with references to abusive majorities, especially their use of paper money to abrogate debts as well as the rapid oscillation of state laws, which legislatures often passed, repealed, and reenacted in such rapid succession that statutes became essentially unknowable.

But these complaints occur in a broader context that requires careful attention in order to arrive at an accurate understanding of Madison's thought. The first indication of that context is that the section of the memorandum that most harshly criticizes local majorities—number 11, "Injustice of the laws of States"—also notes in passing, and without qualification, that "in republican Government the majority however composed, ultimately give the law."[10] At no point does the memorandum implicitly or explicitly question that premise. Majority rule was both the empirical fact and normative ideal that formed borders around any solution to the problem of majority abuse. Indeed, a careful reading of the crucial yet often overlooked preceding sections of "Vices" clearly indicates that his primary concern was the inability of national majorities to decide national issues under the Articles regime.

That is most evident in the striking fact that every specific abuse of which he accused local majorities also involved national or interstate interests. The "Vices" memo actually first cites these abuses not under the heading of "injustices" within the states but rather in an earlier section entitled "Trespasses of the States on the rights of each other":

Paper money, instalments of debts, occlusion of Courts, making property a legal tender, may likewise be deemed aggressions on the rights of other States. As the Citizens of every State aggregately taken stand more or less in the relation of Creditors or debtors, to the Citizens of every other States [sic], Acts of the debtor State in favor of debtors, affect the Creditor State, in the same manner, as they do its own citizens who are relatively creditors towards other citizens. This remark may be extended to foreign nations.[11]

Even in pivoting from interstate to intrastate issues, "Vices" reinforces their interconnectedness:

In developing the evils which viciate the political system of the U.S. it is proper to include those which are found within the States individually, as well as those which directly affect the States collectively, *since the former class have an indirect influence on the general malady* and must not be overlooked in forming a compleat remedy.[12]

Madison's discussion of paper money under the heading "Injustice of the laws of States" thus laments the interstate and even international implications of that policy: "Is it to be imagined that an ordinary citizen or even an assembly-man of R. Island in estimating the policy of paper money, ever considered or cared in what light the measure would be viewed in France or Holland; or even in Massts or Connect.?"[13] Madison adduced similar arguments about paper money on other occasions. Opposing it in the Virginia Assembly, he said that the power to print currency should reside with Congress—that is, the national government—"for the sake of uniformity" and "to prevent fraud in States towards each other or foreigners." Furthermore, he added, paper money "serv[ed] dissentions between States."[14] Similarly, he had complained during the Articles period that state emissions of currency were "manifestly repugnant" to congressional acts on finance and that they rendered states unable to comply with congressional requisitions.[15]

Consequently, the decision of one state to print paper money potentially affected citizens of other states as well as the whole nation. In these cases, local majorities trespassed on the authority of national majorities. These considerations, whose reasoning applies equally to Madison's other complaints about such local abuses as legislative interference in contracts, indicate that his intention was not merely to inhibit local majorities but rather to protect the right of national majorities to decide national issues.

Madison continued to press the case for national majority rule at the Constitutional Convention, where he routinely staked out positions more majoritarian than those of his colleagues. His Virginia Plan, which empowered the first house of the legislature to choose the second and both of them to choose the president, placed so much authority in the hands of the only directly popularly elected branch that Madison himself ultimately objected to some of its features as violating the principle of separation of powers.[16] His riposte to delegates who wanted to base the entire Congress on equal representation of the states was also majoritarian: "Mr. Madison considered the popular election of one branch of the national Legislature as *essential to every plan of free Government.* . . . [Otherwise,] the necessary sympathy between [the people] and their rulers and officers [would be] too little felt." He pursued this argument to the brink of repudiating the very device that Douglass Adair[17] saw as a linchpin of Madison's plan for curbing abusive majorities: a Senate elected by the House and therefore one step removed from public opinion. That idea, Adair writes, was borrowed from Hume's "Idea of a Perfect Commonwealth," which proposed that successive levels of government elect the next higher level, thereby steadily and increasingly filtering the raw material of public opinion. Yet here is Madison early in the convention, opposing a proposal for Congress to be chosen by state legislatures:

> [Mr. Madison] was an advocate for the policy of refining the popular appointments by successive filtrations, but thought it might be pushed too far. . . . He thought too that the great fabric to be raised would be more stable and durable, if it should rest on the solid foundation of the people themselves, than if it should stand merely on the pillars of the Legislatures.[18]

By all accounts, Madison held out longer than any other member of the convention against giving states equal representation in the Senate, a policy that he repeatedly argued would violate the principle of majority rule and preserve the most unjust feature of the Articles. He argued this point with uncharacteristic rhetorical force, declaring on June 7 that such a departure from "the doctrine of proportional representation"—and therefore majoritarianism—would be "evidently unjust."[19] Proportional representation was so much "the proper foundation of Governmt." that "destroy[ing]" it would threaten the remainder of the Constitutional project.[20] Nearly three weeks later, with the convention at risk of imminent collapse beneath the weight of this dispute, Madison—normally a ready and skillful compromiser—"entreated the gentlemen representing the small States to renounce a principle wch. was confessedly unjust, which cd. never be admitted, & if admitted must infuse mortality into a Constitution which we wished to last for ever."[21] A week later, he all but expressed a readiness to force a majoritarian plan on the smaller states:

> He conceived that the Convention was reduced to the alternative of either departing from justice in order to conciliate the smaller States, and the minority of the people of the U.S. or of displeasing these by justly gratifying the larger States and the majority of the people. He could not himself hesitate as to the option he ought to make. The Convention with justice & the majority of the people on their side had nothing to fear. With injustice and the minority on their side they had everything to fear. [He would prefer to conciliate the small States, but] if the principal States comprehending a majority of the people of the U.S. should concur in a just & judicious Plan, he had the firmest hopes, that all the other States would by degrees accede to it.[22]

It is revealing that of all the battles Madison lost in the convention—including the national veto over state laws, which he regarded as the linchpin of the Virginia Plan—the antimajoritarian makeup of the Senate was the only feature he declined to rationalize and defend in *The Federalist*, shunting it aside in Federalist 62 as a necessary compromise that it would be "superfluous to try, by the standard of theory."[23]

Within the convention, once the battle for proportional representation in the Senate was lost, Madison opposed empowering that body to appoint judges, again on grounds of popular rule. The executive, he said at this point, should have a role in appointing judges because he, unlike the Senate as now constituted, would be "a national officer, acting for and equally sympathising with every part of the U. States."[24] Madison thus insisted on a majoritarian influence in the appointment of the judiciary, the branch critics like Charles Beard have most criticized as aristocratic.

Madison also preferred that the president himself be more directly accountable to popular majorities. Smith characterizes the Electoral College as a scheme "to prevent the majority of the qualified voters from choosing the President."[25] But Madison spoke for the prerogatives of exactly such a majority when arguing in the convention for the direct election of the president by the voters at large.[26] Moreover, he joined James Wilson in opposing a proposal to make the executive removable only by a vote of the state legislatures— again, the Articles model—on the grounds that "it would enable a minority of the people to prevent the removal of an officer who had rendered himself justly criminal in the eyes of a majority."[27]

During the ratification debate, Madison continued to argue for the Constitution on majoritarian grounds. Federalist 40, responding to the Anti-Federalist claim that the Constitution should require ratification by all 13 states, assailed "the absurdity of subjecting the fate of twelve states to the perverseness or corruption of a thirteenth," a situation that could hold "fifty-nine sixtieths of the people" hostage to "inflexible opposition given by a *majority* of one sixtieth of the people of America."[28] Madison went further in Federalist 51, embedding a majoritarian argument in the very section of the paper concerned with abusive majorities:

> In the extended republic of the United States, and among the great variety of interests, parties, and sects, which it embraces, a coalition of a majority of the whole society could seldom take place on any other principles, than those of justice and the general good: whilst there being thus less danger to a minor from the will of the major party, there must be less pretext also, to provide for the security of the former, by introducing into the government a will not dependent on the latter: or, in other words, a will independent of the society itself.[29]

At least three times in this passage, Madison emphatically endorsed majority rule even as he implied concern about its potential for abuse. First, the proposed regime was to be tested not merely according to its compliance with justice—which presumably includes minority rights—but rather by whether it served both justice and the general good. There is no evidence in this paper that Madison saw those goals as being in tension with one another; on the contrary, the advantage of an extended republic consisted in alleviating the need to choose between the two. Second, in an argument Madison evidently regarded as unremarkable but that fundamentally challenges contemporary conceptions of rights as exemptions from majority rule, he equated "the society itself" with "its major party." In other words, when the majority spoke, it spoke for the entire community. Third, among the benefits of the new regime was that it removed any pretext even to introduce into the government any will not dependent on the majority.

In Federalist 58, Madison used similar language in opposing a supermajority requirement for action in the House despite explicitly acknowledging its potential for preventing "hasty and partial measures." "Hasty" and "partial" were the very stigmata of majorities that Madison thought were likeliest both to err as to their own interests and to invade the rights of minorities. Madison nonetheless concluded that the necessity of passing measures that served the general good trumped the desire to block errant majorities: "In all cases where justice, or the general good, might require new laws to be passed, or active measures to be pursued, the fundamental principle of free government would be reversed [by a supermajority requirement]. It would be no longer the majority that would rule; the power would be transferred to the minority."[30]

Far from the "neurotic terror" of majorities that Louis Hartz imputed to the Founders, the latent premise here seems to be that the norm is for majorities to pursue the general good.[31] Errant majorities, by contrast, are apparently enough of an aberration that a regime ought not to be structured around them. The alternative reading—that even if hasty and partial majorities are common, one still cannot risk impeding a majority pursuing the general good—would underscore Madison's majoritarianism even more starkly.

These passages may help to explain why the French National Assembly, certainly no bastion of aristocracy, conferred honorary citizenship on Madison and Hamilton for their authorship of *The Federalist*. The revolutionary French understood that work to be a monument to republicanism.[32] Although the particular parameters of republicanism were a subject of intense debate on this side of the Atlantic during the ratification debates, it is also worth observing that Madison's opponents understood the Constitution to empower national majorities as well. Such was often precisely their complaint. To be sure, the fear that the constitutional regime would engender a functional aristocracy was a mainstay of Anti-Federalist argument. But this was, for the most part, an empirical prediction based on the idea that congressional districts would be so large that only the highborn would be able to win election—the assumption, again, being that voting by popular majorities would be the mode of selection. On this point, at least, advocates of the constitution were not accused of hatching such a scheme for the purpose of shielding the privileged from majorities; the assumption was that majorities themselves would select the privileged. Patrick Henry, indeed, argued that most voters would voluntarily turn to the highborn for advice as to how to vote.[33] His portrayal of the commoner so ignorant as to need the tutelage of the upper classes certainly appears to be a more aristocratic, or at least more patronizing, mentality than Madison's.

There is another important sense in which many Anti-Federalists assumed the intention—if not the effect—of the Constitution was to empower national majorities. Those of a communitarian bent, like Henry, George Mason, and Melancton Smith, feared the Constitution would dilute civic identity and participation by removing authority from a comparatively intimate to a diffuse and anonymous level of government.[34] But also implicit in their frequent invocation of Montesquieu's dictum that a republic was only feasible in a small territory was an assumption that the constitutional regime was indeed republican, which was precisely why it was folly to attempt to deploy it over a large country. Moreover, to the extent Anti-Federalists feared the new national regime, it was often because Madison's understanding was theirs: the Constitution would empower national majorities. The dispute pertained to whether the issues to which their authority would extend were actually national in scope as opposed to local.[35] Thus Henry in the Virginia ratifying convention, explicitly acknowledging that the new regime would be based on national majorities but fearing they would be empowered to abolish slavery, which he believed to be a local issue: "And this must and will be done by men, *a majority of whom* have not a common interest with you. . . . The *majority* of Congress is to the north, and the slaves are to the south."[36]

Early in Madison's career as a participant in the system he helped create—most notably his time in the House—his opponents, like subsequent commentators, thought they detected a fundamental shift away from the nationalism he displayed in the 1780s. Substantial grounds for that charge—if it is appropriate to call it an accusation that Madison changed his thought in response to changing circumstances—exist. Madison's concerns about what he took to be abuses of executive power during the early constitutional period—which escalated substantially when President Adams signed the Alien and Sedition Acts—prompted him to join Jefferson in helping to create a party system whose aim was to mobilize public opinion against abuses emanating from the regime. Notice, for example, that in his 1792 opposition essay "Spirit of Governments," Madison says republican regimes derive "their energy [that is, not merely their legitimacy] from the will of the society," a formulation that suggests more active public engagement in politics than Publius seems to have contemplated.[37] John Zvesper sees the party system as sufficiently distinct from Madison's ideas in the 1780s that it constitutes a second "Madisonian system."[38] The question of the "James Madison problem" lies outside the scope of the present study except to observe the consistency of Madison's belief in majority rule. The claim of inconsistency on this point is based largely on misinterpretations of his thought in the 1780s, which cast him as concerned about abusive local majorities but omit his motivation: protecting the authority of national ones. The crucial point is that at all phases of his career, Madison believed national majorities were entitled to decide national issues. The undeniable shifts arise from Madison's changing perception of the greatest threat to that authority. In the 1780s, it was the abuses of local majorities. By the 1790s—rightly or wrongly—Madison had become convinced that figures like Adams were plotting to undermine the authority of national majorities by restricting their liberty. Hence the need to mobilize them.

The consistency of Madison's majoritarianism over the course of his career as an actor within the constitutional order is most evident in his repeated efforts—even while serving in the executive branch—to preserve the policy-making prerogatives of the department he saw as closest to majorities: the legislature. The importance of this fact is that it calls into serious question the claim that Madison attempted to shunt decision making into institutions insulated from public opinion. On the contrary, Madison believed Congress—the

House especially—was the branch most immediately susceptible to popular opinion. He said in the Constitutional Convention that the popular election of the lower house of the legislature was a core principle of free government. House elections were the most majoritarian insofar as they were the contests in which individual ballots had both the most concentrated impact and the most immediate effect. Moreover, the House was the only institution that could be completely remade every two years,[39] thus making it rapidly sensitive to majority views. And in Federalist 52, Madison wrote that "liberty" made it "particularly essential" that the House "have an immediate dependence on, and an intimate sympathy with, the people."[40]

If critics are correct that Madison sought to insulate the regime from majorities, then based on his own description of the House as immediately responsive to public opinion, one would expect him to steer decision making away from it. Yet Madison's record of nearly a quarter century in federal office shows him to be a fierce defender both of congressional prerogatives and, within that institution, the power of the House specifically—the institution, significantly, to which he first aspired.[41]

When Congress undertook its first major discussion of a treaty—John Jay's 1794 Treaty of London—Madison played a decisive role in establishing a precedent, still in place, that the Senate's power to ratify treaties did not trump the House's power to legislate on such matters as commerce and war.[42] In the early Congresses of the 1790s, Madison consistently resisted assertions of executive authority in areas he thought properly legislative. The extent to which he insisted on this point is especially stark in comparison with the broad swaths of authority that have since been delegated to the executive with minimal dissent. Article One of the Constitution, for example, explicitly empowers Congress to appropriate funds for postal roads; Madison opposed even giving the president discretion to designate which roads fit that description. The House, he insisted on this and other occasions, lacked the authority to alienate its own powers even if it wanted to do so.[43] For similar reasons, the Sedition Act was objectionable because it gave the president discretion to define what would make an alien "dangerous" for purposes of deporting him or her, a function Madison took to be legislative in nature.[44] On another occasion, he spoke against a motion asking the executive branch to submit a plan on the public debt for the consideration of the House; the House, he said, should first decide broad questions of policy and only then consider executive plans for implementing them.[45] A proposal to "request the president to submit a plan for the defense of the frontiers" might, he mused, be unconstitutional.[46] Madison denied the slightest executive discretion over spending appropriated funds: except in "extraordinary and pressing" emergencies, the executive owed "an inflexible conformity" to congressional instructions.[47]

Both the extent of Madison's commitment to congressional supremacy and the extent to which the constitutional order has since drifted from it are most evident in the Pacificus–Helvidius debates he held pseudonymously with Alexander Hamilton. The impetus for the debates was the Washington administration's Neutrality Proclamation declaring the nation to take no sides in the European wars sparked by the French Revolution. Madison and Jefferson took exception, partly because they saw the proclamation as a betrayal of both the Franco-American friendship and partly because of their perception at that point of the French Revolution as at least a cousin of the American one. But more broadly, and strikingly in contrast to the contemporary constitutional ethos, Madison also denied the executive branch's authority to make declarations about foreign policy without the assent of Congress.

Madison's Helvidius essays spoke of the executive not as a co-equal policy-making branch but rather as self-evidently subservient to the legislature.[48] Indeed, on Madison's reading of the very nature of legislative power, there would seem to be virtually nothing the executive could do unless Congress acted first. He wrote in the first essay of Helvidius: "The natural province of the executive magistrate is to execute laws, as that of the legislature is to make laws. *All his acts* therefore, properly executive, must pre-suppose the existence of the laws to be executed." Although Hamilton's claim might be seen as a precursor to the contemporary theory of the unitary executive—that is, barring specific exemptions, the president has complete authority where he has any authority—Madison came close to theorizing what might be called a unitary legislature: that is, in areas in which the Constitution gave the national government authority, the legislature was the repository of all powers not specifically allocated to the president. Hence his syllogism, also suggested in Helvidius I, that war represented the highest act of foreign policy, Congress had the power to declare war, and Congress consequently wielded ultimate authority over every power subsidiary to that.[49] The executive, he went on to argue, should neither speak nor be spoken of as "the government" of the United States.[50] Madison singled out Locke and Montesquieu, two philosophers he otherwise admired, for stinging criticism because of their broad views of executive prerogative.[51] It bears further emphasis that all this was apparent to Madison not merely in the technical details of the Constitution but also in the plain meaning of the terms "legislative" and "executive."

Of course, Madison was a member of Congress during this time, and these arguments for legislative supremacy might be seen as self-serving—or, perhaps more charitably, as the kind of institutional self-defense predicted in Federalist 51. But Madison adhered to these views with remarkable consistency even as an official of the executive branch. When President Jefferson suggested deflecting criticisms of judicial vacancies by publishing a docket of cases to demonstrate how little federal judges did, Madison, his secretary of state, demurred because Congress had made "no specific appropriation for the expence" of such a report.[52] He declined a correspondent's request that the administration support his petition for relief in a case of maritime losses, explaining that because Congress had sole authority over the matter, it would be inappropriate for the president even to comment on it.[53] In an act especially difficult to imagine in today's aggrandized executive, Madison resisted as "unconstitutional" a Senate attempt to give the administration—again, it bears emphasis, an administration of which he was a high-ranking official—authority to call up militia troops to defend New Orleans.[54]

When he succeeded Jefferson in 1809, Madison inherited a presidency so modest by contemporary standards that, three weeks into his administration, it was necessary for him to inquire personally of his predecessor "whether the time piece in the sitting room [of the White House needed to be wound] *monthly* or weekly."[55] More significant is that he left the office that way. Many historians have criticized Madison as having blundered into the War of 1812, but nearly all credit him with the substantial feat of being perhaps the only president who led the nation through armed conflict without enlarging his own powers. Madison remained nearly as deferential to Congress as president as he had been as Helvidius. As David J. Siemers notes, Madison discontinued even Jefferson's practice of lobbying members of Congress over dinner: "Madison's own work in political theory had given him a different perspective—one which required the president to defer to Congress's legislative wishes in all cases except those of unconstitutionality."[56] As Siemers argues, it is that commitment—rather than a lack of political skill—that explains Madison's present-day reputation as an unsuccessful president.

On those occasions when he did stretch executive authority, Madison did so self-consciously and took special care to ensure his actions could not be construed as precedents for enlarging presidential power. His 1809 proclamation suspending trade with Great Britain was based not on an assertion of presidential authority over national security, but rather on a generous interpretation of congressional statute.[57] Similarly, Madison's proclamation annexing West Florida—probably his boldest exercise or his greatest abuse of presidential authority, depending on one's perspective—cited statutes that "contemplated . . . an eventual possession of the said Territory by the United States, and are accordingly so framed as in that case to extend in their operation, to the same."[58]

To be sure, it seems likely if not certain that Helvidius would have objected to both proclamations. But whereas modern executives have tended self-consciously to legitimize expansions of their power by declaring them to be implicitly or explicitly constitutional, and thereby enshrining them as precedents, Madison took specific care on these occasions to ensure his actions could not be used to legitimate future aggrandizements of the presidency. His correspondence surrounding both the 1809 trade proclamation and the annexation of West Florida[59] suggested he knew he was stretching the limits of his constitutional authority and that he did not intend for these exceptions to become rules. It was the difference, so to speak, between breaking the speed limit en route to the hospital and declaring speed limits generally to be null and void. In the normal flow of constitutional traffic, Madison believed, the president owed deference to the branch of government more fully reflecting majority opinion.

That Madison did not treat these exceptions as precedents is evident in his June 1, 1812, message to Congress, which documented repeated acts of war on Great Britain's part yet ultimately acknowledged legislative authority:

> Whether the United States shall continue passive under these progressive usurpations, and these accumulating wrongs; or, opposing force to force in defence of their national rights, shall commit a just cause into the Almighty disposer of events . . . is a solemn question, which the Constitution wisely confides to the Legislative Department of the Government. In

recommending it to their early deliberations, I am happy in
the assurance, that the decision will be worthy the
enlightened and patriotic Councils, of a virtuous, a free, and a
powerful Nation.[60]

Madison's rhetoric indicates he hardly considered the question
of the proper course to be an open one. But Congress' subsequent
and bitter debate—the Senate required two votes before it passed a
declaration of war more than two weeks after Madison's message—
also indicates he knew the outcome was uncertain and submitted the
issue to the legislature anyway. Had he operated only on political
convenience, he need not have done so. Because the essence of the
message was that a state of war already existed, he might merely
have retaliated against Great Britain without the arguably superfluous and politically uncertain step of inviting congressional deliberation.[61] That he did not underscores his understanding of congressional authority as supreme.[62]

His majoritarianism is further evident in the paeans to the Constitution he issued as president, a common rhetorical form of the
times. In these statements, the principle he cited as its defining feature was neither individual rights, nor liberalism more generally, nor
the institutional checks that critics understand as impediments to
majority rule. Rather, the central tenet of the Constitution was "respect for the Will of the majority."[63] It was majority rule—not, significantly, individual liberty—that Madison called "the vital principle
of our free Constitution."[64]

During his retirement, he once more affirmed that majority rule
was "the vital principle of republican government" itself.[65] It was
during this period of his life, the most theoretically active since the
1780s, that Madison would be compelled to defend that principle
most fiercely. Once more, the impetus was a threat he perceived to
the rule of national majorities. Southern opponents of the tariff of
1828 seized on Madison's own opposition writings to suggest that
states could legitimately block national acts they took to be unconstitutional—raising once more the specter of local majorities blocking
national ones and bringing Madison's thought in many ways full cir-
cle. Here again he stood with the right of national majorities to decide national issues. This is precisely the position Madison took in
response to the nullification controversy of the late 1820s and early
1830s. Madison understood the nullification doctrine, which asserted

the right of a state to disregard a national law unless three-quarters of the states overruled such an action, to be an assault not merely on the permanence of the Constitution but first and foremost on its defining principle: majority rule: "To establish a positive & permanent rule giving such a power to such a minority over such a majority, would overturn the first principle of free Gov't and in practice necessarily overturn the Gov't itself."[66] It bears emphasis that this "first principle" was decidedly not the rights of individuals or minority groups. On the contrary, interpretations that see Madison's primary objective as protecting inviolable rights against popular abuses find little support in his stark conclusion that an aggrieved minority had no Constitutional recourse. Consider the following passage from Madison's circa 1835–1836 essay, "Notes on Nullification":

> It has been asked whether every right has not its remedy, and what other remedy exists under the Govt. of the U.S. ags't usurpations of power, but a right in the States individually to annul and resist them. The plain answer is, that the remedy is the same under the government of the United States as under all other Govts. established & organized on free principles. The first remedy is in the checks provided among the constituted authorities; that failing the next is in the influence of the Ballot-boxes & Hustings; that again failing, the appeal lies to the power that made the Constitution, and can explain, amend, or remake it. Should this resort also fail, and the power usurped be sustained in its oppressive exercise on a minority by a majority, the final course to be pursued by the minority, must be an object of calculation, in which the degree of oppression, the means of resistance, the consequences of its failure, and the consequences of its success must be the elements.[67]

As will be seen in subsequent chapters, Madison regarded the "first remedy"—that is, constitutional "checks"—as, at root, majoritarian instruments. Moreover, Madison thought abuses possible but "sustained" abuses highly unlikely. At this point, though, the relevance of the passage consists of the following. Contemporary discourse assumes that the very essence of rights is that there are certain basic entitlements individuals or political minorities should not be compelled to defend in the political arena. Madison stands accused by critics like Beard of having erected constitutional barriers that would relieve minorities of precisely such a burden. Yet Madison wrote in the passage just quoted above that appeals to majorities or majoritarian institutions were in fact the only available remedies to minorities. The question at stake is not the extent of Madison's commitment to rights. It is what mechanisms can meaningfully protect them. These were, in sequence, constitutional mechanisms subject to majoritarian pressures ("checks"); elections ("the Ballot-boxes") or public persuasion ("the Hustings"), both of which were subject to the judgment of majorities; or, finally, an appeal to popular majorities acting in their constitutional capacity[68] ("the power that made the Constitution"). If these remedies failed, minorities had no recourse but to exit political society, a radical step that Madison clearly meant to warn was not worth its substantial risks and costs. The relevant distinction, one Madison drew explicitly,[69] was between constitutional rights and natural rights, with the former referring to rights within political society and the latter referring exclusively to the right to rebel, which returned the rebellious party to the state of nature. On Madison's view, minorities had no constitutional rights except appeal to majorities. Failing that, the choices were either sufferance or the natural right of revolt—no more, no less.[70]

This does not mean Madison opposed individual rights, only that he knew no political institution could meaningfully secure them other than a majority seasoned, as will be seen, with time. It is true, of course, that within three decades, a Southern minority that felt oppressed did not blink when confronted with Madison's stark choice between suffering perceived injustice and returning to a state of nature. But stark the choice remained, and Madison framed it as a question of majority rule:

> It has been said that all Govt. is an evil. It wd be more proper to say that the necessity of any Govt. is a misfortune. This necessity however exists; and the problem to be solved is, not what form of Govt. is perfect, but which of the forms is least imperfect; and here the general question must be between a republican Govern't in which the majority rule the minority, and a Govt in which a lesser number or the least number rule the majority.[71]

Madison was not the only figure in this period to see the Constitution in those terms. The foremost theorist of nullification, John C. Calhoun, objected to Madison's interpretation of the Constitution precisely because, like Patrick Henry a generation earlier, he feared it empowered national majorities to rule over a Southern minority. Both Madison and Calhoun were concerned about abusive majorities, but the crucial difference was that Madison was concerned about factious majorities, whereas Calhoun saw all majorities as either inherently factious or as so prone to abusive behavior that they had to be treated as such. Hence Calhoun believed in a "concurrent majority" system by which measures would require the approval of both overall majorities and the majorities they affected. Calhoun claimed that the Constitution enacted a concurrent-majority system and—crucially—that Madison misconstrued the document in assuming the right of national majorities to bind minorities. Calhoun's *Discourse on the Constitution and Government of the United States* grouped Madison alongside Hamilton in a project to "carry out their predilections in favor of a national form of government, as far as, in their opinion, fidelity to the constitution would permit."[72] These predilections, Calhoun concluded, impelled Madison and Hamilton to mischaracterize the proposed government as "partly federal and partly national."[73] The difference between these forms for Calhoun—who believed the regime to be "federal throughout"—was that a federal government operated via a concurrent majority, while a national government operated via a numerical majority. The problem with the latter form, to which Calhoun understood Madison to aspire, was precisely that it accorded national majorities absolute rule.[74]

Calhoun complained that Madison's claim in Federalist 39 that the constitutional regime was simultaneously national and federal was absurd; in the final analysis, Calhoun noted, one or the other form must be supreme. An indication of Calhoun's view of a national regime—again, the form he imputed to Madison—may be found in his statement that had the Constitution been so constructed, "the will of the majority of the whole people of the Union would have bound the minority." This was precisely how Madison saw the Constitution—and precisely why it, and he, must be regarded as majoritarian.

The Property Problem

Even if Madison supported government by majorities of qualified voters, he might still have protected the interests of the wealthy by restricting the voting-eligible population. This commonplace charge against the Founding is refuted in considerable measure by the Constitution's explicit rejection of property qualifications. Charles Beard, singling out Madison by name, imputes economic motives even to this rejection: "Propositions to establish property qualifications [for offices or voting] were defeated, not because they were believed to be inherently opposed to the genius of American government, but for economic reasons—strange as it may seem."[75] Madison, Beard wrote, opposed property qualifications in the convention only because he did not believe that factious activity correlated with property ownership per se, and that these measures therefore would not succeed in protecting minority wealth.

Beard arguably extrapolated excessively from Madison's speeches on this topic, which treat the issue of property qualifications much more ambivalently than his critic suggests. Still, Madison provides some basis for the charge that he sought to restrict political participation on the basis of property. He said in the Philadelphia Convention that he did not object to property qualifications for electors, even if he doubted that a practical and measurable standard could be devised.[76] Even more problematic for the majoritarian interpretation, he not only suggested that one house of the Kentucky legislature be reserved for the propertied, he urged that the Constitution enshrine that protection precisely because a majority of people were likely in time to be landless.[77]

These difficulties must be addressed carefully for, as will presently be seen, Madison himself eventually abandoned his proposal for Kentucky as antimajoritarian. Still, several mitigating factors deserve attention. First, it is both a theoretical and a historical mistake to view "landowner" as a proxy for "wealthy," a point Madison emphasized when he observed in Philadelphia that possession of land provided "no certain evidence of real wealth"; on the contrary, debtor landowners were among the chief proponents of unjust state laws.[78] More important, ownership of land was so widespread, and property qualifications for political participation so liberal, that Bernard Bailyn estimates that "fifty to seventy-five per cent of the adult male white population was entitled to vote" during the Revolutionary era.[79] The relevant conflict, if any, was less between rich and poor than between freeholders and members of the merchant and professional classes.

Second, Madison was as concerned about the wealthy abusing the poor as the other way around. At Philadelphia, he opposed allowing Congress to establish property qualifications for its own membership lest it become "an aristocracy or oligarchy" with "a distinct interest from the people."[80] Even in his remarks on a constitution for Kentucky, Madison took care to limit property qualifications to one house of the legislature: "Give all power to property; and the indigent [will] be oppressed. Give it to the latter and the effect may be transposed."[81] His *National Gazette* essay on "Parties" said an equalization of wealth was to be preferred to the extent such a goal was feasible.[82] During retirement, Madison wrote, "It has been said that America is a country for the poor, not the rich. There would be more correctness in saying it is the country for both, where the latter have a relish for free government; but, proportionally, *more for the former* than the latter."[83]

Finally, during the rapid democratization of the Jacksonian era, Madison, a devotee of Thomas Malthus, came to believe that the poor and landless were destined to become a substantial majority. Precisely for this reason, he abandoned property qualifications in the Virginia Constitutional Convention of 1829–1830. A note he made to himself during the convention says of the landless,

> What is to be done with this unfavored class of the community? If it be, on one hand, unsafe to admit them to a full share of political power, it must be recollected, on the other, that it cannot be expedient to rest a Republican Government on a portion of the society having a numerical & physical force excluded from, and liable to be turned against it; and which would lead to a standing military force, dangerous to all parties & to liberty itself.[84]

Consequently, Madison concluded there was no choice but to trust the "combined numbers" of these masses; individuals who possessed types of property other than land; and the "political & moral influence" provided by what would, by that time, be a lengthy tradition of just behavior on the part of majorities. Here we arrive at a decisive fact for an accurate understanding of Madison's political thought. Power in society ultimately resided with those possessing "numerical & physical force." By definition, the numerical force always resided with the majority. In the republican political culture of America, Madison believed, majorities always possessed the physical force as well. The supremacy of majorities was a defining feature of American political culture, one approaching the status of a physical law, and parchment laws were powerless to alter this fact. On Madison's reasoning, debating whether the majority should rule made no more sense than debating the normative dimensions of the law of gravity.[85]

Inevitability and its Importance

The inevitability of majority rule was the fundamental limiting condition on Madison's democratic thought, and he understood it in direct contradistinction to "parchment barriers." The emptiness of the latter was the defining characteristic of the crucible in which Madison's political views were formed: his service in the Continental Congress. The Articles of Confederation were packed with paper directives—"the states shall," "no state shall"—and yet the repeated experience was that the states did as they pleased.

What experience taught, theory confirmed. David Hume's essay "Of the First Principles of Government" argued that no regime could physically overpower an entire populace, and that "it is therefore, on opinion only that government is founded."[86] Even tyrannical regimes, Hume wrote, could only rule if their subjects believed their authority to be legitimate and obedience to be in their interest. This dictum is, to my knowledge, the only nearly direct quotation from Hume that appears in *The Federalist* in Madison's own hand.[87] He paraphrased it elsewhere as well. His *National Gazette* essay on "Charters" declared: "All power has been traced up to opinion. The stability of all governments and security of all rights may be traced to the same source."[88] "British Government," another essay for the party press, argued that the British regime so admired by Hamilton and Adams derived its "boasted equilibrium" from "public opinion" rather than the institutional distribution of powers.[89] "Public opinion," he also wrote in the party press, "sets bounds to every Government, and is the real sovereign in every free one."[90]

The import of Hume's insight was that it was empirical nonsense to say a people could be ruled against their will. Monarchs did not rule because a charter entitled them to; they ruled because their subjects chose to obey, or at least not to resist. Political power was ultimately derived from physical force, and the physical force of the masses always exceeded that of the rulers. This, as has been seen, was precisely why Madison believed it was ultimately impossible to exclude from political participation a landless majority that possessed the balance of the country's "numerical & physical force."[91] But while Hume deployed this insight to explain why monarchs could rule the masses, Madison invoked it to explain why, in America, they could not. Madison joined his contemporaries in citing the republican "genius" of the people. To contemporary ears, the term sounds like normative praise. In its time, it more closely resembled "genus." To refer to the "republican genius" of the people was to say this was who they were, the type according to which they should be categorized.[92] Madison thus observed that the "genius" of the American people was opposed to monarchy and aristocracy.[93] Elaborate titles for the president and vice president, similarly, could not be reconciled with "the genius of the people."[94] Hume's argument came down to the fundamental fact that all government is more or less majoritarian: it is obeyed if its people believe it is legitimate. In America, Madison wrote, such would only be the case if the government was literally majoritarian.

Throughout his writings, with perhaps more consistency than any other belief, Madison assumed that majorities would exercise power regardless of what strictures were recorded on parchment. Although Federalist 10 has repeatedly been interpreted as the keystone of Madison's plan to corral the masses via constitutional aristocracy, the essay's conclusion was actually—and explicitly—that majorities inevitably ruled and that no institutional mechanism could stop them. The republic had to be extended for precisely this reason. Madison had previewed this observation in Philadelphia: "In a republican government, the majority, if united, have always an opportunity [to abuse minorities]. The *only* remedy, is to enlarge the sphere."[95] The impotence of parchment barriers was also among the reasons that Madison believed Calhoun's doctrines of nullification and concurrent majorities to be impractical. Aggrieved states had no practical recourse except to majority opinion. This belief was evident in Madison's position on the Missouri Compromise. Slaveholding states argued that the compromise was unconstitutional because a state could not be admitted to the union on terms that restricted rights other states enjoyed. Madison was sympathetic to the constitutional reasoning, but observe that the following commentary on the issue says appealing to the Constitution "is"—not "should be," but empirically "is"—the equivalent of an appeal to the majority. There was, Madison wrote, no alternative: "But what is to controul Congress when backed & even pushed on by a majority of their Constituents, as was the case in the late contest relative to Missouri . . . ? *Nothing within the pale of the Constitution* but sound arguments & conciliatory expostulations addressed both to Congress & to their Constituents."[96]

The basis of Madison's belief that power was drawn naturally to the "legislative vortex" was that Congress would be the most majoritarian branch and that majority opinion was the society's most powerful force. Madison therefore worried in Philadelphia that the House's power would overwhelm the Senate's even if their authority was equal on paper and even if senators' terms were extended to seven years.[97] He opposed a proposal to give the executive an absolute veto because it would be pointless to do so. Even the king of Great Britain could not resist a unanimous Parliament, and neither could a president, no matter how powerful, resist a determined Congress.[98] Federalist 48 likewise denied that "a mere demarkation on parchment" could guarantee that each branch of government would have its own will.[99]

A similar belief animated Madison's concern about bills of rights and other constitutional guarantees of liberty, as Chapter 4 will discuss. Most analyses of Madison's opposition have emphasized the arguments Hamilton articulated in Federalist 84, which said that a Bill of Rights was unnecessary because Congress was already limited to the enumerated powers and that a Bill of Rights would actually be dangerous because it would imply authority beyond the strict limits of Article One, Section Eight. Madison more or less shared Hamilton's view, but his assumption that majority rule was inevitable also provoked a unique set of concerns. Such protections would, he argued, be least useful when most necessary—that is, at moments of public passion and uproar—the assumption being that majorities would merely circumvent or ignore them. This, in turn, would create a precedent for violation that would weaken such protections in future situations, triggering a downward cycle.[100] Madison adduced this argument on several occasions. He said in Federalist 41 that it would have been pointless for the Constitution to forbid maintaining troops in peacetime because the people would insist on raising armies if they felt a need to do so: "It is in vain to oppose constitutional barriers to the impulse of self-preservation. It is worse than in vain: because it plants in the constitution itself necessary usurpations of power, every precedent of which is a germ of unnecessary and multiplied repetitions."[101] Madison's comments on Jefferson's draft constitution for Virginia questioned whether it should guarantee the right of habeas corpus to cases of rebellion. "If there be emergences which call for such a suspension, it can have no effect to prohibit it, because the prohibition will assuredly give way to the impulse of the moment."[102] Commenting on a draft constitution for Kentucky, he wrote: "Temporary deviations from fundamental principles are always more or less dangerous. . . . The first precedent too familiarizes the people to the irregularity, lessens their veneration for those fundamental principles, & makes them a more easy prey to Ambition & self Interest."[103]

This need for veneration opens a crucial insight into Madison's posture toward majorities. The contemporary observer, accustomed to Americans' long-standing deference to the courts, may have difficulty imagining a majority simply ignoring barriers to its rule. From today's vantage point, Madison's empirical assumptions seem simply wrong: Americans not only abide but revere constitutional forms, even those that seem to remove decisions further from majority will. But to understand Madison's thought accurately, it is important to examine it from the perspective of his political reality rather than ours.

In Madison's context, majorities could override limitations on their rule in at least three ways. First, Madison had indeed seen factious majorities run roughshod, and without pretense of legality, over state constitutions. Second, and more commonly, majorities employed technicalities and turns of legal phrase to make their abuses seem to abide by constitutional forms. This was the reason Madison insisted that a national veto over state laws reach "all cases *whatsoever.*" States—which Madison believed to be prone to the immediate rule of factious majorities—would exploit any available loophole or technicality, thus trampling constitutional limits while claiming to respect them.

But it is the third means of overcoming constitutional limits on majority rule that is most important for understanding Madison's views on the subject. If majorities believed that limits on their rule were excessive, they would change or abandon the underlying governing agreement—that is, the Constitution—that imposed them. It is true, as critics of Madison have long noted, that the amendment procedure within the Constitution requires a supermajority in order to propose a change.[104] Still, as Martin Diamond has noted, the ratification procedure for amendments requires only a simple majority within each state, thus assuring that an overall majority is nationally distributed. Given Madison's belief that size alone would not create divides between large and small states, it is reasonable to assume he did not foresee a situation in which such splits would persistently enable states with small populations to thwart the will of a national majority comprised mostly of residents of large states.

More important, it could never have been far from Madison's mind that the Constitution itself—and every governing procedure it contained, including those that impeded the immediate expression of popular will—was ratified by simple majorities in the states. If simple majorities could completely replace the Articles of Confederation despite its requirement of unanimity for any change, presumably they could do the same with the Constitution despite its requirement of supermajorities for amendments. In this sense, the Constitution's authority depended at any given moment on the sufferance of simple and often sparse majorities. Indeed, the margins for ratification in many states for which precise records exist were narrow, especially in the more populous states where Madison believed the numerical force of the nation to lie. Massachusetts, for example, ratified by a margin of 187–168, New York by 30–27, and Virginia by 89–78.[105] The importance of these margins is underscored by Madison's belief that the physical survival of the nation—that is, its ability to withstand foreign attack—required the cohesion of all 13 states. Add to this Madison's intimate knowledge that no majority vote had been necessary to call the Philadelphia Convention in the first place, and he must have recognized that the entire edifice rested on the fragile foundation of a simple majority.

The present-day observer, again, will have difficulty imagining a serious statesman fearing a wholesale revision of the Constitution. Madison himself looked forward to an era in which popular reverence for the Constitution would render fundamental alterations to governing procedures unlikely. But even at this point, veneration of the Constitution would only render a simple majority less likely to act on its always looming prerogative to change the form of government. More important, Madison's writings on this topic always conveyed his concern that such a time had not been reached, a point he made most clearly in Federalist 49's critique of Jefferson's proposal to empower any two branches of government to call a constitutional convention: Such a proposal would "deprive the government of that veneration which time bestows on every thing, and without which perhaps the wisest and freest governments would not possess the requisite stability."[106] Time alone could create the constitutional inertia that would make wholesale changes unlikely. At that point, the veneration would still be an expression of opinion and hence of majority will. During the time that Madison wrote, however, it was completely plausible to imagine the country turning back if the majority perceived the Constitution as excessively curtailing its rule.[107] Madison himself had led an effort to do precisely that when the Articles proved unworkable.

The import of these observations, again, is that even to the extent constitutional mechanisms required supermajorities to prevail, the Constitution itself—and hence those mechanisms—rested on the ongoing sufferance of simple majorities. Constitutionalism was, in this sense, a form of self-restraint—but, crucially, a voluntary one that the people could relinquish. In a 1789 congressional debate, Madison characterized constitutionalism as follows: "My idea of the sovereignty of the people is, that the people can change the constitution if they please, but while the constitution exists, they must conform themselves to its dictates."[108] Parchment could not restrain majorities against their will because majorities always retained the power to rewrite it. The success of any aristocratic plot depended on the consent of the very masses the Founders are accused of disenfranchising.

Operating always on these empirical assumptions, Madison never entertained the idea of a constitutional order based on any principle other than majority rule. Even were he inclined to endorse the rule of privileged minorities, the empirical limitations on his thought forbade such an idea.

If, then, Madison believed America would countenance no political regime other than majority rule, what is to be made of a linchpin assumption of his defenders—that Madison sought to curb majority rule only because he was afraid abuses of it would lead to homegrown monarchy? Commentators have broadly understood him to harbor such fears, and with good reason. Douglass Adair related a dramatic narrative of Madison conducting a fevered preconvention search for a theoretical solution to the problem of faction lest the champions of "mixed government" impose order through monarchy.[109] Marvin Meyers portrays Madison as concerned during the opposition period of the 1790s about "a cynical clique of insiders, wielding the power of purse and sword [and] rapidly establishing an oppressive oligarchy on the ruins of the Republic, and even squinting toward monarchy."[110]

Although Madison's writings provide support for this interpretation, subsequent commentators have tended to overstate the extent to which even a constitutional monarchy was considered a realistic option, at least during the preconstitutional period. Were Adair's account true, and had Madison therefore set out for Philadelphia carrying the "glad news" that he had rescued republicanism from monarchy, one might expect this breakthrough to have merited at least a passing mention, if not a dramatic moment at the opening of the convention.[111] Instead, the delegates simply settled into a workmanlike hashing out of the details of a system that all appear to have assumed, whatever their other disagreements, would be republican. Virginia governor Edmund Randolph "opened the main business" of the convention on May 29 by offering the Virginia Plan, and the several days of debate that commenced concerning legislative apportionment provide no reason to believe the delegates were conscious of serious proposals for monarchy or that they contemplated any course other than popular government. When the delegates took up the question of the executive, no proposal for a monarch was heard. Delaware's John Dickenson spoke approvingly of the British system but quickly noted that "a limited Monarchy however was out of the question."[112] It was June 18, by which time the republican die of the convention was already firmly cast, before Alexander Hamilton rose to offer the closest to a monarchical alternative that the delegates heard: a president and Senate with life tenure, subject to good behavior. But far from monarchy being considered a serious alternative, Hamilton apparently understood the notion to be sufficiently outside the mainstream that it was necessary for him to ask "Gentlemen of different opinions [to] bear with him in this,"[113] and the morning after Hamilton's speech, the delegates returned to their previous business as though he had never spoken.

Nevertheless, Madison did harbor fears about despotism, and

in order to establish the idea that he did not consider alternatives to majority rule empirically plausible, they must be confronted directly. The critical fact to observe is that Madison's critics accuse him of seeking to impose an aristocratic or otherwise antimajoritarian regime through the Constitution—that is, peacefully. But when he raised concerns about the American republic terminating in monarchy, they always pertained to the possibility of despotism being imposed by force from either within or outside of the country. The fear was never that the majority would choose monarchy of its own accord.

Madison had, in fact, repeatedly acknowledged that a minority could at least temporarily rule a majority by force.[114] When Anti-Federalists said the Constitution would allow the national government to crush even a democratic rebellion within a state, Madison replied that the power to guarantee each state a republican form of government was necessary for the opposite reason: that an armed junta could use force to impose its will on a popular majority. To the extent Madison feared despotism would arise in the United States, he feared it would arise through similar means.

The chief threat Madison perceived in the preconstitutional period was that monarchy would arrive from overseas. Britain, perceiving the fragile young country as weak, might be tempted to retake the colonies. Similarly, the British crown might piece off individual states through side deals, thereby destroying the solidarity Madison believed necessary to maintaining independence in a dangerous world. Autocrats might arise from within the country too—precisely the reason, he had entreated his colleagues in the Articles Congresses, it was necessary to placate the unpaid revolutionary soldiers who were threatening mutiny. He may have had either scenario in mind when he drafted his address to the states warning of dire consequences if they did not comply with requisitions. We have already encountered the following passage: "The great cause which we have engaged to vindicate, will be dishonored & betrayed; the last & fairest experiment in favor of the rights of human nature will be turned against them; and their patrons & friends exposed to be insulted & silenced by the votaries of Tyranny and Usurpation."[115]

Madison did not say that Americans would choose despotism. Instead, here as elsewhere, he was concerned about the outward image the country projected both because a perception of weakness or chaos might have tempted adversaries and because it might have discouraged other republican movements. Moreover, note that if the American republic collapsed, its friends would have to be "silenced" via "Tyranny and Usurpation"—that is, by force. In neither case did Madison contemplate a majority of the American people throwing themselves into the arms of a tyrant.

A letter Madison posted to Edmund Pendleton in February 1787—the period when Adair places the former in frantic study to avert monarchy—has provided further fodder for the perception that Madison feared a homegrown monarchy chosen in response to chaos: "The late turbulent scenes in Massts. & infamous ones in Rhode Island, have done inexpressible injury to the republican character in that part of the U. States; and a propensity towards Monarchy is said to have been produced by it in some leading minds. The bulk of the people will probably prefer the lesser evil of a partition of the Union into three more practicable and energetic Governments."[116] The following day, Madison conveyed a similar sentiment to Edmund Randolph: "Many individuals of weight particularly in the Eastern district are suspected of leaning towards Monarchy. Other individuals predict a partition of the States into two or more Confederacies. It is pretty certain that if some radical amendment of the single one can not be devised and introduced that one or other of these revolutions, *the latter no doubt*, will take place."[117]

In both cases, Madison explicitly stated that monarchical opinion was festering only among elites and that the majority of the people preferred a partition. There is no indication, in other words, of monarchy voluntarily chosen. The concern Madison evinced here—and during the nullification controversies of the 1820s and 1830s—was that a partitioned union would be unable to defend itself from foreign threats. The only scenarios these letters provide for despotism are its imposition either by domestic elites or foreign tyrants—in either case against the public will.

Madison came closest to predicting homegrown despotism during the administration of John Adams, whom the former accused of harboring monarchical ambitions. Yet even here, what Madison feared was a regime developing interests separate from those of the people and thereby imposing its will by antirepublican means.[118] Madison first began to articulate these concerns when Adams, as vice president, proposed elaborate costumes and titles for high executive officers. Yet Madison also told Jefferson he did not fear titles themselves because they, like parchment, could not confer power against the will of the people.[119] What he did come to fear was that Adams and his ilk would impose monarchy. Madison's opposition essay "A Candid State of Parties" cast his opponents as "more partial to the opulent than to the other classes of society; and having debauched themselves into a persuasion that mankind are incapable of governing themselves, it follows with them, of course, that government can be carried on only by the pageantry of rank, the influence of money and emoluments, and *the terror of military force.*"[120] Whether Madison portrayed Adams and other Federalists fairly is questionable at best, but it is clear that in no case did Madison contemplate the possibility that the American people would choose any system of government other than majority rule.

The foregoing analysis has endeavored to establish two points. First, Madison was normatively committed to majority rule. Second, he never considered another system plausible. The distinction between these points is subtle but, for the analysis that follows, crucial. As has been seen, it is the second point that more persuasively refutes critics who cast Madison as an aristocrat, for on his reasoning, they charge him with aspiring to absurdity. Detached from his empirical assumptions, Madison's normative commitment to majority rule cannot conclusively rescue him from the charge of aristocratism. Because Madison also expressed serious concerns about majority rule in certain circumstances, the most that could be said would be that he favored popular government more often than he opposed it. Finally, and most important, once Madison's critiques of majority rule are examined in the context of his belief that majority rule was inevitable in a republic as a matter of empirical fact, it becomes clear that he was not criticizing majority rule per se, but rather specific majorities under specific circumstances.

We are now in a position to consider the question of which majorities, and which circumstances, these were.

Chapter Two

Time and Tranquility

In 1798, Madison wrote brief notes for a toast to be delivered at a Fourth of July dinner celebrating the twenty-second anniversary of the young nation's independence. The precise context of the toast is unknown, but its contents are instructive: "To the P[resident] & V[ice] P[resident] may the former never feel the passions of J.A. [John Adams] nor the latter be forsaken by the philosophy of T.J. [Thomas Jefferson]."[1] Nearly every written comment Madison ever made about Adams included a specific denunciation of what he took to be the latter's impulsive temperament. As early as February 1783, Madison reported that "Congress yesterday received from Mr. Adams [then an American envoy] several letters dated September not remarkable for any thing unless it be a display of his vanity, his prejudice against the French Court & his venom against Doctr. Franklin."[2] Similarly, during Adams's presidency, Madison compared him unfavorably to Washington: "The one cold considerate & cautious, the other headlong & kindled into flame by every spark that lights on his passions."[3] Even eulogizing Adams, Madison recalled the former president's proclivity to become carried away: "That he had a mind rich in ideas of his own, as well as its learned store; with an ardent love of Country, and the merit of being a colossal champion of its Independence, must be allowed by those most offended by the alloy in his Republicanism, and the fervors and flights originating in his moral temperament."[4] Whether he described Adams fairly is open to dispute, but the contrast Madison drew was clearly a central dichotomy in his attitude toward popular majorities as well as political figures: those governed by reason and those governed by passion.

Madison did not define these terms precisely, but some suppositions of his meaning may be derived by the context in which he used them. In the passages that follow, Madison used reason in a sense akin to what Aristotle calls "rational calculation": the ability to use the reasoning part of the mind to choose correctly among available alternatives.[5] For Madison, reason carried an instrumental connotation in that it was the faculty one used to identify the course of action likeliest to achieve a given end. Passion, by contrast, was an emotional influence that obscured or distorted reason. It referred not merely to ardent flights of emotion or temper, but also more broadly to irrational appetites. Greed, for example, was a passion insofar as instant gratification was not in one's long-term interest.

Understood in these terms, Madison believed majorities or their leaders should prevail when cold, considerate, and cautious; those heated by passion should be stalled. Federalist 37 thus laments the "misfortune, inseparable from human affairs, that public measures are rarely investigated with that spirit of moderation, which is essential to a just estimate of their real tendency to advance, or obstruct, the public good."[6] This was why Madison warned Jefferson that an immediate convention to consider amendments to the new Constitution would be unwise: "At present the public mind is neither sufficiently cool nor sufficiently informed for so delicate an operation."[7] Not long after, he wrote to Benjamin Rush:

> If we are to take for the criterion of truth the majority of suffrages, they ought to be gathered from those philosophical and patriotic citizens who cultivate their reason, apart from the scenes which distract its operations, and expose it to the influence of the passions. The advantage enjoyed by public bodies in the light struck out by the collision of arguments, is but too often overbalanced by the heat proceeding from the same source.[8]

This dichotomy between reason and passion operates across Madison's democratic theory from his first public writings in the 1780s to his death over half a century later. He hardly ever criticized a potential or actual majority as errant or unjust without also diagnosing it as being motivated by passion rather than reason. His pre–Constitutional Convention essay "Vices of the Political System of the United States" located the danger of majority abuse in those united by "an apparent interest or common passion."[9] Majorities were "liable to err," he said in Philadelphia, "from fickleness and passion."[10] Similarly, numerous bodies were "actuated more or less by passion."[11]

So closely interwoven were passion and abuse that Madison linked them almost causally in his definition of faction in Federalist 10: a group "united and actuated by some common impulse of passion, or of interest, adverse to the rights of other citizens, or to the permanent and aggregate interests of the community."[12] Federalist 49 worries that Jefferson's proposal for occasional appeals to the people to correct abuses of the Constitution poses the danger "of disturbing the public tranquillity, by interesting too strongly the public passions."[13] The House, Madison predicted to Pendleton, would be susceptible to "capriciousness," a quality that, significantly, Federalist 57 associated with "wickedness."[14] "Passion," Madison said during the convention, was also associated with "fickleness."[15] Extensive assemblies were inherently prone to passion because normal psychological controls collapsed in large groups. "In all very numerous assemblies, of whatever characters composed," he warned in a famous passage of Federalist 55, "passion never fails to wrest the sceptre from reason. Had every Athenian citizen been a Socrates, every Athenian assembly would still have been a mob."[16]

Madison continued to embrace this dichotomy in the 1790s, even as his priority shifted toward mobilizing majorities as a control on the regime. In a 1790 congressional debate, Madison denied that a proposal of his had been "dictated by passion," insisting that "he considered it as a cool, as well as a proper measure, and believed, that the more coolly it was examined, the more proper it would appear."[17] During another debate, he criticized his opponents for making emotional appeals: "Warmth and passion should be excluded from a discussion of a subject, which ought to depend on the cool dictates of reason for its decision."[18] An essay for the party press warned against consolidation of power in the executive because "uncontrouled power, ever has been, and ever will be administered by the passions more than by reason."[19]

As tensions with Britain swirled early in Madison's presidential term, he noted that republics considered national "degradation" to be the only fate worse than war, but that dispassion might avert the need to choose: "To avoid, if it be possible amidst the unbridled passions which convulse other nations, both of these alternatives, is our true wisdom, as well as our solemn duty."[20] When war erupted, Madison wrote that eastern states opposed to the conflict would mistake their true economic interest if they left the Union. Consequently, "I have never allowed myself to believe that the Union was in danger, or that a dissolution of it could be desired, unless by a few individuals, if such there be, in desperate situations or of unbridled passions."[21]

The passions were understood in direct contrast to reason, the "cool" faculty with which majorities or leaders could correctly identify their interests and the courses of action likeliest to attain them. Federalist 41 expresses confidence that while Anti-Federalists nitpicked the proposed Constitution, "cool and candid" people would focus on the overall improvement it represented rather than its smaller imperfections.[22] One of his *National Gazette* essays similarly predicted that a "temperate observer" would recognize that the republican majority of Americans would eventually rise up against what Madison believed to be the monarchical ambitions of the Adams regime.[23]

Reason, in turn, was associated with two interrelated qualities: an openness of mind that considered facts and opposing ideas rather than reaching conclusions in advance, and impartiality, according to which decisions would be made on the basis of objective facts and principles rather than being bent to one's interest or preconceptions. Madison's initial concerns about political parties and factions centered in large measure on his belief that they lacked these reasoning qualities. The first time he expressed concern about factions pertained to the 1780 congressional attempt to recall Benjamin Franklin as minister to France. The faction associated with Virginia's Lee dynasty was, Madison believed, making decisions on the basis of personal animus rather than reason. Significantly, this first use of the term "faction" applied to a situation in which Madison believed the interests of the whole nation, not the rights of a minority, were at risk. Hence Madison wrote that he felt "great anxiety lest the flame of faction" overtake Congress.[24] In Federalist 49, Madison argued that Jefferson's occasional appeals "would inevitably be connected with the spirit of preexisting parties, or of parties springing out of the question itself." The defining feature of these parties was their adherents' devotion to charismatic individuals who would have made their decisions in advance: "The *passions*, therefore, not the *reason*, of the public, would sit in judgment. But it is the reason of the public alone, that ought to control and regulate the government. The passions ought to be controled [*sic*] and regulated by the government."[25] After ratification, Madison argued against calling an immediate second convention to consider a bill of rights because it would "be the offspring of party & passion, and will probably for that reason alone be the parent of error and public injury."[26]

The reason–passion dichotomy also provides another thread of consistency during Madison's transition from the nationalism of the 1780s to the party system of the 1790s. He was always the most concerned about the institutions or entities he perceived as most under the sway of passion. During the late 1790s, the same period during which Madison shifted his concern about abuses from popular majorities to leaders within the regime, he also began describing the latter, especially Adams, as impassioned. Signs of this concern preceded the Adams administration, most clearly in Madison's claim that extensive assemblies were inherently prone to passion because normal psychological controls collapsed in large groups. "In all very numerous assemblies, of whatever characters composed," he warned in a famous passage of Federalist 55, "passion never fails to wrest the sceptre from reason. Had every Athenian citizen been a Socrates, every Athenian assembly would still have been a mob."[27] Moral or religious motives "lose their efficacy in proportion to the number combined together."[28] Character could only be counted upon as a restraint in groups "so small, that a sensible degree of the praise and blame of public measures may be the portion of each individual."[29]

By 1798, Madison feared this concern had been realized. It was impossible to make predictions about the outcomes of legislative battles, he told Jefferson, because "there [was] too much passion it seems in our Councils."[30] He rued Adams's successful use of newspapers "in kindling a flame among the people, and of the flame in extending taxes[,] armies & prerogatives," adding he hoped these "solemn lessons [would] have their proper effect when the infatuation of the moment is over."[31]

Unreason also manifested itself in majorities or leaders with a personal interest in a given question.[32] The only majorities Federalist 10 spoke of inhibiting were those united by a "co-existent passion or interest." When factions reigned, the essay observed, disputes were settled by "the superior force of an interested and overbearing majority," a manner of resolution Madison counterposed to "*rules* of justice," that is, objective standards accessible by reason, and minority rights.[33] Notice, in the well-known phrase of Federalist 10, the explanation for why a man cannot judge his own cause: "No man is allowed to be a judge in his own cause, because his interest would certainly bias his *judgment*."[34] Latent in this claim is an assumption of moral objectivity. Most questions have a "right answer" discoverable by reason so long as it is not distorted by interest. In this sense, reason corresponded with "impartiality," a standard evoking the moral philosophy of Adam Smith, for whom the criterion of moral conduct was the hypothetical judgment of an "impartial spectator."[35]

One recognizable mark of interested or impassioned majorities and leaders was that they formed and sought to act quickly, a fact important for understanding Madison's attempt to control them through the use of time. Madison, as we have seen, portrayed passion through metaphors that suggested rapid and uncontrolled spread, including those of fires, fevers, pestilence, and contagions. For example, factious leaders would attempt to "kindle a flame," but under the right circumstances, that flame would not "spread a general conflagration."[36] Among the defects of ancient and modern republics were "popular assemblages, so quickly formed, so susceptible of contagious passions, so exposed to the misguidance of eloquent & ambitious leaders; and so apt to be tempted by the facility of forming interested majorities, into measures unjust and oppressive to the minor parties."[37] The demand for paper money was always a popular "rage."[38]

Madison often linked "passion" with "precipitancy,"[39] a term whose connotation as "rushed" is evident from his use of it elsewhere as the opposite of "procrastinate."[40] During a 1782 legislative battle in Virginia, for instance, he hoped the Senate would have the "perseverance" to act as "a check to the *precipitate* acts of a single Legislature."[41] Virginia's assembly passed "*sudden* resolutions" so imprudent that members of that body would often "repent" and lobby the state Senate to block them.[42] Majorities might "under *sudden* impulses be tempted to commit injustice on the minority."[43] As this memorandum indicates, acts based on "interest and passion" were frequently the result of "impulses," a term that also suggests rapid formation and execution before the intellect can be consulted.[44] A senate was thus needed to counteract "the propensity of all single and numerous assemblies, to yield to the *impulse* of *sudden* and violent passions."[45] One reason republics were more volatile in small than in large territories was the danger in the former of "easy combinations under the *impulse* of misinformed or corrupt passions."[46]

Madison's concern with impulsivity is evident in his retirement as well. Writing to his old adversary John Adams in 1817, Madison noted with satisfaction that all the American states "placed the powers of Government in different depositories, as a means of controlling the *impulse* and sympathy [that is, spread] of the passions, and affording to reason better opportunities of asserting its prerogatives."[47] That exchange was prompted by Condorcet's critique of bicameralism. Madison sounded a similar note in warning the British reformer John Cartwright against the latter's proposal for a one-house legislature: "The infirmities most besetting Popular Governments, even in the Representative Form, are found to be defective laws which do mischief before they can be mended, and laws passed under transient impulses, of which time & reflection call for a change."[48] Also in retirement, Madison speculated that the United States probably would be subject to partisan fervor at some point: "The most, perhaps, that can be counted on, & that will be sufficient, is, that the occasions for party contests in such a Country & Gov't as ours, will be either so slight or so *transient,* as not to threaten any *permanent* or dangerous consequences to the character & prosperity of the Republic."[49] Therein, as will now be seen, lay Madison's solution to the problem of impulsive politics: time. It was, in the phrase of Montaigne that the young Madison recorded in his commonplace book, "the sovereign physician of our passions."

Temporal Republicanism

The fact that Madison endorsed bicameralism as one outlet for "transient impulses" suggests that the diversity of interests he discussed in Federalist 10 did not exhaust the entirety of his concern about abusive majorities.[50] Diversity reduced the likelihood that factious majorities would form, but as Madison acknowledged in Federalist 63, "this advantage ought not to be considered as superseding the use of auxiliary precautions."[51] To the extent that impassioned majorities formed, then, we seem to encounter a puzzle that may be summarized as follows:

Madison was concerned about impulsive or impassioned majorities.

Madison believed persistent majorities always prevailed, regardless of institutional attempts to restrain them.

Madison was confident impulsive or impassioned majorities
would not prevail in the United States.[52]

This formulation helps to reveal the latent premise that reconciled these views: by their very nature, impassioned majorities were
not persistent. It is true that the "fit characters" of Federalist 10
played an important role in resisting popular abuses, a fact that such
commentators as Willmoore Kendall, George W. Carey, and Isaac
Kramnick have properly emphasized.[53] But even more than others at
the Philadelphia Convention, Madison also believed these leaders
should be directly dependent on the public, so it seems difficult to
assume they were to bear the primary burden of disciplining the
public's passions. Unless some other mechanism was presumed, the
best for which Madison could hope was that impulsive majorities
would postpone their abuses until the next election, at which time
they would prevail. On this model, relief from majority abuse would
only be temporary. Madison in fact presumed the opposite: that
abuses would be temporary and relief would be sustained.

He must have assumed, then, that public passions themselves
would dissipate of their own accord if given time to do so. Although
there may have been a role for moral tutelage in disciplining the passions, Madison was largely silent on this point. His premise was not
that elected leaders would resist public passions until they were defeated at the polls; it was that passions would burn out before leaders
stood for reelection.[54] This was the import of Montaigne's observation that time achieved its ends by supplying the mind with new di-
versions. Time itself was the leavening agent.

Commentators have often scoured Madison's thought for a
more active mechanism for controlling the passions. Martin Diamond, for example, understands Madison to have favored the proliferation of commercial interests as a comparatively safe outlet for
the public's energies.[55] Colleen Sheehan stresses Madison's discussion of civic virtue in his opposition writings of the 1790s.[56] Gary
Rosen's thoughtful treatment of Madison's attempt to enlarge the
public's conception of interest concludes that he was able to do so
only because the pursuit of individual interest added up, without
conscious intent, to a coherent whole.[57] Although temporal republicanism is compatible with these interpretations, it also suggests that
time diminished the need for more active mechanisms. Because individuals acted against the public interest only under the influence

of passion, delay could carry a substantial part of the weight in the Madisonian system, a fact evident in his observation that "opinions whose only root is in the passions must wither as the subsiding of these withdraws the necessary pabulum."[58]

He frequently described passion or impulsiveness in a manner that suggested these qualities were inherently fleeting. Federalist 10's classification of factions underscores the point. As Douglass Adair has noted, Madison's taxonomy appears to be compatible with David Hume's analysis in the latter's essay "Of Parties in General."[59] Hume, for instance, divided parties into those that were "real" and "personal." Real parties were in turn subdivided into those based on interest, principle, or affection. Madison, in a parallel analysis, distinguished between factions based on "a zeal for different opinions concerning religion, concerning government, and many other points" (Hume's parties of principle); those based on "an attachment to different leaders" (Hume's personal parties); and those based on "the various and unequal distribution of property" (Hume's parties of interest).

Adair notes that Madison "greatly expanded the quick sketch of the faction from 'interest' buried in the middle of the philosopher's analysis."[60] But Madison did more than this; he accepted Hume's categories but completely reversed the Scottish philosopher's analysis of them. Hume described parties based on interest—Madison's economic factions—as "the most reasonable, and the most excusable." By contrast, those based on "*principle*, especially abstract speculative principle" were irrational and dangerous. The human propensity to convince others to conform to such principles was "the origin of all religious wars and divisions."

Madison, by contrast, located his primary concern in factions based on property. The particular route by which he reached this conclusion is instructive. Factions based on religion or personal attachment had "divided mankind into parties, inflamed them with mutual animosity, and rendered them much more disposed to vex and oppress each other, than to co-operate for their common good." Indeed, Madison, here echoing Hume, observed that "where no substantial occasion presents itself, the most frivolous and fanciful distinctions have been sufficient to kindle their unfriendly passions, and excite their most violent conflicts." Yet despite this vivid description, Madison did not join Hume in placing emphasis on this kind of faction. The reason was that such factions—again, note the metaphor—

"kindle[d] [mankind's] unfriendly passions." These were naturally fleeting and hence less dangerous. The reason special consideration had to be given to factions based on property was that they were both "common" and, crucially, "durable." That is, by their nature, the passions on which religious or personal disputes were based were transient. But property was not, to use Hume's epithet, "abstract"; hence, disputes based on it did not vanish as quickly.[61]

Similarly, in his retirement, Madison wrote to the English constitutional reformer John Cartwright that the impulses to which bicameralism gave vent were transient. Party conflicts in the United States, he told Monroe, would be "transient" and hence would not cause "permanent" damage.[62] Amid the tariff dispute of 1828, he hoped Southern agitation for disunion would be "as transient as [it was] intemperate."[63]

In turn, because impulses were transient, time was healing. Madison, as has been seen, thus resisted efforts to call a postratification constitutional convention to consider a bill of rights, arguing that even a brief delay would induce a calmer and therefore more reasoned atmosphere: "An early Convention is in every view to be dreaded in the present temper of America. A very short period of delay would produce the double advantage of diminishing the heat and increasing the light of all parties."[64] The key to preventing impulsive politics, then, was to delay the point of decision long enough for passions to evaporate. Conversely, the foremost indicator of whether a majority was ripe to prevail was the length of time it had cohered.

This mechanism operates throughout Madison's thought, most clearly in his treatment of the Senate, which was necessary "to protect the people agst. the *transient* impressions into which they themselves might be led."[65] A senate's use, he said in Philadelphia, was "to consist in its proceeding with more coolness, with more system, & with more wisdom, than the popular branch."[66] In the *Federalist* essays concerning the Senate, the most important reason that body would serve a cooling function was the longer terms of its members, which allowed them to resist public passions on the assumption they would dissipate before senators faced reappointment or, in contemporary terms, reelection. Federalist 62 said a body whose purpose was to resist "the impulse of sudden and violent passions" should "possess great firmness, and consequently ought to hold its authority by a tenure of considerable duration."[67] Although Madison unquestionably believed the Senate would be populated with even fitter characters than the House, this passage attributes their "firmness" not to superior character but rather to the longer duration of their terms. This assumption might be explicable in two ways. Longer tenures might mean senators would only want to serve a single term and that they would therefore be unburdened of any concern for public opinion. But this was clearly not Madison's view. The Virginia Plan specified that senators were to be eligible for reelection,[68] and while Madison believed the Senate would help to ripen public opinion, he nevertheless regarded the public's considered views to be "the real sovereign in any free [government]."[69] The second possibility is that senators could firmly resist public impulses in the moment while reasonably anticipating those passions would dissipate before they next faced reelection or reappointment. This latter explanation seems to be what Madison had in mind, which helps to explain his persistent interest in the length of senatorial terms. Commenting, for example, on Jefferson's draft of a constitution for Virginia, Madison argued that "the term of two years [for senators] is too short. Six years are not more than sufficient. A Senate is to withstand the occasional impetuosities of the more numerous branch."[70] At the convention, Madison went as far as saying he would not object to a term of nine years.[71] Federalist 63, an entire paper devoted to the length of senatorial terms, goes on to make the temporal function of that body explicit. The framework of this argument has already been discussed above:

> As the cool and deliberate sense of the community ought, in all governments, and actually will, in all free governments, ultimately prevail over the views of its rulers: so there are particular moments in public affairs, when the people, stimulated by some irregular passion, or some illicit advantage, or misled by the artful misrepresentations of interested men, may call for measures which they themselves will afterwards be the most ready to lament and condemn.

Now, the importance of Madison's explanation of precisely how the Senate would serve that function may be seen. It would be a speed bump, so to speak, rather than a roadblock: "In these critical moments, how salutary will be the interference of some temperate and respectable body of citizens, in order to check the misguided career, and to *suspend* the blow mediated by the people against themselves, *until* reason, justice, and truth, can *regain* their authority over the public mind?"[72]

The chronology Madison implies is crucial for understanding why critics are mistaken when they portray the Senate as an aristocratic body whose purpose was to foil public opinion. The passage just quoted suggests that the people ordinarily act on the basis of reason, justice, and truth. It is only at "particular moments" that either "passion" or "advantage" clouds their reasoning. By a temporary suspension of these impulses, reason, justice, and truth regain their authority. Madison's latent assumption about the calming effect of time was herein made explicit, and again, it was apparently time itself—not what happened in the interim, which Madison did not specify—that served this function. There was no indication of moral tutelage by leaders; on the contrary, the tacit premise was that public opinion was the primary force to which the Senate reacted. Nothing would have occurred except the passage of time, and this alone, Madison suggested, was sufficient to defuse the passions.[73]

Of course, by this analysis, the Senate would still be subject to convulsions of passion every six years at the moment of reelection. That was, in fact, how the Maryland senate operated, a fact that elicited Madison's anxiety when the state debated the issuance of paper money:

> The Senate of Maryd. has hitherto been a bar to paper in that State. The clamor for it is now universal, and as the periodical election of the Senate happens at this crisis, and the whole body is unluckily by their constitution to be chosen at once, it is probable that a paper emission will be the result. If in spite of the zeal exerted agst. the old Senate a majority of them should be reelected, it will require all their firmness to withstand the popular torrent.[74]

During the ratification process, Madison cited this mechanism as one reason that adoption of the Constitution would make it less likely that rights to navigation of the Mississippi would be bargained away to Spain. Six years were necessary to change the entire membership of the entire Senate, whereas the Articles Congress "undergoes a revolution once in three years."[75] Because, as will be seen below, Madison regarded a sacrifice of the Mississippi to be an impassioned idea motivated by the eastern states' short-term greed, the

Scattered 6 yr terms

longer period made it less likely that the majority in favor of such an action would persist long enough to prevail. The importance of staggered terms in this context was that an impassioned majority would have not simply to cohere for six years—a scenario in which it could presumably be allowed to smolder for most of that time and be inflamed only at the time of elections or appointments; it would also have to remain uniformly passionate because changing the membership of the entire Senate would require it to prevail in three successive political cycles.[76]

Generally, then, Madison's constitutional theory required majorities to cohere for long enough intervals to ensure they were guided by reason rather than passion. He did not specify the length of this interval, but it was generally proportional to the gravity of the topic under consideration. A clear majority favoring a comparatively routine matter of policy could prevail quickly, for example, while a close contest involving fundamental constitutional questions required a longer period. The idea was to act as a metronome setting a tempo appropriate to a given circumstance. Sometimes, as in the case of basic constitutional change, the tempo was to be slow and leisurely. At other times, when reasonable decisions had been reached and only needed execution, allegro was appropriate. This metronome, in turn, applied to the process of deliberation, not decision. As Madison's frustration with the Articles period showed, some decisions needed to be executed quickly once a deliberate majority had emerged.

This inherent power of time to defuse passions helped to make the Constitution a self-regulating system whose dependence on parchment barriers was minimal. To be sure, temporal republicanism relies to some extent on institutional mechanisms like the Senate, but it also minimizes the weight these parchment barriers must bear.[77] On Madison's assumptions, parchment needed to hold up only for as long as it took for the passions tearing at it to dissipate. Even were a majority determined to trample constitutional barriers, it was likely to lose interest before it succeeded.

By this analysis, critics misread Madison by judging the extent of his republicanism according to a snapshot of any one moment in time at which a majority seems not to prevail. The relevant measure is a time-lapse photograph. This lateral perspective, in turn, makes it possible to address the following objection: to say Madison was a majoritarian because he favored the rule of dispassionate majorities but not impulsive ones may simply be a fatuous way of saying he favored those majorities with which he agreed. In other words, why should one majority prevail because it is motivated by the head while another fails simply because its impetus is the heart?[78] By projecting Madison's democratic theory across time rather than isolating it at a single moment, it is possible to see that he did not favor some majorities over others; nor did he pose a choice between majorities and minorities at discrete points in time. His democratic theory addressed at what point the same majority should rule. The question was not who rules, but when.

By agreeing or tacitly consenting to the Constitution, then, a majority did not give up its right to rule; it agreed to rule on the basis of reason. A *Gazette* essay Madison wrote critiquing Rousseau's ideal of a "Universal Peace" made this point by way of explaining that it was easier to prevent wars based on a sovereign's will than it was to end those based on the public's will: "As wars of the first class were to be prevented by subjecting the will of the government to the will of the society, those of the second, can only be controuled by subjecting the will of the society to the reason of the society; by establishing permanent and constitutional maxims of conduct, which may prevail over occasional impressions, and inconsiderate pursuits."[79]

A majority acting in its constitutional capacity is thus much in the position of a bar patron who, in a sober moment, entrusts the bartender with his or her keys, a decision better understood as an exercise of freedom rather than a surrender of it. As Viscount James Bryce would later observe, this is the very essence of constitutionalism:

> Along with the principle of Liberty, a Constitution embodies also the principle of Self-restraint. The people have resolved to put certain rules out of the reach of temporary impulses springing from passion or caprice, and to make these rules the permanent expression of their calm thought and deliberate purpose. It is a recognition of the truth that majorities are not always right, and need to be protected against themselves by being obliged to recur, at moments of haste or excitement, to maxims they had adopted at times of cool reflection.[80]

Bryce, like Madison, refers to the majority recognizing its own propensity to passion and thereby protecting itself. Madison's thought provides several reasons the majority might agree to delaying measures as a means of self-protection. In the course of dissipating passions, time seasoned majorities in at least three ways: by reorienting their view from immediate gratification to long-term interest; by ensuring they were relatively settled rather than capturing their oscillating views at one arbitrary moment in time; and by providing the benefit of maximum information before a decision is reached.

Perhaps the greatest passion to which human beings were susceptible was instant gratification. One purpose of delay was to rectify what Drew McCoy, citing Hume's essay "On the Origin of Government," calls "the calamitous inversion of the proper hierarchy between the immediate and the remote."[81] The concepts of the immediate and the ultimate operate in Madison's thought as almost exact parallels to passion and reason. Reason, again, encompasses the idea that it is rarely in a majority's own long-term interest to invade the rights of a minority. Consequently, Madison often qualified his descriptions of majority "interests," referring instead to their "apparent" interests. His preconvention "Vices" essay, as has already been seen, observed that it was difficult to restrain a majority when united by "an *apparent* interest or common passion."[82] That difficulty, according to Federalist 10, arose in turn from the difficulty of "taking into view indirect and remote considerations, which will rarely prevail over the immediate interest which one party may find in disregarding the rights of another, or the good of the whole."[83]

In the following passage in Federalist 42, the desire to gratify immediate appetites is associated with impatience: "The mild voice of reason, pleading the cause of an enlarged and permanent interest, is but too often drowned before public bodies as well as individuals, by the clamours of an impatient avidity for immediate and moderate gain."[84] This tendency to ignore the remote at the expense of the immediate was the basis of Madison's objection in Federalist 50 to correcting constitutional abuses by "periodic appeals" to the people. If the appeals were held in the immediate aftermath of an abuse, the same passions that produced it would continue to reign. If the appeals were less frequent, "a distant prospect of public censure would be a very feeble restraint on power from those excesses, to which it might be urged by the force of present motives."[85]

Delay could help overcome short-term temptations in part by bringing the remote into closer and therefore clearer view, a dynamic evident in Madison's 1786 comments on the intensely controversial Jay–Gardoqui treaty. These are among his most widely quoted—and perhaps most widely misunderstood—statements of concern about majority abuse. The treaty, which would have given Spain exclusive rights to the Mississippi for five years, sparked fierce opposition among the western states. Westerners believed that Jay had bargained away their livelihoods in exchange for concessions chiefly benefiting the east. Madison argued in a letter to Monroe that the scheme was not vindicated by the fact that an overall majority of states supported it:

> The progression which a certain measure [the Jay–Gardoqui treaty] seems to be making is an alarming proof of the predominance of temporary and partial interests over those just & extended maxims of policy which have been so much boasted of among us and which alone can effectuate the durable prosperity of the Union. Should the measure triumph under the patronage of 9 States or even of the whole thirteen, I shall never be convinced that it is expedient, because I cannot conceive it to be just. There is no maxim in my opinion which is more liable to be misapplied, and which therefore more needs elucidation than the current one that the interest of the majority is the political standard of right and wrong. Taking the word "interest" as synonimous [sic] with "Ultimate happiness," in which sense it is qualified with every necessary moral ingredient, the proposition is no doubt true. But taking it in the popular sense, as referring to immediate augmentation of property and wealth, nothing can be more false. In the latter sense it would be the interest of the majority in every community to despoil & enslave the minority of individuals; and in a federal community to make a similar sacrifice of the minority of the component States.[86]

At first glance, the statement seems starkly at odds with Madison's claims elsewhere that majority rule was the first principle of republican government. Madison even appears to share Calhoun's inherent suspicion of majorities, and many commentators have indeed understood this passage to pit majority rule against individual rights.[87] John O. McGinnis, for example, points to the letter as support for his assertion that "Madison believed that the protection of natural rights, rather than the promotion of democracy, was the end of government."[88] For James T. Kloppenberg, the passage is evidence that America's primary political tradition is liberalism rather than merely majority will.[89] Ralph Ketcham similarly interprets the letter as an indication of Madison's belief that "concepts of right and justice were paramount to expressions of majority rule."[90]

These commentators are not wrong to identify this passage as an important statement of Madison's concern about abusive majorities. But fully considered, it is in fact an affirmation of majority rule or, more precisely, temporal republicanism. Temporal overtones pervade the passage: an abusive majority emphasizes the "temporary" over the "durable," seeking an "immediate" augmentation of its wealth, a modifier Madison contrasts with its "ultimate" happiness. The majority's long-term interest is not to despoil and enslave the minority, which matters precisely because the "ultimate happiness" of the majority is "the political standard of right and wrong." A majority was to be delayed under these circumstances not because it was abusing minorities, but because it was mistaken about its own interests. The fact that Madison valued the general good over the very minority rights to whom this passage is often understood to apply is evident in his complaint that the treaty sacrifices "partial" interests to those of "the Union."[91]

Madison's underlying point was not that the majority had no right to infringe the rights of the minority, but rather that the interest of both was the same,[92] a fact that only a near-sighted and therefore distorted view could obscure. During the Articles period, for example, Madison said it was safe to empower a majority of states to enact trade policy because "the fact is that a case can scarcely be imagined in which it would be the interest of an ⅔ds of the States to oppress the remaining ⅓d."[93] This belief forms a pattern across Madison's thought: He almost never perceived conflicts to be binary struggles between abusive majorities and victimized minorities. Rather, the problem was almost always the majority's inability to perceive its own interest accurately—an interest that, clearly perceived, would often reveal that there was no conflict at all. Time and the easing of immediate appetites would bring this perspective into view.

A snapshot perspective of Madison's letter to Monroe could easily misperceive it as a commentary on majority–minority conflicts, as Roberto Gargarella apparently does in interpreting it to mean that "Madison's distrust of majority rule had achieved its high-est point."[94] Madison's protégé and biographer, William Cabell Rives, however, understood that the relevant perspective was lat-eral—the majority's ability across time to perceive its true interest:

> Of the republican statesmen of America, Mr. Madison was undoubtedly the one who saw, the earliest and most clearly, the indispensable necessity of providing, the scheme of the new government, some safeguard for the rights of the minority, which should not be inconsistent with the fundamental principle itself of popular institutions. In a letter . . . to Mr. Monroe, he had expressed his sentiments most forcibly with regard to the abuses of the maxim which makes the *temporary* will of the majority the criterion of right and wrong.[95]

Rives did not suggest an inherent tension between majority rule and minority rights. On the contrary, he characterized Madison as believing the two must be reconciled in order to guard rights without violating republican principles. They could be reconciled because the apparent conflict arose from the majority temporarily misperceiving its interest. Moreover, even in those cases in which the majority was wrong, nothing in this letter suggested they should not rule. The question was whether they ruled immediately; but in any case, Madison entertained no alternative to their ultimate authority. Recall here that majority rule and liberalism address different choices. The first pertains to how decisions are made and the second to how they are evaluated. Even in those cases in which majorities reach illiberal decisions, there is no evidence that Madison believes any other de-cision-making mechanism would reach better ones or would itself be a more just procedure. On the contrary, a passage that has been called "the first time Madison discussed his fear of majority tyranny"[96] in fact identifies the long-term happiness of the majority as the proper object of political society.

Time also addresses the following dilemma of democratic the-ory. During periods of ongoing oscillation in public opinion, enshrin-ing a view in policy at any one given moment seems arbitrary. Tem-poral republicanism helps to alleviate this dilemma by postponing decisions until the public has coalesced around an opinion and per-sisted in it for an interval proportional to the gravity of the issue in question. In his *National Gazette* essay "Public Opinion," Madison thus drew a distinction between fixed and fluctuating majorities: "As there are cases where the public opinion must be obeyed by the government; so there are cases, where, not being fixed, it may be influenced by the government. This distinction, if kept in view, would prevent or decide many debates on the respect due from Government to the sentiments of the people."[97]

Finally, time served the additional purpose of ensuring that decisions were made on the basis of experience and adequate information, both of which were central to Madison's idea of Aristotelian prudence. The problem with mutable laws in the states consisted not simply in the fact that the laws were unknowable, but also in the fact that legislators could not possibly have made them with an adequate understanding of whether or how the laws had actually worked. One reason for the Senate, and the longer terms of its members, was that the public was liable to be led into "temporary errors, thro' want of information as to their true interest."[98] Similarly, Madison argued repeatedly against a second constitutional convention because delay would produce a better sense of what amendments were needed. A convention might be appropriate "as soon as time shall have somewhat corrected the feverish state of the public mind, and trial have pointed its attention to the true defects of the system."[99]

The fuller scope of information that could be collected during delays also included a comprehensive rather than partial sense of public opinion. During his House tenure, Madison worried that a rush to enact legislation placed more urban areas, where information spread and opinion formed quickly, at an advantage. He was concerned about a rush to ratify the Jay treaty in 1796 because "there was not time for distant parts where the treaty was most odious to express their sentiments before the occasion was over."[100] In the first bank debate, he therefore sought delay so the public would have time to reflect: "The public opinion has been mentioned: If the appeal to the public opinion is suggested with sincerity, we ought to let our constituents have an opportunity to form an opinion on the subject."[101] In the aftermath of the XYZ affair, during which French agents attempted to extort bribes in exchange for diplomatic concessions, the eruption of prowar opinion stimulated by the press in urban areas should not be considered the true public sentiment: "There has not been time for any impressions on the public sentiment in this [rural] quarter. . . . [The initial public reaction was prowar, but] the final impressions will depend on the further & more authentic developments which can not be far behind."[102]

Incrementalism

Madison's concern about sudden convulsions, his emphasis on moderation, and his respect for legislative supremacy were also conducive to a political incrementalism whose clearest explication arose from his most direct discussion of the role of time in politics: his reply to Jefferson's "earth belongs to the living" epistle in 1789. Their exchange of letters on the topic reveals a subtle yet deep difference in the two men's approaches to politics and, more specifically, their attitudes toward reason. Jefferson emerges from the exchange as a devotee of what might be called a constructivist Enlightenment perspective that views reason as an unbounded tool of progress or insight, while Madison's reply underscores his more classical understanding of reason as prudence.

The conversation began with Jefferson's inquiry into the extent to which each generation had the right to incur debts or enact other measures that imposed obligations its descendants would inherit without having had the opportunity to consent to them. Jefferson wrote from Paris in September 1789, with the revolution there in full bloom:

> The question Whether one generation of men has a right to bind another, seems never to have been started either on this or our side of the water. Yet it is a question of such consequences as not only to merit decision, but a place also, among the fundamental principles of every government. . . . I set out on this ground, which I suppose to be self-evident, *"that the earth belongs in usufruct to the living"*: that the dead have neither powers nor rights over it. The portion occupied by any individual ceases to be his when himself ceases to be, & reverts to the society.[103]

Jefferson sought to apply this observation to generations rather than merely individuals. Acknowledging that generations consisted of individuals who came and went in "a constant course of decay & renewal," he nonetheless insisted that it was possible to affix a term

for each generation's authority "beginning at the date of their contract, and ending when a majority of those of full age at that date
shall be dead." Calculating on the basis of mortality tables, Jefferson
set the upper limit for each generation's lifespan at nineteen years.
On this basis, no generation had the right to contract debts or otherwise make commitments beyond that term. Moreover, "on similar
ground it may be proved that no society can make a perpetual constitution, or even a perpetual law. . . . The power of repeal is not an
equivalent." Jefferson urged Madison to enshrine the nineteen-year
term in the preamble to the new Congress' first appropriations law.
"Besides familiarising us to this term, it will be an instance the more
of our taking reason for our guide, instead of English precedent."

Madison, who at the time was working to erect a constitutional
government on the basis of enduring fundamental law, could not
oblige, for Jefferson's argument amounted to a claim that any such
law, at least for any significant duration, was illegitimate. The difference in his and Jefferson's perspective is evident in the fact that Jefferson wanted a constitution to last no more than nineteen years,
while Madison advised a friend that the new state of Kentucky would
need an introductory period of at least fifteen to twenty years of trial
and experience before it could thoughtfully consider even revisions
to its constitution.[104] Even worse, on Madison's terms, Jefferson's proposal would put the nation through regular eruptions of sudden
change—a concept with which Madison was already uncomfortable,
and one from which he had just seen the nation barely emerge intact.

Madison later flattered Jefferson by observing that the latter's
theory was gaining ground in the face of Edmund Burke's "extravagant doctrines" to the contrary. But Madison's own views on the
topic were far more Burkean than Jeffersonian. In addition to its careful and compelling rebuttal to Jefferson's argument, Madison's initial
reply[105] deserves attention as a theoretical justification for a gradual,
cautious pace for politics.[106] Much of its contents were already evident in his thought, but this letter gathered them into a concise and
theoretical whole. He began by observing that a short-lived Constitution would never achieve "those prejudices in its favor which antiquity inspires, and which are perhaps a salutary aid to the most rational Government in the most enlightened age." This emphasis on
constitutional veneration evoked the linchpin of so much of Madison's democratic theory: parchment is meaningless without the support of the people it purports to govern. At the same time, Madison's

subtle use of "prejudices" as a positive or at least necessary contrast to the "rational" and "enlightened" drew boundaries around what reason could achieve; even in "the most enlightened age," the most rationally constructed regime still needed the assistance of prejudice.

Madison next offered a Lockean narrative of property: to the extent that the earth belonged to the living, they were entitled to it only in its natural state. "The *improvements* made by the dead form a charge against the living who take the benefit of them." A similar argument applied to debts, which "may be incurred for purposes which interest the unborn, as well as the living," so the only limitation on transgenerational debts could be that they could not exceed the value of the advances made when they were contracted. Moreover, the idea of obligations being dissolved at regular intervals would have the effect of making "most of the rights of property" defunct. The only means of avoiding these undesirable conclusions was the device of tacit consent, without which, Madison noted, there would be no inherent justification for majority rule.

This emphasis on tacit consent had three implications for Madison's thought. The first was to establish a prejudice in favor of existing institutions and therefore against sudden change. Second, and related, the idea of rapid and constant change ignored the complexities and interwoven obligations evident when political issues are viewed across time rather than in a snapshot of a given moment. This much was evident in Madison's praise of the Senate as the one institution of government that could most effectively deal with and be held accountable for policies whose effect could only be known over an interval of several years.[107] Finally, Madison recognized, and gently suggested to Jefferson while the latter was enthralled with Enlightenment rationality, that attempts to devise ideal or unassailable institutions on the basis of unbounded reason would inevitably run aground on the shoals of political reality. This, he wrote in Federalist 37, was why the draft Constitution could not be tested by a priori theories of government alone. Science, he wrote, could fix laws of nature precisely. However,

> When we pass from the works of nature, in which all the delineations are perfectly accurate, and appear to be otherwise only from the imperfection of the eye which surveys them, to the institutions of man, in which the obscurity arises as well from the object itself, as from the

organ by which it is contemplated; we must perceive the necessity of moderating still further our expectations and hopes from the efforts of human sagacity.[108]

The model of Madisonian reason suggested by these arguments is the application of the intellectual faculties to the choices presented by reality rather than the heuristic construction of idealistic regimes or policies from the ground up. These more modest hopes for reason may help to explain why, in sharing the letter with a Jefferson biographer, Madison redacted a closing phrase lamenting that "the spirit of philosophical Legislation" evident in Jefferson's proposal had not yet permeated the United States.[109] The lament was almost certainly no more than Madison's occasional habit of opening and closing his writings about Jefferson with effusive praise while thoroughly deconstructing his arguments in between.[110] But excerpted out of context, it would have appeared to endorse a kind of reason that was not only foreign, but also dangerous, to Madison's prudential thought.[111]

Madison on Human Nature

The perspective of temporal republicanism suggests one final dimension of Madison's thought that merits attention. Commentators of several stripes have typically treated Madison as a pessimist deeply skeptical of human nature. Louis Hartz casts him as a Hobbesian whose idea of experience "seems to be exhausted by the human propensity to fight," a view echoed by Robert Dahl, while Richard K. Matthews describes Madison's worldview as a Calvinist belief that "humans are usually lazy and often unreasonable."[112]

What we have seen above, however, suggests that Madison's view was more nuanced. The picture that emerges from his discussion of passion and reason appears to assume that reasonableness is the normal or healthy state of affairs and that passion is the irregular and distorting influence. Indeed, Federalist 55 characterizes this nuanced view as reasoned and excessive pessimism about human nature as a "passion." Anti-Federalists who assumed the darkest scenario of perfidy in elected officials

renounce every rule by which events ought to be calculated, and to substitute an indiscriminate and unbounded jealousy, with which all reasoning must be vain. The sincere friends of liberty, who give themselves up to the extravagancies of this passion, are not aware of the injury they do their own cause. As there is a degree of depravity in mankind, which requires a certain degree of circumspection and distrust: so there are other qualities in human nature, which justify a certain portion of esteem and confidence. Republican government presupposes the existence of these qualities in a higher degree than any other form.[113]

The fact that Madison gave little overt attention to cultivating these qualities has led some observers, especially of the civic republican school, to assume that virtue vanished as a priority between the revolutionary and constitutional eras. Gordon Wood, for example, understands Madison to have believed that individually selfish pursuits would add up to a general good, and that, by contrast, "the really great danger to liberty . . . was that each individual may become insignificant in his own eyes—hitherto the very foundation of republican government."[114] A related interpretation, offered charitably by Martin Diamond and less favorably by George Will,[115] portrays Madison as actively favoring the proliferation and pursuit of individual interests, perhaps at the deliberate expense of loftier ideals.

Temporal republicanism calls many of these assumptions into question. Its passive character, again, is key to understanding how the doctrine operates. Reasonable people would ordinarily perceive their own interest in respecting the rights of others and pursuing the public good—again, what Tocqueville called "self-interest rightly understood." It was only the distorting influence of passion—which was amplified by the group dynamics inherent in politics—that obscured this exercise of reason. The passage of time would help to restore focus—if not total clarity, at least enough of it to give fit characters in public office sufficient space to craft or identify measures that served the public good.

On this model, no heroic exertions of character were necessary to achieve civic-mindedness, nor did interests have to be set against one another in political combat.[116] In the sense that Madison understood it, civic-mindedness was the healthy perspective, one that could be depended on as long as the diseased condition—passion—had time to heal. A snapshot view might well show human beings behaving badly, but a time-lapse image was likely to show them being reasonable over the longer term.

To the extent that Madison's words portrayed human nature negatively, he was often describing the diseased rather than the normal state. Federalist 10, for example, said men are "inflamed with mutual animosity, and . . . much more disposed to vex and oppress each other, than to co-operate for their common good"—but this condition occurred only when "zeal" kindled "the human passions."[117] If that zeal could be dissipated by time, the healthy state—self-interest rightly understood—would be restored.[118] Consequently, when Patrick Henry demanded to know what place virtue occupied in the constitutional order, Madison's reply suggested it need not be provided for because the basic conditions of reasonableness already existed:

> I have observed, that gentlemen suppose, that the general legislature will do every mischief they possibly can, and that they will omit to do every thing good which they are authorised to do. If this were a reasonable supposition, their objections would be good. I consider it reasonable to conclude, that they will as readily do their duty, as deviate from it: Nor do I go on the grounds mentioned by gentlemen on the other side—that we are to place unlimited confidence in them, and expect nothing but the most exalted integrity and sublime virtue. But I go on this great republican principle, that the people will have virtue and intelligence to select men of virtue and wisdom. Is there no virtue among us? If there be not, we are in a wretched situation. No theoretical checks—no form of government can render us secure.[119]

None of this adds up to an enthused portrait of human nature. Madison was a realist, not a Rousseauian. But neither was Madison the Hobbesian pessimist he is often assumed to have been. It is only by viewing human nature over time that, on Madison's grounds, a balanced and realistic perspective may be gained. Men were not angels, but neither were they necessarily devilish.

———

To recapitulate, Madison's democratic thought contains an implicit doctrine that I have called "temporal republicanism," according to which the primary criterion for whether a majority should prevail is the length of time it has cohered. This doctrine is fully compatible with Madison's commitment to majority rule because it asks not whether a majority should prevail over a minority at any one moment, but rather at what point the same majority's opinion should be considered authoritative. Time is a passive mechanism whose foremost purpose is the dissipation of passions, which induce a diseased state that obscures the normal and healthy condition in which people are able to use reason to perceive their long-term interests.

The fact that reason was the ever-present underlying state therefore allowed Madison, from the perch of retirement, to express serene confidence in the American political system. He wrote to the Marquis de Lafayette in 1830:

> Here, we are, on the whole, doing well, and giving an example of a free system, which I trust will be more of a Pilot to a good Port, than a Beacon warning from a bad one. We have, it is true, occasional fevers, but they are of the transient kind flying off thro' the surface, without preying on the vitals. A Govt. like ours has so many safety-valves giving vent to overheated passions, that it carries within itself a relief agst. the infirmities from which the best of human institutions cannot be exempt.[120]

We may now see those safety valves in operation in several areas of Madison's thought.

Chapter 3

Time and the Tenth Federalist

On July 14, 1787, a Saturday, the residents of rural towns surrounding Philadelphia converged on the city for market days, only to find banks and merchants suddenly unwilling to accept paper money as payment for basic necessities. Panic ensued, and a riot nearly followed. Desperate and enraged, the holders of paper—a form of currency on which the poor disproportionately depended—were poised to take matters into their own hands.[1] Madison recorded the scene in a letter to Jefferson:

> The paper money here ceased to circulate very suddenly a few days ago. . . . The entire stagnation is said to have proceeded from a combination of a few people with whom the Country people deal on market days against receiving it. The consequence was that it was refused in the market, and great distress brought on the poorer Citizens. Some of the latter began in turn to form combinations of a more serious nature in order to take revenge on the supposed authors of the stagnation. The timely interposition of some influencial [*sic*] characters prevented a riot, and prevailed on the persons who were opposed to the paper, to publish their willingness to receive it. This has stifled the popular rage, and got the paper into circulation again. It is however still considerably below par, and must have received a wound which will not easily be healed. Nothing but evil springs from this imaginary money wherever it is tried.[2]

Incidents of this type were precisely why Madison considered paper money to be the archetype of factious activity, and his derogatory or at least fretful characterization of the protest as a "popular rage" is exactly the kind of rhetoric that has led Progressive critics to conclude that his fear of faction was, in effect, fear of majority rule.[3] But history presents a paradox, or at least an irony: as mobs formed in the marketplace of Philadelphia that Saturday, Madison stood inside the cloistered quarters of Independence Hall making a strenuous argument for majoritarian government. That day, Maryland's cantankerous Luther Martin moved for a vote on whether the Senate should be constituted on the basis of population or equality of the states, and Madison rose to make a final appeal for proportional representation, which, we have seen, he viewed as a proxy for majority rule. Indeed, the first objection he stated to the small-state view was that if each state had an equal number of votes in the Senate, "the minority could negative the will of the majority of the people," an arrangement that would "destroy" the "proper foundation of Government." This plea failed to convince his colleagues, whose first business upon reconvening after a Sunday respite was to approve a committee report that included what Madison had described as an unjust and undemocratic design for the Senate.

To be sure, this issue was unrelated to the currency dispute unfolding on the streets of Philadelphia. There is no reason to believe Madison was even aware of the mob forming in the marketplace when he spoke. But this confluence of events in the same city on the same date—outdoors, a factious mob of exactly the type Madison believed should not rule, yet indoors, a spirited defense of majoritarian government—illuminates an essential feature of his thinking on the issue of faction: majorities should not rule when proximity allows them to do so immediately and impulsively; distance, by contrast, adds the seasoning element of time, enabling majorities to rule thoughtfully and in accordance with their long-term interests. Here again, we recall that the choice was not between majority and minority rule; it was at what point the majority would rule. Authority remained always in the majority's hands. This was where time and majority rule converged in Madison's most famous contribution to political theory: the extended republic theory of Federalist 10.

As Lance Banning has noted, Federalist 10 should not be regarded as the sole linchpin of Madison's thought. Nevertheless, it requires our sustained attention for several reasons. First, Madison himself regarded the extended republic theory to be highly important, even if he would agree that it should not be considered the end-all, be-all of his thought. He took the unusual step of explicating the theory at length twice in *The Federalist,* once in Federalist 10 and again in Federalist 51. It was the basis of his proposal for a national negative on state laws, which he clearly did regard as a linchpin of the constitutional system he envisioned—so much so that the failure of the negative prompted him to predict to Jefferson that the Constitution would fail, an argument he made by deploying the extended republic theory.[4] Second, the essay was among Madison's signal contributions to political theory, and the sheer volume of literature concerning it requires an extended treatment. Third, one strain of that literature has consistently used Federalist 10 to portray Madison as antimajoritarian.

In this chapter, I endeavor to counter that portrayal and establish the centrality of temporal republicanism to the ideas that found their foremost although not exclusive expression in Federalist 10. In order fully to draw together Madison's views on such issues as injustice, I shall draw also on other writings roughly contemporaneous with that essay. In doing so, we shall first see that the concerns about rights and injustices that prompted the extended republic thesis, especially as they pertained to property, were in fact complaints about how majorities achieved certain ends, not what ends they pursued. On Madison's view, majorities could do mostly as they wished, including regulating property, provided they did so in accordance with the rule of law—a case bolstered by Madison's tendency to use "justice" in a procedural rather than substantive context. Next, we shall see that the power of time lies at the heart of the extended republic theory. Federalist 10 is, at its core, an essay about temporal republicanism. One of the core insights of Federalist 10 is that the unique conditions of an extended republic naturally defer decisions until after passions have cooled, thereby enhancing the likelihood that national majorities will respect minority rights.

Finally, we shall explore the interplay of both issues—majority rule and temporal republicanism—in the specific institutional proposal that arose from the logic of Federalist 10: the proposal for a national negative on state laws. As we proceed, we shall again encounter Madison's writings in multiple stages of life—primarily those surrounding the framing and ratification of the Constitution as well as his retirement-era "Detached Memorandum"—showing that even as his thought evolved in other areas, it remained relatively consistent where temporal republicanism was concerned.

Federalist 10 and Justice

At the outset of Federalist 10, Madison lamented abuses committed by popular majorities of the sort we have seen him decry in the "Vices" memorandum. He wrote in Federalist 10:

> Complaints are every where heard from our most considerate and virtuous citizens, equally the friends of public and private faith, and of public and personal liberty, that our governments are too unstable; that the public good is disregarded in the conflicts of rival parties; and that measures are too often decided, not according to the rules of justice, and the rights of the minor party, but by the superior force of an interested and overbearing majority.[5]

This does indeed sound like an indictment of majority rule written from the perspective of one who wants to protect the property of the minority, and it helps to explain why Federalist 10 has long been the linchpin of critiques of Madison's thought. Even redemptive readings of Madison have more or less accepted the idea that Federalist 10 sought to balance majority rule and minority rights, calibrating the system so as to maximize both—or, conversely, restrict each the least. There is, of course, much to support those interpretations, and Madison was clearly concerned about majorities trampling the rights of minorities, especially at the state level. Yet Federalist 10 itself identifies majority rule as the limiting condition of its analysis: "To secure the public good, and private rights, against the danger of [a majority faction], and at the same time to preserve the spirit and the form of popular government, is then the great object to which our inquiries are directed."[6] Madison had earlier said in Philadelphia that enlarging the sphere of the union was "the only defence agst the inconveniences of democracy consistent with the democratic form of Govt,"[7] a formulation that appears to exclude institutional limitations on majority rule. Federalist 39 reinforces the point that majority rule trumps other constitutional concerns, apparently including rights: "If the plan of the convention, therefore, be found to depart from the republican character, its advocates must abandon it as no longer defensible."[8] That essay goes on to identify republicanism with government accountability to the community—which, we have seen, Madison equated with the majority.

Nonetheless, while Madison was clearly not a proto-Marxist, it is equally clear that the economic dimensions of Federalist 10 were paramount. There can be no question that Madison's writings during this period and on these topics more generally—from his earliest broadsides against paper money to the preconvention "Vices" memo to his remarks in the convention itself—show acute concern about redistributionist and leveling schemes in the states.[9] If writings like Federalist 10 form a theory of injustice that substantively precludes certain economic outcomes, his majoritarianism would be situational at best. Even if Madison had good reasons to favor property rights, such a conception of them would still leave him privileging liberal over republican values. A careful assessment of Madison's reflections on property rights in Federalist 10 and elsewhere reveals, however, that he objected not to the economic outcomes that would have resulted from policies like paper money but rather to the manner in which those outcomes were to be achieved. Madison's "rights of property," to use Federalist 10's phrase, were largely procedural rights meant to secure the rule of law.[10]

The extended republic theory, like Madison's concerns about factious activity in the states, applies to a specific kind of scenario: majorities exerting pressure directly on the regime.[11] As we have just seen, Federalist 10's concern lay with the exertion of "the superior force of an interested and overbearing majority." A critic of Madison might reasonably ask whether such situations are not the very definition of majority rule. But the scenario Madison had in mind was the majority using the apparatus of the state as a weapon—"a mere instrument," he wrote to Jefferson while summarizing the argument of Federalist 10[12]—to steamroll the minority. Madison believed one of the first purposes of government was to avoid precisely this kind of situation—that is, individuals being constantly exposed to coercion merely on the basis of superior force, unbound by any known or predictable standard. On Madison's view, this exposure to arbitrary force was among the defining features of the state of nature, a situation government was instituted by unanimous choice precisely to avoid. The point is implicit in a well-known passage of Federalist 51:

> Justice is the end of government. It is the end of civil society.
> It ever has been, and ever will be, pursued, until it be
> obtained, or until liberty be lost in the pursuit. In a society,
> under the forms of which the stronger faction can readily

unite and oppress the weaker, anarchy may as truly be said to reign, as in a state of nature, where the weaker individual is not secured against the violence of the stronger.[13]

Madison justified the Constitution's restrictions on bills of attainders, ex post facto laws, and legislative interference with contracts—crucially, the only surviving constitutional provisions traceable to the concerns about majority abuses within the states elucidated in Federalist 10—on similar grounds. According to Federalist 44, such measures violated "the first principles of the social compact."[14] The first principles were derived from the compact's purpose, which was, first and foremost, to establish the security and predictability that were elusive in the state of nature. The rule of law therefore held the status of something like a natural right. Property, by contrast, was a political invention that could be regulated by political processes. To what, then, was the individual or minority group inviolably entitled? Two things only: the right to consent, vindicated through voting and persuasion within a system of majority rule, and the right to know the rules. Note, then, the kinds of rights Madison described as "essential exceptions" to the legislative power, and therefore that of majorities, when Kentucky was considering its constitution not long before the drafting of the federal one:

> The Constitution may expressly restrain them from medling with religion—from abolishing Juries—from taking away the Habeas corpus—from forcing a citizen to give evidence against himself—from controuling the press—from enacting retrospective laws at least in criminal cases, from abridging the right of suffrage, from taking private property for public use without paying its full Value, from licensing the importation of Slaves, from infringing the confederation, &c &c.[15]

With the exception of religious freedom, which Chapter 4 will show occupied an analytically unique category, and restrictions on the slave trade,[16] these exceptions amount to two broad rights. The first is consent (the rights to vote and persuade, as well as the restriction on laws infringing the confederation, whose purpose was to protect the right of national majorities to decide national issues), and the second are procedural guarantees for the rule of law (habeas corpus, self-incrimination, ex post facto laws, and compensation for takings) rather than to substantive outcomes. Madison's complaints about factious majorities pertained to this second category rather than to the rights of consent; the states were not, generally speaking, accused of curtailing suffrage or interfering with elections.

The catalog of complaints elucidated in Federalist 10 as well as the "Vices" essay were thus not directed against majority rule as such, but rather against arbitrary majority rule. Put otherwise, the problem was not that majorities trespassed on property, it was that they did so arbitrarily—a problem to which the solution was the rule of law. It was this end—majority rule in accordance with the predictable standards necessary to the rule of law—with which Madison was concerned in Federalist 10, not protecting minorities from substantive outcomes.

The arbitrariness of majorities was the consistent complaint of the "Vices" essay, Madison's most detailed statement of concern about factious activity within the states. The essay lists Madison's concern as threefold. The first is the "multiplicity" of state laws, whose sheer volume was "a nuisance of the most pestilent kind": "The short period of independency has filled as many pages as the century which preceded it. Every year, almost every session, adds a new volume. . . . A review of the several Codes will shew that every necessary and useful part of the least voluminous of them might be compressed into one tenth of the compass, and at the same time be rendered ten fold as perspicuous."[17]

Significantly, the quality lacking in these voluminous state laws was perspicacity: Madison's complaint that the useful parts of the state codes were needles scattered in haystacks of presumably gratuitous legislative acts suggests that the law was difficult for the average person to know. It will not surprise us to learn that the majorities enacting this multiplicity of laws did so in a fevered rush, passing statutes quickly enough to fill a volume at least every year. These were also the qualities Madison observed in his second complaint, one that was "intimately connected" with the first: the "mutability" of state laws. "We daily see laws repealed or superseded, before any trial can have been made of their merit, and even before a knowledge of them can have reached the remoter districts within which they were to operate. In the regulations of trade this instability becomes a snare not only to our citizens, but to foreigners also."[18]

Significantly, according to Federalist 62, it was the minority, not the majority, that profited from the mutability of laws. Constant change provided an advantage "to the sagacious, the enterprising, and the monied few, over the industrious and uninformed mass of the people."[19] Again, this rapid oscillation in laws made them unknowable—so much so that by the time notice of a new law reached areas distant from the state capitals, it was likely already to have changed. Madison's use of the metaphor of a snare indicates his concern that those unaware of these laws risked being entrapped and harmed by them.

It seems readily clear how both multiplicity and mutability undermine the rule of law at its most fundamental level: the requirement that laws be propagated and known in advance. But Madison's third complaint—the "injustice" of state laws, the theme to which he would return in Federalist 10—presents a more complex difficulty for evaluating his commitment to majority rule. If he believed the requirements of justice made it illegitimate for majorities to reach certain conclusions, there is no avoiding the conclusion that—whether for good reasons or bad—he intended to curtail majority rule at least in those cases.

What, then, does Madison mean by *injustice* in Federalist 10? The answer is that justice, like multiplicity and mutability, was a procedural standard guaranteeing that decisions would be made according to known rules. The error we must avoid in this context is conflating "property rights" with "property." Madison never suggested that regulating or even confiscating property would be unjust in and of itself. The problem arose when majorities did so arbitrarily, unpredictably, or on the basis of sheer force.

To see why, we must look beyond Federalist 10 to other occasions on which he used that term. Throughout Madison's writings, justice is generally associated with fairness and rules rather than the substance of political decisions.[20] This is not to say that Madison never objected to the substance of decisions; clearly he did. The point is that Madison used *justice* in a specific context and *injustice* as a particular kind of critique pertaining far more often to procedure than to substance. Federalist 10 refers twice to the "rules" of justice, and "Vices" to its "rules and forms." The convention's debate on whether to comprise Congress on the basis of population was a matter of justice precisely because it pertained to the rules according to which future disputes would be decided.[21] In the Virginia ratifying convention, Madison said the Articles regime produced injustice in part because the lack of congressional taxing authority forced public needs to be financed through arbitrary seizures of property:

> Is it not known to every member of this committee, that the great principles of a free government, were reversed through the whole progress of that scene? Was not every state harassed? Was not every individual oppressed and subjected to repeated distresses? Was this right? Was it a proper form of government, that warranted, authorized, or overlooked, the most *wanton* deprivation of property? Had the government been vested with complete power to procure a regular and adequate supply of revenue, those oppressive measures would have been unnecessary.[22]

The fact that this entire passage laments the lack of compulsory taxing authority indicates that confiscating private property did not inherently violate property rights. The problem was "wanton" deprivations, which in this context referred to the sudden and arbitrary impressments of private property that became necessary during the Revolution.[23] These "wanton" impressments were contrasted with a "regular"—that is, rules-based and therefore predictable—revenue.

Madison's frequent critiques of paper money similarly demonstrate that his concern was maintaining the rule of law rather than protecting property per se. From the Revolutionary period through the ratification debates, few issues more consistently provoked Madison's ire than what he saw to be the states' promiscuous printing of currency as a substitute for precious metals. It was the subject of a lengthy circa 1780 essay in which Madison assailed paper money on economic grounds yet did not, significantly, describe the issue as one of rights. As the use of paper money became more rampant, his rhetoric escalated. By the time the ratification debates were complete, Madison had deployed a battery of harsh adjectives against paper, calling it, at various times, "pernicious"[24] and "pestilent,"[25] the cause of "numerous ills"[26] and the product of "wickedness and folly."[27] This is strong language, especially in contrast to Madison's normally mild rhetorical style. Several commentators—most persuasively the historian Woody Holton[28]—have argued that the opposition of the landed class to paper was less about macroeconomic policy or questions of justice than keeping poorer Americans trapped in endless debts that the crisis-level shortage of hard currency left them unable to pay. But the question of debts also illustrates why Madison described paper money as not only unwise but "unrighteous"[29] and "unjust"[30] as well. His complaint is difficult to see from a contemporary vantage point in which paper money commands widespread faith as legal tender. At Madison's time, though, it was quite literally an IOU that could be exchanged for specie, which was the only trusted and universally accepted currency. To make matters more problematic, the issuing governments were notoriously unable to redeem their own notes. The result was in effect to change contracts after they had been agreed to—a clear violation of the rule of law, and one that made political conditions unpredictable. The scenario was akin to the following: Person A loans money to Person B, and Person B repays A with an IOU he has received from Person C—who was not party to the first transaction and who is, to boot, widely known to be unable to pay his debts. Person A, to make matters worse, is legally bound to accept the IOU as payment. This was why Madison likened paper money to the practice, also widespread, of state laws that abrogated contracts.[31] The importance of this issue to the rule of law, and thus to predictability, is also evident in Federalist 44's lament that paper money had destroyed "the necessary confidence between man and man" and "the necessary confidence of the public councils" and that, were states allowed to issue paper under the new regime, they might make "retrospective alterations in its value."[32]

Justice, by contrast, required conformity to rules agreed upon in advance. This is also the suggestion of Madison's 1792 essay "Property," which was published in the opposition press—during the period when he began his shift toward mobilizing public opinion to correct abuses by the regime—and which closely tracks Locke's *Second Treatise*.[33] Madison wrote:

> This term [property], in its particular application, means "that dominion which one man claims and exercises over the external things of the world, in exclusion of every other individual." In its larger and juster meaning, it embraces everything to which a man may attach a value and have a right, and *which leaves to every one else the like advantage*. In the former sense, a man's land, or merchandise, or money, is called his property.[34]

Notice that the essay gives property an explicitly and inherently public rather than private meaning. Far from being the exclusive dominion of the individual, property exists because of a reciprocal agreement with other members of the community. This definition, combined with Madison's obvious debt to Locke, indicates that when the former spoke of the right to property, it was a civil as opposed to a natural right. As we have already seen in Madison's claim that there was a "natural" right to rebel but no "civil" right for nullifiers to resist constitutional authority, this distinction makes a decisive difference in his thought. On Locke's as well as Madison's account, it is only in the state of nature that individuals can assert an absolute right to property in the sense of claiming that no legitimate authority can violate it. By contrast, political society is founded on the exchange of that absolute natural right for a civil right whose distinguishing feature is that the majority can regulate its boundaries so long as it does so in accordance with rules known and agreed upon in advance.[35] The "Property" essay makes clear that Madison's objection was to property being seized or otherwise violated arbitrarily. Three times, it employs the word *arbitrary* to characterize violations of property rights, indicating that they included "arbitrary seizures of one class of citizens for the service of the rest," "arbitrary restrictions, exemptions, and monopolies," and "arbitrary taxes." These objections to arbitrary measures tacitly acknowledge the community's right to regulate property, provided it does so in a nonarbitrary way—that is, in accordance with the rule of law.[36]

Viewed through the prism of the rule of law, it is also clear why Madison believed that violating minority rights was never in the majority's interest. One could easily imagine scenarios in which seizing or regulating property genuinely serves the interests of the majority, but there is never a situation in which it serves anyone's long-term interest to abandon the rule of law. Every individual, in all situations, retains an unchanging interest in predictability, as witnessed by the fact that—again, on the Lockean account to which Madison apparently referred—individuals unanimously formed political society to secure precisely that.

Madison's emphasis on just dealings with minorities, then, does not mean they were to be preferred over the majority's good or that the majority was to be prevented from reaching certain conclusions. Of course, a cynic might object that this analysis merely defines the problem away: rather than admit to elevating minority interests over majority rule, Madison simply declared by fiat that what was good for the minority was good for the whole. But by the logic of Federalist 10, Madison could not have meant that majorities and minorities (or different minorities) always had the same interests. Were such the case, it would have been superfluous to specify that the good of the whole should be measured by the good of the majority. It is only in cases of justice that majority and minority interests are equivalent. One reason embedded in the logic of Federalist 10 is that majorities and minorities in American society are fluid, so the members of a majority today may belong to the minority tomorrow and hence maintain an interest in establishing precedents for fairness.[37] But Madison's concern about justice cuts to the even more fundamental issue of predictability. The problem, again, was not that majorities regulated or otherwise affected property; it was that they did so arbitrarily and unpredictably, and no one—majority or minority—had an interest in an unpredictable political condition.

Moreover, far from protecting an aristocratic class, Madison's few writings about the propertied elite support preventing them from accumulating wealth. To see this most clearly, we must move forward in time to his circa 1819 "Detached Memorandum," a loosely knit collection of observations on a variety of subjects. Written after his political career concluded—and therefore presumably free of any populist motives—Madison explicitly endorsed the regulation of property for, it is crucial to note, the express purpose of preventing the very same excessive accumulations of property that critics accuse him of protecting. The sale of public lands to individuals should be respected, he wrote, because such grants were made "according to rules of impartiality, for a valuable consideration" and because all citizens who purchased public lands held them in perpetuity—that is, the sales were made according to the standards of impartiality and equality. However, Madison was sensitive to the concern that the wealthy might establish a de facto aristocracy. Consequently, "the evil of an excessive & dangerous cumulation of landed property in the hands of individuals is best precluded by the prohibition of entails, the suppression of the right of primogeniture, and by the liability of landed property to the payment of debts. In Countries where there is a rapid increase of population as the U.S. these provisions are evidently sufficient."[38]

Madison here sounds very unlike part of an aristocratic elite.

He calls the "excessive" accumulation of property "evil" and "dangerous," and he proposes preventing it by restricting entails and primogeniture—precisely the devices used to maintain the European aristocracies, and ones whose abolition, incidentally, Tocqueville predicted would lead to widespread economic equality in the United States. In addition, the fact that Madison believed that holding the wealthy liable for debts would disperse their property indicates that his concern about the rights of creditors cannot be regarded as code for protecting the rich against the poor.[39] Most important, the devices Madison endorses for promoting economic equality are preventive: they are enforced before agreements are executed or property is transferred, and thus they comport with his conception of the rule of law.

The "Detached Memorandum" takes a similar tack in warning against allowing "ecclesiastical corporations" to stockpile unlimited wealth lest their political influence become disproportionate: "But besides the danger of a direct mixture of Religion & civil Government, there is an evil which ought to be guarded agst in the indefinite accumulation of property from the capacity of holding it in perpetuity by ecclesiastical corporations. The power of *all* corporations, ought to be limited in this respect. The growing wealth acquired by them never fails to be a source of abuses."[40]

Although this passage is directed at ecclesiastical corporations, the memorandum's discussion of other types of corporations—including banks—suggests he refers to all of them, as the logic he employs surely would. Madison notes that corporations are subject to unique restrictions because they are creations of the community and therefore subordinate to its good. But equally important, these restrictions must be made clear in advance in an entity's articles of incorporation. He laments that the acts of incorporation often "*give* this faculty [the right to acquire property], without limit either as to time or as to amount."[41] The fact that the community "gives" this right demonstrates Madison's belief that at least in the case of corporations, there is no entitlement to acquire property separate from the public good. An 1824 letter to Jefferson—again referring to ecclesiastical corporations, but also again employing logic that would apply to others—makes the point even more explicitly. The context is a discussion of whether public charters granted to religious or charitable institutions should be considered irrevocable, and the letter emphatically denies that they should be. The public good is, of itself, an adequate justification for regulating property, whose owners are entitled only to compensation for any loss: "The time surely cannot be distant when it must be seen by all that what is granted by the Public Authority for the Public good, not for that of individuals, may be withdrawn and otherwise applied, when the Public good so requires; with an equitable saving or indemnity only in behalf of the individuals actually enjoying vested emoluments."[42]

Madison does, to be sure, specifically refer to an equal distribution of property in Federalist 10 as a "wicked project." But equalization of property inherently involves confiscation without full compensation—a clear case of procedural justice. The case with abolitions of debts, which Federalist 10 calls "unjust," is similar.

The public nature of property, as well as the procedural nature of justice, is also suggested by the following question: if the analysis of Federalist 10 was directed against unjust laws in the states, and if "unjust" meant the government interfering in areas in which it had no business, why—not merely in Federalist 10, but also in the considerable trove of correspondence and other writings surrounding it—did Madison never mention the one right he held to be most inviolable and that, by his standards, the states commonly violated: the right of conscience? Chapter 4 will explore Madison's views on this subject in more detail, but it is sufficient for purposes of understanding Federalist 10 to observe that scarcely two years before composing that essay, Madison's "Memorial and Remonstrance" described state assessments to pay for religious instruction as violations of the principle of religious liberty. Such assessments were commonplace in the preconstitutional states, as were other measures that Madison regarded as violations of religious liberty, including religious tests for officeholders.[43] Yet his catalog of state injustices in "Vices" does not mention them.[44] Conversely, the "Memorial and Remonstrance" employs the term "justice" only once. The reason is that freedom of conscience was a matter of liberty but not a matter of justice, which was instead a public and procedural quality.

This particular context in which Madison used the terms "justice" and "injustice" is also evident in the Virginia Report of 1800, Madison's lengthy attempt to explain the Virginia Resolutions of 1799, which had—or at least he now claimed—sought to rouse public opinion against the Alien and Sedition Acts. Commentaries have tended to focus on the Sedition Act, but Madison's assessment of the Alien Act is equally important for understanding his political thought. Significantly, the Virginia Report discusses justice in the context of the Alien Act but not the Sedition Act. The reason is that the Alien Act delegated broad swaths of what Madison regarded to be arbitrary authority to the president to detain or expel foreigners without procedural guarantees to ensure fairness.[45] Aliens were entitled, Madison insisted, to "the judgment of some judicial authority" as well as guarantees like habeas corpus. That he did not describe the Sedition Act as unjust hardly means he did not object to it. On the contrary, the Virginia resolutions describe the Alien and Sedition Acts combined as "evil." The confusion arises if we think of "unjust" as a synonym for "objectionable." Instead, Madison generally used "justice" and "injustice" in the particular context of procedural guarantees. Their use in Federalist 10 therefore suggests his concern was not to prevent majorities from reaching substantive outcomes, but rather to ensure they did so fairly rather than arbitrarily.

These considerations suggest that, contrary to the bulk of both critical and redemptive interpretations of Federalist 10, he believed the majority could treat property more or less as it decided the public interest required, so long as it did so in accordance with rules and procedures known in advance. These procedures themselves, Madison assumed, were subject either to definition by majorities or, in cases in which the Constitution prescribed them, the ongoing sufferance of majorities.[46] Majorities consented to this arrangement because securing a stable and predictable environment was the very reason political society was instituted to begin with.

Indeed, not only did Madison believe private rights to be compatible with the public good; he also did not regard the two as analytically distinct. He did, of course, express repeated concern that minority rights would be sacrificed to the majority's immediate appetites. Moreover, he equated the good of the majority with the good of the whole community. But Madison did not regard transient majority appetites as an expression of the public's genuine long-term good. Far from making a choice between majority rule and individual rights, his writings knit them together in a mutually reinforcing relationship that more closely resembles a double helix than separate strands of thought. He rarely mentioned either of the two without simultaneously mentioning the other, and he repeatedly described the two concepts as though they reinforced, rather than undermined, one another.

Federalist 10 directly challenges the idea of a fundamental opposition between the public good and private rights, famously defining factions as groups whose agendas are "adverse to the rights of other citizens, or to the permanent and aggregate interests of the community."[47] The grouping of the public good and private rights in this context—a measure is factious if it violates either, or, conversely, to be nonfactious it must satisfy both—refutes the idea that he assumed one might have to pick between the two. This is why Federalist 10 says a statesman needs both "patriotism"—that is, a commitment to the whole—and a "love of justice," which pertains to treatment of minorities.[48] Further, Madison repeatedly and without feeling any evident need for further explanation described the public good and private rights as simultaneous goals. Abuses in the states were to be especially regretted because they caused skeptics to question whether popular majorities could protect both the "public Good and private rights."[49] New York's Council of Revision provided "a valuable safeguard both to public interests & to private rights."[50] Federalist 14 praises American innovations "in favour of private rights and public happiness."[51] The separation of powers was to be maintained in order to secure both "private rights" and "public liberty."[52] And perhaps most starkly, Federalist 51 states that justice is the "end" of government while majority rule is the "means" of securing it. Conversely, Madison rarely discussed individual rights outside the context of the "public good," "common good," or "public liberty."[53]

This interconnectedness of the public good and private rights is underscored by the striking fact that Madison almost never described as "unjust," "factious," or a violation of "rights" any policy that he had not also classified as harmful to the public good. Note the interrelatedness of "moral," "political," and "economic" problems in this passage from a 1786 letter to Jefferson:

> Another unhappy effect of a continuance of the present anarchy of our commerce, will be a continuance of the unfavorable balance on it, which by draining us of our metals furnishes pretexts for the pernicious substitution of paper money, for indulgences to debtors, for postponements of taxes. In fact most of our political evils may be traced up to our commercial ones, as most of our moral may to our political.[54]

On this analysis, the issues which Federalist 10 explicitly describes as factious exhibit moral, political, and economic features that are woven into a set of concerns encompassing both private rights and the public good. Referring to many of the same issues, Federalist 10 groups paper money with abolitions of debts and equal division of property as "wicked project[s]"[55] that are matters of "justice."[56] But both in the essay and elsewhere, Madison also explicitly described these policies as averse to the public good. Paper money again supplies a compelling illustration. Although it clearly implicated questions of justice, it also threatened the community as a whole by making it impossible to repay the public debt, impeding commerce, and causing internecine disputes between states or residents of different states.

If factious policies contravened both private rights and the public good, one should expect majorities deliberating in calm circumstances to arrive at just and reasonable conclusions. So it is no surprise, again, that Madison described factions as the products of "rage" and "commotion," as well as other dynamics that fueled passion and distorted reason. Nor, consequently, is it surprising that one of the primary mechanisms on which Madison relied to thwart these dynamics was time.

Time and Majority Formation

Madison's diagnosis of factious majorities lays the basis for time as a treatment: these majorities were "united and actuated by some common impulse of passion, or of interest, adverse to the rights of other citizens, or to the permanent and aggregate interests of the community."[57] Federalist 10 specifies that its object is only those majorities whose judgment was warped by "co-existent passion or interest."[58] In other words, the factious majority was driven by passion or interest rather than reason. Support for measures that arose purely or primarily from passion would dissipate naturally of its own accord, which was why Madison listed these—a "zeal for different opinions concerning religion, concerning government, and many other points," "an attachment to different leaders," and so forth—yet set them aside as though they presented no serious difficulty.[59] These were apparently the kinds of conflicts Madison had in mind when

he said of mankind that "the most frivolous and fanciful distinctions" could "kindle their unfriendly passions and excite their most
violent conflicts."[60] Once kindled, these disputes flamed dramatically
and burned out rapidly.

Property, on the other hand, belonged to a different category:
factions based on "interest," the tangible manifestation of which
made them more "durable" than the passions. Durability, in turn,
made property-based factions more dangerous because they could
cohere long enough to prevail but remained subject to the same problem that plagued impassioned majorities: interest, like passion, distorted reason, leading those under its sway to make not only unjust
decisions about the rights of others but also short-sighted judgments
about their own needs. Factious majorities were apt to sacrifice their
own long-term and true interests to immediate appetites, a point evident in Madison's lament that "enlightened statesmen" could not
always be relied upon to elevate "indirect and remote considerations" over "the immediate interest which one party may find in disregarding the rights of another, or the good of the whole."[61]

That was especially the case when government was called
upon, as it frequently was, to adjudicate conflicts over property.
These controversies, again, concerned "the rights of large bodies of
citizens" and should be decided on the basis of "justice." When majorities were directly involved and were also parties to the conflict,
they were called upon to judge their own causes,[62] yet interest distorted their judgment and was liable to "corrupt their integrity."
Hence the central difficulty: the rights of minorities could not be
safely entrusted to interested or impassioned majorities. This was the
theme to which Madison returned on every occasion on which he adduced the extended republic theory.[63] "Vices" is illustrative:

> Place three individuals in a situation wherein the interest of
> each depends on the voice of the others; and give to two of
> them an interest opposed to the rights of the third. Will the
> latter be secure? The prudence of every man would shun the
> danger. The rules and forms of justice suppose and guard
> against it. Will two thousand in a like situation be less likely
> to encroach on the rights of one thousand?[64]

The answer, Federalist 10 observes, is no:

> Complaints are every where heard from our most considerate
> and virtuous citizens, equally the friends of public and
> private faith, and of public and personal liberty, that our
> governments are too unstable; that the public good is
> disregarded in the conflicts of rival parties; and that measures
> are too often decided, not according to the rules of justice,
> and the rights of the minor party, but by the superior force of
> an interested and overbearing majority.[65]

Consequently, Federalist 10 continues, factious majorities pose a fundamental difficulty:

> With equal, nay, with greater reason, a body of men are unfit
> to be both judges and parties, at the same time; yet, what are
> many of the most important acts of legislation, but so many
> judicial determinations, not indeed concerning the rights of
> single persons, but concerning the rights of large bodies of
> citizens? and what are the different classes of legislators, but
> advocates and parties to the causes which they determine?[66]

Madison's primary solution to this problem was to observe that the multiplicity and diversity of interests made it unlikely that a majority could form "upon any other principles, than those of justice and the general good."[67] Madison did not propose any mechanism for breaking up extant majorities; his point was that factious majorities often would not exist at all. Such a situation is, by definition, irrelevant to the question of whether Madison favored majority rule, for without a majority, there is no rule either to favor or oppose. But Madison obviously assumed majorities, even factious ones, would emerge. In an important sense that literature on Federalist 10 has tended to overlook, interested majorities were not the exclusive problem of the essay; or, stated conversely, Madison's solution was not to curtail their authority. The central problem of Federalist 10 was that the rule of interested majorities was unavoidable.

To be sure, Madison did express reservations about interested majorities. But recall that criticizing how majorities behave in certain circumstances is not tantamount to criticizing their rightful authority. To impugn Madison's majoritarian credentials, it would be necessary to show that he believed majorities should not be permitted to make

decisions in cases in which their judgment might be biased by interest. Federalist 10 actually says precisely the opposite. Individuals are
not allowed to judge their own causes, whereas in republican politics, there is no alternative: "What are many of the most important
acts of legislation, but so many judicial determinations. . . . Justice
ought to hold the balance between [parties to such decisions]. Yet the
parties are, *and must be,* themselves the judges."[68]

Here again is Madison's ever-present assumption that majorities that formed and persisted were bound to prevail. In the case of
a dispute between a majority and minority, the majority "must"—
that is, "will always"—win out. Nothing in the succeeding analysis
of Federalist 10 or Madison's other writings on the problem of faction
repudiates this opinion. Quite the contrary: Federalist 51's reiteration
of the extended republic theory reinforces it. That essay warns that
if majorities continued to abuse minorities in a small territory like
Rhode Island, "some power altogether independent of the people,
would soon be called for by the voice of the very factions whose mis-
rule had proved the necessity of it."[69] Madison understood the Constitution to be the alternative to such an arrangement. Under the
Constitution, factious conflicts would be adjudicated by a power dependent on the people—that is, derived from majority opinion.

However, such a majority—the majority that is to decide any
given controversy—is not an organic entity. It must form; in Madison's phrase in Federalist 51, a majority must "take place."[70] In an extended republic, some gravitational force must attract the disparate
elements of a majority together, and it is difficult to see any such
force other than a reason to care about the outcome of the dispute—
in other words, an interest. On Madison's reasoning, the fact that a
national majority coheres indicates it has an interest in the outcome.
Otherwise, it would have no incentive to form or, if it does, to incur
the political risks that are inevitable in controversial disputes. The
nation's interest in minimizing conflict between states might exert
enough gravitational force for a national majority to coalesce. In any
case, this national majority is not disinterested per se; its interest is
merely less immediate and intense than a minority that is directly involved.

Why, as Robert Dahl asks, can this type of majority form but not
a factious one?[71] Its interest is exactly the reason. The "public good"
to which Madison referred was certainly not a metaphysical and perhaps not even an outwardly moral concept.[72] He spoke instead of the

"common" good and the "aggregate interests" of the community. If these interests are truly commonly held or aggregated from smaller political units, the building blocks of a national majority need only act on what appears to them as self-interest, which was why Madison could predict in Federalist 51 that in an extended republic, "a coalition of a majority of the whole society could seldom take place upon any other principles than those of justice and the general good," a formulation whose converse indicates that majorities would commonly take place on those principles.[73] Madison, again, assumed individuals or groups could gauge their own interests and good accurately barring distorting forces like passion or temptation. An extended republic naturally filters out proposals based on those forces because the time required for a majority to coalesce and prevail across broad expanses of territory exceeds the lifespan of a typical eruption of passion; thus the idea of temporal republicanism.

In that sense, Madison's challenge was not how to divert power from an interested majority to an impartial authority, at least not literally so. This is clear from the fact that Federalist 10 does not even contemplate property rights being protected by the courts. The essay assumes their fate rests in the hands of interested majorities. The question was how to ensure the interested majority ruled as impartially as possible. An essential feature of Madison's answer was that the natural conditions of an extended republic imposed delays that, rather than shifting authority from majorities, postponed decisions until a point at which those same majorities were likely to feel less intensely about their immediate temptations and thus to perceive their true interests more clearly. The perspective is lateral rather than vertical. The issue is not whether, but rather when, the majority should rule. If the point of decision could be deferred until passions had cooled and immediate appetites had ebbed, the interested majority was likelier to rule in accordance with both justice and the public good.

The complaints about injustice in the states that stimulated Madison's thought on the problem of faction make this temporal dimension of his analysis clear. One of the most consistent stigmata by which arbitrary and factious majorities could be identified was the speed at which they formed and acted. The history of the preconvention period, too, was rife with examples of mobs descending on legislatures and demanding passage of laws within days or even hours. We recall that Madison tended to describe this factious behavior in temporal terms. A majority, for example, "might under *sudden impulses* be tempted to commit injustice on the minority."[74] Similarly, writing to Jefferson, he described "interest" and "passion"—the characteristic features of faction in Federalist 10—as "impulses."[75] Writing in retirement—although by way of defending majority rule—Madison's diagnosis of mob rule in "the ancient republics" was that "popular assemblages [were] so quickly formed, so susceptible of contagious passions."[76]

Passion and impulse, in turn, were related to proximity. The comparatively small size of the states, he wrote in the "Detached Memorandum," facilitated the "contagion & collision of the passions,"[77] triggering demands for instant and unrelenting change. The compression of time in a small territory accelerated this process. Given the proximity of individuals to one another and of factions to the seat of government, scarcely any time passed, and therefore no passions cooled, between a factious proposal arising, its embrace by a popular majority, and its translation into policy.[78] By contrast, he wrote in an 1817 letter to Adams, "the extent of our Country . . . prevent[ed] the contagion of evil passions."[79]

The relevance of the country's large geography was the time required to traverse it.[80] Madison argued that extensiveness fundamentally altered the dynamics of majority formation in several ways. According to Federalist 10, if a factious majority cohered, extensiveness would render its elements unable "by their number and local situation . . . to carry into effect schemes of oppression."[81] In an extended republic, it would be difficult for the widely dispersed local components of a national majority "to discover their own strength." One reason was the fact that "where there is a consciousness of unjust or dishonourable purposes, communication is always checked by distrust," but the fact that Madison introduced this remark with the word "besides" suggests that distrust was not the primary reason a national faction would be unable to feel its own strength.[82] The primary reason was apparently that members of such a faction in a dispersed territory simply would not know that one another existed.

But this assumption does not cohere without another: the effect of time. Communication was hardly impossible, a fact established by the more than 30 volumes of correspondence Madison carried on with contemporaries stretching from Vermont to South Carolina. His point was not that communication was impossible. It was that communication was slow and the life expectancy of factions was short.

Such was Madison's assumption about impassioned or impulsive majorities. This was the pivotal reason majority factions were unlikely to prevail in an extended republic. By the time they discovered one another, communicated their ideas to the capital, and engaged in debate back and forth, their impulsivity would have dissipated.

One additional assumption is necessary to ensure the length of the process: Madison's ideal of the "fit" representative, another feature of his thought that has provoked charges of aristocratism. Gordon Wood, for example, writes, "Considering the Federalist desire for a high-toned government filled with better sorts of people, there is something decidedly disingenuous about the democratic radicalism of their arguments."[83] Emery G. Lee III ascribes "an elitist understanding of representation" to Madison.[84] These commentators, like the Progressives, place Madison in largely the same position as did his contemporary detractors in the Anti-Federalist camp. Brutus, for example, said large electoral districts would only produce representatives from "the natural aristocracy of the country,"[85] while the minority of the Pennsylvania ratifying convention feared that "from the nature of the thing, men of the most elevated rank in life, will alone be [elected to Congress]. The other orders in the society, such as farmers, traders, and mechanics, who all ought to have a competent number of their best informed men in the legislature, will be totally unrepresented."[86]

These essayists adhered to what might be called a "reflective" model of representation whose assumption was that the representatives should precisely mirror their constituents and therefore their opinions. Thus the Federal Farmer: "A fair and equal representation is that in which the interests, feelings, opinions and views of the people are collected, in such manner as they would be were the people all assembled."[87]

To be sure, Madison was explicitly opposed to such a model, but a closer look at his own theory of representation indicates that it, too, was derived from public opinion. However, rather than merely reflecting his or her constituents' views, Madison's ideal elected official focused popular opinions via what may be called a "refractive" model of representation, in which its purpose was to focus rather than mirror. He wrote in Federalist 10: "The effect of [representation] is . . . to refine and enlarge the public views, by passing them through the medium of a chosen body of citizens, whose wisdom may best discern the true interest of their country, and whose patriotism and love of justice, will be least likely to sacrifice it to temporary or partial considerations."[88]

The temporal dimension of Madison's thought is again evident in the assumption that support for factious proposals tends to be "temporary." Consequently, in the case of popular movements pressuring the legislature, the representative's role is less to defy than to delay. Moreover, Madison did not envision representatives routinely exercising judgment independent of the wishes of their constituents. On the contrary, his writings generally suggest he believed that cases in which representatives would have to resist their constituents would be rare. During his service in the Articles Congress, for example, Madison was acutely embarrassed when Virginia abruptly withdrew its support for giving the national legislature direct taxing authority. The incident prompted him to reflect on the role of the representative: "Although not only the express instructions, but even the declared sense of constituents as in the present case, were to be a law in general to their representatives, still there were occasions on which the latter ought to hazard personal consequences from a respect to what his clear convictions determine to be the true interest of the former."[89]

Observe here that the "general" case is the representative adhering to the wishes of his or her constituents, whereas risking one's popularity by resisting them occurs only on "occasions." Federalist 63 similarly describes situations in which the representative would resist the will of his or her constituents as "particular moments" deriving from "irregular passions."[90] Even in such cases, the foremost factor separating Madison from the aristocratic model of representation imputed to him is that the representative was to base his or her decisions on the public's "true interest" and "views."

Jack Rakove likens this idea of representation to Edmund Burke's,[91] but Madison's and Burke's views actually differ substantially and in illuminating ways. To illustrate the point, compare Madison's dictum that the representative should "refine and enlarge the public's views" with Burke's "Speech to the Electors of Bristol." Burke expressed the hope that a representative would "live in the strictest union" with his constituents but nonetheless said "his unbiased opinion, his mature judgement, his enlightened conscience" could not be sacrificed because these were derived from neither constituents nor even the Constitution, but rather were "a trust from Providence, for the abuse of which he is deeply answerable."[92]

On Burke's quasi-Platonic view, the representative's judgment is ultimately directed toward a fixed and exterior objective good. Madison's, by contrast, is directed inward with a goal of focusing the public's views. There remains, of course, substantial distance between Madison's views and those of the Anti-Federalists. For purposes of evaluating whether Madison was a majoritarian, the point is that both the reflective and refractive models of representation depend on majority opinion. Madison, after all, wanted representatives to "refine and enlarge," not discard or ignore, the public's views. Comparing Washington favorably to Adams, Madison found it to be a cause for praise that the former was "ever scrutinizing into the public opinion, and ready to follow where he could not lead it," whereas the latter was "often insulting [public opinion] by the most adverse sentiments & pursuits."[93]

Even when an enlightened statesman differed with his or her constituents, he or she could prevail only by persuading rather than thwarting them, and the most potent tool at the representative's disposal was time. This was why Madison so often emphasized not merely the wisdom of fit characters but also their "firmness"—the quality they needed to resist factious proposals long enough for the passion behind them to cool. Here is Madison in the convention, reflecting on what conclusions a people deliberating "in a temperate moment" might reach about the structure of government: "Another reflection equally becoming a people on such an occasion, wd. be that they themselves, as well as a numerous body of Representatives, were liable to err also, from fickleness and passion. A necessary fence agst. this danger would be to select a portion of enlightened citizens, whose limited number, and firmness might seasonably interpose agst. impetuous counsels."[94]

Because Madison believed a majority that clung to its beliefs would inevitably prevail, this "interposition" could only serve the purpose of persuasion—in which case a majority would have changed its own opinion, thus removing any pretense for questioning his commitment to majority rule—or of delay, which served much the same purpose. The time required for a factious proposal to travel to the capital, the representative's reply to travel back, and the majority to insist on its view—through election if necessary—created a built-in mechanism for dissipating the passions: the physical extent of the republic and the time required to travel it.

These dynamics help to explain why a factious majority could not cohere in an extended republic. For Madison, the converse was also true. If a proposal could survive the time necessary for a majority to form, its idea to be communicated to the capital, negotiations to be completed, and so forth, it was highly likely that it was compatible with "justice and the general good." The barriers that inhibit factious majorities therefore do not impede worthy ones.

All these factors were at work in Madison's only proposal for a specific constitutional mechanism that flowed directly from the logic of the extended republic thesis: his much maligned idea for a national veto on state laws.

Temporal Republicanism and the National Negative

Madison's proposal to empower Congress with a veto over all state laws remains perhaps his most vilified—and, critics claim, antimajoritarian—idea. Madison described it as a republican alternative to the British king's prerogative to veto acts of Parliament,[95] but critics ranging from contemporaries like Jefferson to subsequent commentators like J. Allen Smith have described it as an overly blunt instrument whose purpose or at least effect would have been to limit self-government at the local level. They seem, by Madison's own arguments, to have a point. Although one major purpose of the veto was to protect the jurisdiction of the national government against incursions by the states—the very problem that rendered the Articles regime impotent and necessitated the Philadelphia Convention—Madison also repeatedly cited its promise for taming unjust majorities inside the states. His case to Washington is typical:

> Another happy effect of this prerogative would be its controul
> on the internal vicissitudes of State policy; and the
> aggressions of interested majorities on the rights of minorities
> and of individuals. The great desideratum which has not yet
> been found for Republican Governments, seems to be some
> disinterested & dispassionate umpire in disputes between
> different passions & interests in the State. The majority who
> alone have the right of decision, have frequently an interest
> real or supposed in abusing it. In Monarchies the sovereign is
> more neutral to the interests and views of different parties;
> but unfortunately he too often forms interests of his own

repugnant to those of the whole. Might not the national
prerogative here suggested be found sufficiently disinterested
for the decision of local questions of policy, whilst it would
itself be sufficiently restrained from the pursuit of interests
adverse to those of the whole Society?[96]

This passage presents several difficulties from the perspective
of majority rule. One is that Madison himself described the policies
subject to the veto as "internal" and "local." Consider, by way of illustration, a local dispute that genuinely does not affect jurisdictions
beyond the one deciding it: say, for example, whether to invoke the
power of eminent domain to seize a privately owned plot of land for
an exclusively local purpose such as building a new city hall.[97] Referring that decision to Congress for review may be more republican
than referring it to a hereditary monarch, especially insofar as the jurisdiction in question would at least be represented on Capitol Hill,
but the residents of the town in question are unlikely to feel their
right to self-government is vindicated by their comparatively minus-
cule representation in Congress. From their point of view, the neutrality and "disinterestedness" Madison desires would be precisely
the problem: an issue with which they are closely concerned could
be decided by a distant body that is almost entirely disconnected
from it.[98] Such a body may be in a position to resolve abstract claims
of rights and justice, but it would be wholly incompetent to the crucial task of applying them to local questions such as the extent to
which the community actually needs the land in question. If this is
the kind of scenario Madison contemplates, the national negative
may not violate the republican principle, but it certainly would place
considerably more distance between public opinion and public policy than has been seen thus far.

To compound the difficulty, Madison's repeated insistence that
the veto's jurisdiction extend to "all cases whatsoever" has prompted
critics to charge that regardless of whether he intended the device to
encompass purely local cases, it surely would have empowered Congress to interfere with them. Jefferson thus assailed the proposal:

Prima facie I do not like it. It fails in an essential character,
that the hole and the patch should be commensurate. But this
proposes to mend a small hole by covering the whole
garment. Not more than 1. out of 100. state acts concern the

confederacy. This proposition then, in order to give them 1.
degree of power which they ought to have, gives them 99.
more which they ought not to have, upon a presumption that
they will not exercise the 99.[99]

Indeed, many commentators have cited the universal jurisdiction of the veto as evidence that Madison intended it to be used primarily to control injustices within the states, not to protect the national government against incursions of its authority. Garry Wills
echoes Jefferson:

> Some have tried to minimize this call for central power,
> saying it was to be used only defensively by the national
> legislature, to fend off invasion of its authority. If that were
> the case, Madison should have [limited its jurisdiction]; but
> he went on to say that *all* laws fall under this power, with no
> norm but the *opinion* (judgment) of the national legislator. He
> was an experienced enough legislator to know that this was
> no way to frame a *limited* power.[100]

And, finally, Michael Zuckert draws a distinction between
"Madison Federalism"—equipped with a universal veto directed at
the "national ends" of securing justice and protecting rights—and
"Randolph Federalism," based on the Virginia Plan's call for a negative limited to constitutional violations affecting the distribution of
power between the state and federal governments.[101]

These analyses require careful attention, for they seem to square
in major respects with Madison's own description of the veto. It is
worth observing at the outset that in nearly every description of the
negative Madison offered, protecting national jurisdiction was paramount and taming local majorities was ancillary. Moreover, his foremost motive in making its jurisdiction universal was to prevent
states from evading it through legal technicalities. Contrary to Wills's
analysis, Madison was an experienced enough legislator to know
there was no other way to frame the power successfully. But more to
the point of the present study, many commentators mistake Madison's analysis in one important respect: he did not regard the local
abuses to which he objected and the national issues for which the
veto was also necessary as entirely distinct. In Jefferson's terms,
Madison believed that far more than one of a hundred local issues

did affect the confederacy; in Zuckert's, Madison believed the national end of preventing injustice and the federal end of protecting national jurisdiction were intertwined. By describing majority abuses as "local" or "internal," he referred to the jurisdiction in which the decisions were made, not to the scope of their impact; and by calling national majorities "disinterested," he meant that their interest was vastly diluted compared to that of local majorities, not that the interest did not exist. On the contrary, as we have seen in Chapter 1, every specific abuse of which he accused local majorities also involved national or interstate interests.

The purpose of the negative was thus to ensure an issue was decided by the largest majority that shared an interest in it. One might argue that a dispute between, say, two states should therefore be decided only between the two of them.[102] But such an approach would require an infinite proliferation of governing institutions, and given Madison's repeated assumption that all 13 states had to cohere to achieve and maintain independence—a belief he first articulated during the Revolution but reiterated at the end of his life[103]—Congress was a logical locus of decision because any dispute between two or more states could be reasonably said to involve the interests of national majorities. Madison supplied several reasons to believe these national majorities would make more temperate decisions. One is that their interest in the outcome of such disputes would be highly diluted compared to the intense and immediate interests of local majorities. This is what Madison meant by describing them as disinterested or neutral. In addition, the time required for these larger majorities to cohere enhanced the probability that they would render decisions on the basis of reason rather than passion.

Still, this analysis does not entirely answer Jefferson's complaint, reiterated by Wills, that the universal jurisdiction of the veto merely assumed that Congress would not exercise it in cases that did not involve national issues. It does indeed seem unlike Madison to propose a power on the belief that it would often not be used. Yet this is in fact Madison's assumption, and it arises clearly from the logic of Federalist 10. Recall that given the empirical conditions of an extended republic, national majorities will arise only in response to issues of general interest. By the same analysis, one ought not expect Congress to insert itself in a local dispute unless the national interest is at stake. Again, a majority—whether of the public or of Congress—is not a preexisting, organic entity. It must form, and there is no reason to believe a majority would form in favor of overturning a popular local measure (a step that would involve substantial political risk) without some interest beyond the state concerned—that is, on Madison's reasoning, a national interest. The fact that majorities form for a reason (their own interest) was why Madison could be confident that natural political dynamics would confine the veto to genuinely national issues.

Following this reasoning further, however, one might lodge another objection to the veto: that it would have been the flimsiest of parchment barricades, something that Madison repeatedly disdained. The relevant question is this: if Madison's assessment of the relative interests between national and state majorities is correct—that the former would be dilute and the latter intense—why would the states comply with a congressional veto? Moreover, not only would the national government be only weakly interested, it would also be naturally weak in power. Madison predicted in Federalist 46 that popular opinion—the source of power, he believed, in free societies—would lie with the states over the national government, at least until such time as the latter proved its superior administrative skills.[104] This would seem to leave a weak and weakly interested national government in the unenviable position of merely asking the states—which were already more powerful than it—to desist in implementing a popular policy in which their interest was intense. This would have been precisely parallel to the impotence of the Articles Congress. In fact, the following argument, one of many Madison made in Philadelphia in his futile attempts to secure support for the veto, all but openly suggests the national government would be unable to enforce a negative:

> A negative was the mildest expedient that could be devised for preventing [state abuses]. The existence of such a check would prevent attempts to commit them. Should no such precaution be engrafted, the only remedy wd. lie in an appeal to coercion. Was such a remedy eligible? was it practicable? Could the national resources, if exerted to the utmost enforce a national decree agst. Massts. abetted perhaps by several of her neighbours? It wd. not be possible. A small proportion of the Community, in a compact situation, acting on the defensive, and at one of its extremities might at any time bid defiance to the National authority. Any Govt. for the U. States

formed on the supposed practicability of using force agst. the unconstitutional proceedings of the States, wd. prove as visionary & fallacious as the Govt. of Congs. The negative wd. render the use of force unnecessary.[105]

What purpose, then, would the negative serve if it could not be imposed by force? The answer may lie in Madison's prediction that such a power would "prevent" state–national conflicts. The idea was for a conflict involving the negative never to reach a point at which force was necessary. On his own assumption that persistent majorities always prevailed, the only reason to believe a veto would divert such conflicts is that it would impose a delay between a local majority making a factious decision and that decision being implemented—a delay across which the majority in fact would not persist because it would have been initially motivated by short-lived passion. Presumably, the passion that would have initially motivated an unjust majority—passion that would also have been necessary for it to resist a decree of the national government—would dissipate in the time required for a local law to be communicated to the capital and Congress' decision to be communicated back. In these senses, we may see that Madison's call for a national negative on state laws "in all cases whatsoever," far from an attempt to curtail majorities, instead affirmed temporal republicanism at the national level.

So, as will presently be seen, was another device widely understood to be a Madisonian restraint on popular majorities: the Bill of Rights.

Chapter Four

Constitutional Metabolism

By its critics as well as its admirers, the Bill of Rights—the other American political device of which Madison is awarded paternity— is generally regarded to be countermajoritarian: its purpose is to establish what H. B. Mayo has called "no trespassing" zones, areas of autonomy in which the majority is prevented from legislating.[1] The judiciary—and, indeed, the text of the Constitution more broadly— is generally regarded in the same light. In this chapter, I argue that all these devices are in fact agents of temporal republicanism. Again, we shall endeavor at all turns to establish two points with respect to the Bill of Rights, the judiciary, and the broader text of the Constitution: that they were both majoritarian devices and pacing mechanisms. Madison's intent was to slow and guide, rather than preempt, majority deliberation in cases of rights—once more, to establish speed bumps rather than roadblocks.

Madison's analysis is substantially at odds with a contemporary ethos that tends to see rights as wholly exempt from the cognizance of majorities. According to this understanding, the claims of majorities are irrelevant in cases of rights; or, conversely, individuals need not justify their exercises of rights to the majority. Ronald Dworkin, for example, understands this immunity from public claims to be the very definition of a right: when we say someone has a right to do something, "we mean that he is entitled to do so even if this would not be in the general interest."[2] Madison, by contrast, affirmed majority rule even when assertions of individual rights were at stake, a point that will be shown in the narrow basis on which he defended the two freedoms with which he is most prominently associated: those of conscience and political expression. In the former case, Madison's near absolutist position derives not from any inherent zone of individual autonomy but rather from his Lockean conclusion that the public good cannot rationally be served by regulating the realm of conscience.[3] In the latter, his defense of political expression is also based not on individual autonomy but rather on the essential role of open debate in majoritarian government. In each instance, Madison reaches his conclusions by way of, rather than by circumventing, majority rule.

Moreover, Madison believed that disputes over rights were ultimately to be settled by majorities, not the courts. In exploring this feature of his thought, it is important to remember that the issue at stake is not the extent of Madison's commitment to what have come to be called "individual rights"[4]—on the contrary, his views of legitimate legislative authority were often narrower than those of his contemporaries, especially where freedom of conscience was concerned—but rather how best to protect them. Madison's derision for "parchment barriers" was especially acute in the case of institutional protections for rights. His simultaneous beliefs that majorities would inevitably prevail in the United States and that they would present the most serious threat to rights in the American system compelled him to think in terms not of dictating protections from on high but rather of creating conditions in which majorities were likeliest to behave tolerantly. Madison believed a Bill of Rights could facilitate those conditions both by encouraging majorities to pause in what might otherwise be headlong rushes to trample the rights of minorities and by providing a common vocabulary that would make discussions of rights productive in the political realm. The Bill of Rights was, in this sense, a device of temporal republicanism.

From there, we shall explore Madison's view of constitutional interpretation. Here again, the contemporary assumption is typically that constitutional interpretation lies beyond the reach of majorities, assigned instead to a judicial branch designed to be insulated from them. Madison envisioned the judiciary playing a comparatively limited role. The ultimate arbiters of the Constitution were those who made it: popular majorities. And once again, the criterion for whether a majority's interpretation was authoritative was the length of time it cohered. In this regard, Madison believed the authoritative meaning of the Constitution could change, but only gradually and on the basis of persistent consensus: It was, so to speak, a living Constitution with a slow metabolism.

Rights and Majorities

Freedom of Conscience: The "Memorial and Remonstrance"

Madison's most famous statement on freedom of conscience is his "Memorial and Remonstrance against Religious Assessments," a petition he wrote in 1785 amid his mounting concern about Patrick Henry's plan to provide public funds for Christian religious instruction. As Robert W. T. Martin notes, the proposal produced a frenzy of public opinion on both sides of the issue. Henry's side was expected to prevail when Madison was encouraged to take up his pen for what turned out to be a notably majoritarian rather than individualist argument for freedom of conscience.[5] In summarizing Madison's doctrinaire view of religious freedom, commentators have tended to emphasize the frank conclusion of the "Memorial and Remonstrance's" first article: "We maintain therefore that in matters of religion no man's right is abridged by the institution of Civil Society, and that religion is wholly exempt from its cognizance."[6] At first glance, the argument appears conducive to a liberal state of nature account in which the authority of the government is limited by the purposes for which it was established. Thomas Paine typifies that perspective:

> The natural rights which [man] retains are all those in which the *power* to execute is as perfect in the individual as the right itself. The natural rights which are not retained, are all those in which, though the right is perfect in the individual, the power to execute them is defective. . . . The power produced from the aggregate of natural rights, imperfect in power in the individual, cannot be applied to invade the natural rights which are retained in the individual, and in which the power to execute is as perfect as the right itself.[7]

We are not concerned here with contrasting Madison's and Paine's views on freedom of conscience. On the contrary, they were, for the most part, substantively compatible. But the different paths by which they reached those conclusions are illuminating. Note that while Paine's analysis in the passage just quoted leads him to defend freedom of conscience, it does not depend on any qualities especially unique to that right. Paine claims that individuals do not need the protection of society in order to follow their own religious convictions, so society—in a republic, the majority—cannot regulate that realm of life. That standard might apply to any number of rights.

By contrast, the analysis that leads Madison to conclude that religion is "wholly exempt" from political authority applies only to conscience and could not, consequently, establish a standard for exempting other rights from majority review. The "Memorial and Remonstrance" begins by reprising Locke's argument—much acclaimed in America—that religious observance demands purity of intention, which the sovereign cannot, as a matter of rational possibility, compel.[8] Thus Madison, quoting the similarly Lockean Virginia Bill of Rights:

> We hold it for a fundamental and undeniable truth, "that religion or the duty which we owe to our Creator and the manner of discharging it, can be directed only by reason and conviction, not by force or violence." The religion then of every man must be left to the conviction and conscience of every man, and it is the right of every man to exercise it as these may dictate. This right is in its nature an unalienable right. It is unalienable because the opinions of men, depending only on the evidence contemplated by their own minds, cannot follow the dictates of other men.[9]

The crucial word is "cannot." The literal impossibility of compelling inward religious belief separates conscience from property—indeed, from every right expressed through outward action—because there is no public good that can rationally be served by regulating it. This makes conscience uniquely unalienable—that is, it alone cannot be alienated. Such is clearly not the case with, for example, the right to property. As opposed to property—charters to which, again, could be both granted and withdrawn for the public good—society has no claim to make, no balancing act to perform, in the case of conscience. Although the theoretically richest portion of the "Memorial and Remonstrance" is its first article's analysis of political obligation, the bulk of the document is in fact devoted to disproving claims made by proponents of the religious assessment that it would serve the public good. The fifth through fourteenth articles oppose the assessment on prudential grounds such as the sovereign's incompetence in matters of conscience and the corrupting influence of public funding on religious institutions.[10] What Madison never argues, as Dworkin might, is that claims of the public good are irrelevant: The point of the "Memorial and Remonstrance" is that they are inherently unsuccessful, which was why Madison's draft of what became the First Amendment specified that the rights of conscience could not be "on any pretext" infringed.[11] Conscience is therefore the only right Madison establishes on the grounds of the innate autonomy of the individual.

None of these observations is intended to suggest that Madison would have countenanced state involvement in religion were it capable of fulfilling a hypothetical public purpose.[12] Madison generally foreclosed that possibility on the basis of equality. Because "all men are to be considered as entering into Society on equal conditions, as relinquishing no more and therefore retaining no less, one than another of their natural rights," it was unfair to force any of them to subsidize a religious practice with which they disagreed—a possibility that, on Madison's account, any state involvement in religious affairs could scarcely avoid.[13] Significantly, Madison's proposal for the Bill of Rights forbade the national and state governments from infringing the "equal rights of conscience," not the right of conscience simply.[14] This concern with equality was the basis of his opposition to official chaplains in both Congress and the military.[15] In a similar vein, Madison objected to presidential proclamations calling on the people to fast or practice other religious observances, especially when these used, in his words, "the language of *injunction*" rather than recommendation. The particular problem with these proclamations was not the inherent incompatibility of religion and politics, but rather the fact that they "lost sight of the equality of *all* religious sects in the eye of the Constitution."[16] But notice, first, that Madison never allowed this observation alone to resolve the argument without simultaneously rebutting claims that a given measure would serve the public good, and, second, that his choice of equality as the basis for this objection gives it an interpersonal and distributive character that further belies any suggestion that he meant substantively to isolate assertions of individual rights from the social realm. The "Memorial and Remonstrance" cautions: "Whilst we assert for ourselves a freedom to embrace, to profess, and to observe the religion which we believe to be of divine origin, we cannot deny an equal freedom to those whose minds have not yielded to the evidence which has convinced us." The first phrase in the sentence would be unnecessary if Madison intended merely to isolate the individual from the majority. In that case, he would merely have said conscience was none of the majority's business. Instead, the obligation to respect others' freedom of conscience arises not from their autonomy but rather from reciprocity. We are bound to respect others' freedom of conscience because they respect ours, not because their individuality is inviolable.[17] Again, Madison clearly did believe individuals were inviolable in the case of conscience. The relevant point here is how he arrived at that conclusion.

Madison's denial that political interference in religion could serve a public purpose—especially combined with his invocation of equality—would be sufficient to conclude the point, but the "Memorial and Remonstrance" extends his argument in a way that further confines it to freedom of conscience. Religion, to put the matter simply, outranks politics. Observe the particular basis of that claim:

> It is the duty of every man to render to the Creator such homage, and such only, as he believes to be acceptable to him. This duty is precedent, both in order of time and degree of obligation, to the claims of Civil Society. Before any man can be considered as a member of Civil Society, he must be considered as a subject of the Governor of the Universe. And if a member of Civil Society, who enters into any subordinate association, must always do it with a reservation of his duty to the general authority, much more must every man who becomes a member of any particular Civil Society do it with a saving of his allegiance to the Universal Sovereign.[18]

Whereas Paine's argument protects the internal realm of the individual, Madison's is based on a ranking of external obligations. Religion is exempt from civil society not because the individual is autonomous but, on the contrary, because the individual is obligated to two external entities—the Creator and society—the first of whom trumps the second. The fact that religious obligation precedes political obligation in time cannot of itself establish Madison's point, especially because the entire basis of the Lockean social contract theory to which he is obviously indebted is that a broad array of rights that become subservient to society—such as property—antedate it as well. The key to Madison's argument lies in its syllogistic hierarchy of associations and the obligations that attend them. These rise from "subordinate associations" to the "general authority" to the "Universal Sovereign." Conscience is the only assertion of right that logically outranks the general authority on this scale. Conversely, and equally important, every other right deals with associations or activities—such as the individual's possession of property—that would be located below the general authority on the same scale, and thus be regulable by it. That is not to say the individual is at the mercy of the general authority—that is, the majority. Again, the majority is obliged to maintain the rule of law, including in its regulation of rights. The relevant point for the present analysis is that the individual's right of conscience actually derives from the individual's obligation to an authority that outranks society. For another right to be comparably immune from majorities, it would have to entail obligations exceeding the individual's obligation to society as well. No other right contemplated in Madison's writings meets that criterion. The point, in sum, is not that society is not entitled to interfere with the individual. Madison indicates clearly that it can. What society is not entitled to do is interfere with the Creator's superior claim to the individual's allegiance.

The majoritarian basis of Madison's argument is further evident not merely in its content but also in the fact that he makes an argument to begin with—and to whom it is addressed: namely, the legislature. Recall that one consistent feature of contemporary rights discourse is the assumption that the individual is not obligated to explain himself to the majority. The assertion of a right constitutes its own explanation. But the preamble to the "Memorial and Remonstrance" plainly assumes the burden not just of "declar[ing] the reasons by which we are determined" to oppose the policy in question, but also of persuading a political institution—the legislature—of their justice.[19] Even in the course of describing the proposed religious assessment as a potential violation by the majority of minority rights, the "Memorial and Remonstrance" acknowledges the legitimacy of majority rule: "True it is," the first article says, "that no other rule exists, by which any question which may divide a society can be ultimately determined, but the will of the majority; but it is also true, that the majority may trespass on the rights of the minority."[20] The point of the document was to declare that the majority would be making such a mistake, not to deny its authority to do so. Jefferson's "Virginia Statute for Religious Freedom"—which Madison steered through the legislature and later described as the best synopsis of the principle of religious liberty that "words can admit"—announced a similar purpose for itself:

> And though we well know that this Assembly, elected by the people for their ordinary purposes of legislation only, have no power to restrain the acts of succeeding Assemblies, constituted with powers equal to our own, and that therefore to declare this act to be irrevocable would be of no effect in law; yet we are free to declare, and do declare, that the rights hereby asserted are of the natural rights of mankind, and that if any act shall be hereafter passed to repeal the present or to narrow its operations, such act will be an infringement of natural right.[21]

Significantly, Madison praised this statute as "having been the result of a formal appeal to the sense of the Community and a deliberate sanction of a vast majority," whereas the "Memorial and Remonstrance" warned that the community's views on the religious assessment were not yet fully known, and "a measure of such singular magnitude and delicacy [as the religious assessment] ought not to be imposed, without the clearest evidence that it is called for by a majority of citizens."[22] The need to appeal to the community on matters of religious freedom was especially important because public support was the only reliable protector of the right of conscience.[23]

This self-conscious appeal to the community to resolve questions of rights refutes the assumption that Madison believed the purpose of declaring individual liberties was to isolate them from popular majorities. Commentators would later assume that Madison drafted the national Bill of Rights to empower the courts to break the force of public opinion,[24] but the "Memorial and Remonstrance"—which repeatedly invokes the Virginia Bill of Rights—conspicuously lacks any reference to the judiciary. On the contrary, it assumes that the proper forum for debating whether a religious assessment would violate the right of conscience is the legislature. The "Memorial and Remonstrance" does, to be sure, deny that "the will of the Legislature is the only measure of their authority," but his choice of the word "will" is revealing. Madison has already been seen to counterpose "will" unfavorably to "reason."[25] The suggestion may be that one purpose of appealing to the legislature on questions of rights is to slow its deliberations and enable reason to prevail over an impulsive will. Failing that, the "Memorial and Remonstrance" says its purpose is to appeal to the very entity Madison is often assumed to be trying to thwart: the majority itself. The document warns that the views "of the Representatives or of the Counties" (that is, of public officials) may not yet reflect that of "the people," but in any case, "our hope is that neither of the former will, after due consideration, espouse the dangerous principle of the Bill. Should the event disappoint us, it will still leave us in full confidence that a fair appeal to the latter will reverse the sentence against our liberties."[26]

This passage in many ways encapsulates Madison's treatment of rights. "Due consideration" may relieve a legislature's impulse to violate rights. If the legislature violates rights anyway, the result is "disappointing" but not illegitimate—and the proper remedy is an appeal to the people at the next election. Such was also the remedy Madison sought to what he believed to be the young republic's first major test of freedom of political expression: the Alien and Sedition Acts of 1798.

Freedom of Expression: The Alien and Sedition Acts

Madison's views on the freedoms of speech and press, especially as he expressed them in reaction to the Alien and Sedition Acts, initially seem as doctrinaire as those he espoused on the right of conscience. The acts were passed in a political environment dominated by tensions with France, which had escalated since Washington's decision to maintain neutrality in the conflict between Great Britain and the French Republic. Tensions boiled over into a quasi-war of naval skirmishes, and the sense of alarm accelerated with the intrigue of the XYZ Affair. Apologists for President John Adams have characterized the Alien and Sedition laws as an understandable reaction to genuine instability. Moreover, they have emphasized that the Sedition Act liberalized the common law of sedition. Cynics, by contrast, have seen the laws as both a power grab and an attempt to silence the administration's critics. [27]

Our particular concern at this point is with the Sedition Act, which made it a crime to publish untrue statements that defamed the government or discouraged unrest against it. Madison's writings on the topic generally include two documents and correspondence surrounding them: the Virginia Resolution of 1798, which asserted the right of states to "interpose" against the Alien and Sedition laws—a nebulous authority whose boundaries he never clearly explained—and the Virginia Report of 1800, an extended legislative commentary penned in reaction to criticism of the resolution. We shall use these writings as a window into Madison's views on rights and popular majorities.

The Virginia Report argued against the Sedition Act on the grounds that the First Amendment was "a denial to Congress of all power over the press."[28] The freedoms of press and conscience, he added, "rest equally on the ground of not being delegated by the constitution, and consequently withheld from government."[29] By this Madison did not mean that press and freedom were withheld from government inherently, only from the national government, which was one of enumerated powers. But press and conscience were also equal in another sense: Madison reflected the broad consensus of his time in assuming the parameters of each were to be determined by the community and that majorities retained ultimate authority to settle disputes regarding them.

Indeed, it could hardly be any other way, for the phrases "freedom of speech" and "freedom of the press" already require definition, and hence parameters, that could only come about from the deliberation and prudential judgment that Madison associated with the legislative branch of government. The need for definition makes absolutism on these rights something of a non sequitur—what Mary Ann Glendon describes as "the illusion of absoluteness."[30] Alexander Meiklejohn frames the problem in the following way: "[The First Amendment] *does not forbid the abridging of speech.* But, at the same time, *it does forbid the abridging of the freedom of speech.* It is to the solving of that paradox, that apparent self-contradiction, that we are summoned if, as free men, we wish to know what the right of freedom of speech is."[31]

That paradox was known to Madison's contemporaries. Benjamin Franklin, a printer who must have reflected on the matter in his professional capacity, candidly admitted that "few of us, I believe, have distinct Ideas of its [freedom of the press] meaning," adding that he personally would be willing to exchange his own right to libel others in exchange for protection from others libeling him.[32] Such an exchange was precisely what distinguished the civil right of free speech from its natural counterpart. In the state of nature, the natural law permitted individuals more or less to do as they pleased but also restrained them from injuring one another. Because individuals possessed property in their reputations, libel constituted an injury in the same way theft of physical property would.[33] Civil society arose from the difficulty of enforcing those restraints, just as it arose from the impossibility of resolving property disputes peacefully. Philip Hamburger argues that Americans broadly understood civil law to permit the limits natural law already placed on freedom of speech in the prepolitical condition, including restraints on libel and obscenity. As Hamburger notes, the Virginia ratifying convention of 1788 thus saw no inconsistency in recommending that the Constitution be amended to protect the freedom of speech and provide legal remedies for individual injuries to one's "person, property, or character."[34]

The fact that Madison cited the convention's resolution on freedom of speech in the course of arguing against the Sedition Act suggests his familiarity with and approval of it.[35] The question, of course, was where precisely the boundaries of political expression were to be fixed, not whether limits were permissible. The Virginia Report acknowledges this fact explicitly. What it denies is the claim, made by adherents of the Sedition Act, that British common law was the relevant regulative standard:

> The committee [that produced the report] are not unaware of the difficulty of all general questions which, may turn on the proper boundary between the liberty and licentiousness of the press. They will leave it therefore for consideration only, how far the difference between the nature of the British government, and the nature of the American governments, and the practice under the latter, may show the degree of rigour in the former to be inapplicable to, and not obligatory in the latter. . . . [In the United States], magistrates are not held to be infallible, nor the legislatures to be omnipotent; and both being elective, are both responsible. Is it not natural and necessary, under such different circumstances, that a different degree of freedom, in the use of the press, should be contemplated?[36]

Note that Madison declined to defend freedom of speech on the basis of individual autonomy. Its relevance—and, crucially, the standard for judging its proper extent—lies in the purpose it serves in society, which is to facilitate majority deliberation. For that reason,

Madison continued, the British enjoyed especially wide-ranging free-dom of the press when commenting on "the responsible members of the government, where the reasons operating here [that is, the need for free commentary to facilitate public deliberation on officeholders the people have the power to remove], become applicable there."[37]

Similarly, Madison's draft of the Bill of Rights, like the state bills of rights on which it was based, justified itself with exactly the type of apologia contemporary discourse assumes is unnecessary where individual liberties are concerned: the freedom of the press would be inviolable not in and of itself but rather *because* it was "one of the great bulwarks of liberty."[38] The Sedition Act, Madison further ex-plained in the Virginia resolutions, should arouse "universal alarm, because it is leveled against that right of freely examining public characters and measures, and of free communication among the peo-ple thereon, which has ever been justly deemed, the only effectual guardian of every other right."[39] Equally important, these benefits had to be weighed against the risks of an abusive press. In observing that it had been the American practice to resolve these questions on the side of license rather than restriction, much as he had advocated should be done in the case of freedom of conscience, Madison tacitly acknowledged their prudential character: "Some degree of abuse is inseparable from the proper use of everything; and in no instance is this more true, than in that of the press. It has accordingly been the practice of the states, that it is better to leave a few of its noxious branches to their luxuriant growth, than by pruning them away, to injure the vigour of those yielding the proper fruits."[40]

The dispute, again, concerned how much latitude the social purposes of freedom of speech required. But when Madison denied Congress any power over the press—rejecting the Federalist argu-ment that the freedom of political expression could be regulated so long as it was not abridged—he did not mean that the freedom in question was inherently boundless. He meant that once the bound-aries were determined—and freedom of the press or speech was thereby established—it was to receive absolute protection.[41]

The fact that such decisions required prudential judgments made the task of adjusting the boundaries of rights the proper sphere of the legislature, and therefore of popular majorities. The case of British common law, which supporters of the Alien and Sedition Acts invoked in their defense, supplies an illustration. Madison consis-tently argued that it was up to the legislature, and thus majorities, to determine the content of a uniquely American common law. Madison thus objected that empowering courts to undertake that endeavor "could confer on the judicial department a discretion little short of a legislative power."[42] In an unrelated context that nonetheless illuminates Madison's belief that areas requiring detailed or prudential judgments were appropriate for the legislature alone, the Virginia Report warns that "those who place peculiar reliance on the Judicial exposition of the constitution, as the bulwark provided against undue extensions of the Legislative power" should resist excessively broad interpretations of the necessary and proper clause because it would thereby no longer be "sufficiently precise and determinate for judicial cognizance and control." If the necessary and proper clause was rendered unlimited, its scope would involve "questions of mere policy and expediency, on which legislative discretion alone can decide, and from which the judicial interposition and control are completely excluded."[43] These were the kind of questions involved in determining the latitude guaranteed by the freedom of political expression—questions it was up to the community, acting through the legislature, to resolve.

Indeed, one of the most striking features of the debate over the Alien and Sedition Acts is that it seems not to have occurred to even their most strident opponents to ask the courts to overturn them. Madison did hope, as will be seen in more detail below, that individual judges and juries would derail prosecutions under the Sedition Act—a hope frustrated by a fiercely partisan and pro-Adams judiciary—but he never contemplated the courts setting aside the law per se.[44] On the contrary, the entire purpose of his Virginia Report was to rebut resolutions passed by other states that said Virginia had no business rousing public opinion against an act of the national government. Rhode Island, for example, had claimed that the Constitution "vests in the federal courts exclusively, and in the Supreme Court of the United States ultimately, the authority of deciding on the constitutionality of any act or law of the Congress of the United States."[45] Madison, however, insisted that the Virginia Resolutions were intended not to disrupt the constitutional operation of the government but rather simply to appeal to public opinion. They were "expressions of opinion, unaccompanied with any other effect than what they may produce on opinion, by exciting reflection."[46] The Virginia Report concluded on a similarly rhetorical note: The Virginia Assembly "do hereby renew their protest against 'the alien and sedition acts' as palpable and alarming infractions of the constitution."[47] Madison would later insist that the Virginia Resolutions and Report meant to serve no other function than urging the people to undo the Alien & Sedition Acts by majoritarian processes:

> Concert among the States for redress against the alien & sedition laws, as acts of usurped power, was a leading sentiment, and the attainment of a concert the immediate object of the course adopted by the [Virginia] Legislature, which was that of inviting the other States "to *concur* in declaring the acts to be unconstitutional, and to *co-operate* by the necessary & proper measures in maintaining unimpaired the authorities rights & liberties reserved to the States respectively & to the people." That by the necessary and proper measures to be *concurrently* and co-operatively taken, were meant measures known to the Constitution, particularly the ordinary controul of the people and Legislatures of the States over the Gov't of the U.S. cannot be doubted; and the interposition of this controul as the event showed was equal to the occasion.[48]

His determination to limit the Virginia Resolutions' scope to this rhetorical purpose is accentuated by Madison's self-conscious choice not to join Jefferson's Kentucky Resolutions in declaring the Alien and Sedition Acts to be "utterly void and of no force."[49] Madison would later say that even his somewhat more conservative approach of interposition was appropriate in "extreme cases only, and after a failure of all efforts for redress under the forms of the Constitution."[50] The "form of the Constitution" under which Virginia sought redress was an appeal to public opinion. Madison had, in fact, wanted both the Virginia Resolutions and the Virginia Report to be offered in the name of the people of the state alone so as to avoid any suggestion that the state was objecting to the Alien and Sedition Acts in its corporate capacity.[51] He argued to Jefferson at the time that the power to determine the constitutionality of an act of the national government lay with the "states"—whose people had consented to the Constitution via conventions—but not their "legislatures." Phrasing the claim in this way "would leave to other States a choice of all the modes possible of concurring in the substance [of the Virginia Resolutions], and would shield the Genl. Assembly agst. the charge of Usurpation in the very act of protesting agst. the usurpations of Congress."[52] The Virginia Resolution and Report were ultimately, he insisted, an appeal by the people of Virginia to the national majority to settle the boundaries of the right of political expression liberally. That strategy, Madison later reflected, succeeded, triggering a backlash against the Adams administration that resulted in its ouster, the Sedition Act's expiration, and presidential pardons for those convicted under it. Significantly for this study, Madison—in the course of denying Calhoun and other nullifiers the right to his legacy—would later describe Virginia's appeal to popular majorities as a *"constitutional* remedy" available against any unwarranted assertion of national authority: An aggrieved state had recourse to "constitutional remedies such as have been found effectual; particularly in the case of alien & sedition laws, and such as will in all cases be effectual, whilst the responsibility of the Gen'l Gov't to its constituents continues: Remonstrances & instructions—recurring elections & impeachments; amend't of Const. as provided by itself & exemplified in the 11th article limiting the suability of the States."[53] Madison's reference to aggrieved states and to the Eleventh Amendment pertained to the nullification controversy specifically. For present purposes, the point to observe is that he believed complaints over the Alien and Sedition Acts—and thus the proper boundaries of the right of political expression—were appropriately, and successfully, settled by an appeal to the majority.

The power of delay is also latent in Madison's analysis, which may be seen by asking the following question: Given his repeated assertions that majorities would present the most serious threat to rights, why would he seek to redress those violations by an appeal to the same majorities? The answer is twofold. First, in the specific instance of the Alien and Sedition Acts, Madison believed power was being usurped by a cabal in Washington that genuinely did not reflect majority opinion.[54] However, and second, in a case in which a majority supported such a measure, it might be possible to slow its consideration and overcome its impulsiveness by reminding it that it was trampling rights that all had agreed to abide. Such an appeal might work if it occurred against a backdrop of broad consensus on what those rights were. Madison hoped a national Bill of Rights might facilitate precisely that.

The Bill of Rights

Many, if not most, twentieth-century commentators have assumed that the Bill of Rights was intended as a tool the judiciary could use to protect individuals against popular majorities. Beard described the judiciary as the antimajoritarian linchpin of the entire constitutional enterprise. "The radicals of 1788," Charles Warren adds, including Madison among that number, "knew full well that *only through the Courts of law could these rights be enforced*. One does not have to infer such knowledge; for they themselves [again including Madison] specifically stated that the chief value of the Bill of Rights lay in the existence of the Judiciary."[55] Warren joins many other commentators in citing what does, it must be acknowledged, seem to be a rather emphatic endorsement of judicial review on the basis of the Bill of Rights. Madison said in introducing the proposal before Congress: "If [these protections] are incorporated into the Constitution, independent tribunals of justice will consider themselves in a peculiar manner the guardians of those rights; they will be an impenetrable bulwark against every assumption of power in the Legislative or Executive; they will be naturally led to resist every encroachment upon rights expressly stipulated for in the Constitution by the declaration of rights."[56]

But if Madison intended the Bill of Rights to be available to the judiciary as such a weapon, the courts were remarkably slow to take up the sword. As Charles Epp documents, the Supreme Court decided almost no cases on the basis of the Bill of Rights before the twentieth century.[57] Madison himself was reticent at best about the Bill of Rights and especially about the judiciary's role in applying it. When Jefferson first confronted him about the absence of a Bill of Rights in the proposed Constitution, Madison replied with essentially the same argument Hamilton had made in Federalist 84: A Bill of Rights would be dangerous, first, because it might imply that rights not specified were not held, and second, because prohibiting the government from exercising powers it had not been explicitly granted might imply the existence of latent powers beyond the enumeration of Article One, Section Eight.[58] By the time he introduced the Bill of Rights, the best Madison could say for his own proposal was that it might not be "altogether useless."[59] "It was," Donald S. Lutz reflects, "perhaps the most lukewarm introduction in political history."[60] Even by late in life, when the Bill of Rights had taken hold and attained a degree of public veneration, Madison's view of his achievement was hardly more aggrandized. The amendments enshrined in the Bill of Rights were, he reflected in 1821, "safe, if not necessary" and "politic if not obligatory."[61]

Before considering the limited uses Madison believed a Bill of Rights might serve, it may be worth pausing to observe that the fact that he introduced the amendments to begin with reflects his commitment to majority rule. We are accustomed to dismissing any action politicians take in response to public opinion as crass pandering, but far from the image of Madison as an aristocrat who believed a representative's function was to resist majorities, he took his campaign promise to introduce a Bill of Rights to be a serious obligation. Although Madison's speech introducing the proposed amendments did speak of the need to protect minorities against majorities—although not in quite the sense in which those remarks are typically understood—he did not invoke that explanation for the Bill of Rights again in the extensive congressional debate that followed. The majority of times he engaged in debates over wording, he argued at least in part—and often primarily—that a given alternative should be preferred not because it would do more to control majorities but rather because it was the language the public seemed to prefer. His speech of August 14, 1789, was typical: He "insisted that the principal design of these amendments was to conciliate the minds of the people."[62] True to his belief that the only dependable guarantor of the Constitution was establishing public opinion in its favor, Madison counseled his colleagues repeatedly that the amendments were advisable in order to build support for the new regime, as he did on August 13: "If this is an object worthy the attention of such a numerous part of our constituents, why should we decline taking it into our consideration, and thereby promote that spirit of urbanity and unanimity which the government itself stands in need of for its more full support?"[63]

Still, Madison did believe a Bill of Rights might serve a purpose beyond mollifying the lingering suspicions of Anti-Federalists—a purpose directly relevant to temporal republicanism: In those cases in which majorities were directly involved in policy making, a Bill of Rights might help to establish a political culture that would disincline them to abuse and provide a common understanding of rights that would facilitate appeals to the majority's sense of fair play. Once this common understanding was established, it would also serve a delaying function that would help defuse any passions that were fueling attempts to violate rights. In these senses, Madison viewed the Bill of Rights less as a control on majorities than as a majoritarian instrument—one that both reflected and, as Patrick J. Deneen notes, came to enhance his comfort with "the democratic capacities of the populace."[64]

This rhetorical and educational as opposed to judicial function of the Bill of Rights is first evident in the fact that many of Madison's proposals—the ones, in fact, that he placed under the heading "Bill of Rights"—could scarcely serve any other purpose, and least of all could they be legally enforceable. Madison proposed a list of nine amendments, one of which—his fourth—contains most of the provisions we today identify as the Bill of Rights. His first would have amended the preamble to the Constitution—a section whose contents he elsewhere said could not trump the main body of the document[65]—with such obviously rhetorical declarations as, "That all power is originally vested in, and consequently derived from, the people," and "that Government is instituted and ought to be exercised for the benefit of the people."[66] Interestingly, after listing all nine of his proposals, Madison said: "The first of these amendments"—that is, the explicitly rhetorical one—"relates to what may be called a bill of rights,"[67] a description he did not apply to the more specific and therefore enforceable protections that today have come to be called by that name.

Why, then, did he describe the courts, empowered with a Bill of Rights, as "an impenetrable bulwark"? To understand the phrase, careful attention must be paid to the structure of the speech in which he made the remark, using a contemporaneous dispatch to Jefferson to clarify some key phrases. In doing so, one theme to notice is that those instances in which he claimed a role for the courts did not apply to situations of direct majority engagement. The speech and letter identify two distinct threats to individual liberties—a distinction that has already been seen via Federalist 51 and that will be seen once more in exploring the separation of powers below: first, abuses arising from within the regime and committed against the people; and second, abuses committed against the minority by majorities using the apparatus of government as a weapon. The first kind of abuse, in turn, he subdivided into threats presented by the executive and those presented by the legislature. The state Bills of Rights, for example, were directed "sometimes against the abuse of the Executive power, sometimes against the Legislative, and, in some cases, against the community itself; or, in other words, against the majority in favor of the minority."[68] Bills of Rights had traditionally been directed against the plenary power of monarchs, but the American system of government presented different threats. This classification of dangers requires close attention:

> In our Government it is, perhaps, less necessary to guard
> against the abuse in the Executive Department than any
> other; because it is not the stronger branch of the system, but
> the weaker. It therefore must be leveled against the
> Legislative, for it is the most powerful, and most likely to be
> abused, because it is under the least control. Hence, so far as a
> declaration of rights can tend to prevent the exercise of undue
> power, it cannot be doubted but such declaration is proper.
> But I confess that I do conceive, that in a Government
> modified like this of the United States, the great danger lies
> rather in the abuse of the community than in the Legislative
> body. The prescriptions in favor of liberty ought to be leveled
> against that quarter where the greatest danger lies, namely,
> that which possesses the highest prerogative of power. But
> this is not found in either the Executive or Legislative
> departments of Government, but in the body of the people,
> operating by the majority against the minority.[69]

The first thing to notice is Madison's tacit assumption—suggested by the use of the transitional word *but* in the sentence beginning "but I confess"—that Bills of Rights naturally apply to abuses committed by the regime against the people, not those committed by majorities against minorities. Writing privately to Jefferson, Madison in fact used this distinction not as a reason to enact a Bill of Rights, but rather as a reason why he did not believe a Bill of Rights to be necessary: It would not deal effectively with abuses committed by majorities:

> I have not viewed [a Bill of Rights] in an important light . . .
> because experience proves the inefficacy of a bill of rights on
> those occasions when its controul is most needed. Repeated
> violations of these parchment barriers have been committed
> by overbearing majorities in every State. . . . Wherever the
> real power in a Government lies, there is the danger of

oppression. In our Governments the real power lies in the majority of the Community, and the invasion of private rights is *cheifly* [*sic*] to be apprehended, not from acts of Government contrary to the sense of its constituents, but from acts in which the Government is the mere instrument of the major number of the constituents.[70]

Despite his skepticism, Madison proceeded in the congressional speech to speculate that a Bill of Rights might help restrain majorities:

It may be thought that all paper barriers against the power of the community are too weak to be worthy of attention. I am sensible they are not so strong as to satisfy gentlemen of every description who have seen and examined thoroughly the texture of such a defence; yet, as they have a tendency to impress some degree of respect for them, to establish the public opinion in their favor, and rouse the attention of the whole community, it may be one means to control the majority from those acts to which they might otherwise be inclined.[71]

In other words, the purpose a Bill of Rights might serve in cases of majority abuse was to facilitate appeals to the majority, and it would do so by means of temporal republicanism: A Bill of Rights might both prevent majority abuses by instilling a common understanding of rights and providing occasion for majorities to stop and think. Again, one need not assume a long delay. If a common understanding of rights enables even a moment's reflection, that might be sufficient to, as it were, break the majority's trance. Moreover, this educative function would perform a key role in facilitating constructive majority deliberation on the issue of rights.[72] One reason contemporary conversations about rights are often unproductive is that the consensus Madison envisioned building on what precisely constitutes a right, something that requires definition and therefore deliberation, has broken down—in no small part because the courts have, in assuming this role, relieved majorities of the necessity of engaging in the conversation. In the absence of such a consensus, rights discourse consists primarily of parties lobbing assertions of rights at one another with no common vocabulary to guide the conversation and help them evaluate one another's claims.

This temporal dimension became even more explicit when Madison made the same point to Jefferson. A Bill of Rights might, he wrote, serve two purposes:

> 1. The political truths declared in that solemn manner acquire by degrees the character of fundamental maxims of free Government, and as they become incorporated with the national sentiment, counteract the impulses of interest and passion. 2. Altho' it be generally true as above stated that the danger of oppression lies in the interested majorities of the people rather than in usurped acts of the Government, yet there may be occasions on which the evil may spring from the latter sources; and on such, a bill of rights will be a good ground for an appeal to the sense of the community.[73]

Notice that Madison pivoted between points one and two from his concern with abusive majorities to his concern with abusive regimes. He made the same turn at the identical point in the speech and, crucially, did not return to the theme of abusive majorities—so that when he reached the description of the judiciary as an "impenetrable bulwark," he referred not to its impenetrability against popular majorities, something he never believed either empirically or normatively, but rather to its potential to control abuses arising from within the regime. The exception, and a significant one, might be cases in which the public backed the judiciary, as might have been the case had the courts declined to permit prosecutions under the Alien and Sedition Acts.

The first issue Madison tackled in this next section of the speech was whether Congress, having only been granted 18 enumerated powers, needed to be restrained from exercising what would seem to be extraneous ones. His answer was yes, because Congress' discretion to implement its enumerated powers could lead to the kinds of abuses against which a Bill of Rights might protect. Madison supplied one specific example: Congress might enact a law providing for general warrants—as opposed to those directed against specific premises on specific evidence—in order to ensure taxes were properly collected. It is this kind of abuse that one can readily imagine the judiciary overturning and to which Madison referred in describing the courts as an impenetrable bulwark. By contrast, the kinds of abuses that majorities might commit against minorities—such as violating the right of conscience—are ones that Madison thought best handled by appeals to the majorities themselves.[74] We are now in a position to see the significance of Madison's remark about the judiciary quoted in full context: "[The courts] will be an impenetrable bulwark against every assumption of power *in the Legislative or Executive*"[75]—not every assumption of power by an abusive majority. Indeed, had Madison meant to refer to majorities rather than the regime, he would be guilty not simply of inconsistency but of incoherence, for in the same speech—as in the same letter—he denied the possibility of restraining majorities by any means other than appealing to them directly.

Reflecting on the Alien and Sedition Acts during his retirement, he reiterated both the distinction between abuses committed by the majority and those committed by the regime, as well as his belief that majorities could be controlled only by appeals to their own reason. Note the use of the word "recollections"—that is, reminding people of the mutual promises they had made via the Bill of Rights—in this passage, as well as Madison's assumption that an aggrieved party had no choice ultimately but to acquiesce to majorities:

> In seeking a remedy for [abuses of the Constitution], we must not lose sight of the essential distinction, too little heeded, between assumptions of power by the General Government, in opposition to the Will of the Constituent Body, and assumptions by the Constituent Body through the Government as the Organ of its will. In the first case, nothing is necessary but to rouse the attention of the people, and a remedy ensues thro' the forms of the Constitution. This was seen when the Constitution was violated by the Alien and Sedition Acts. In the second case the appeal can *only* be made to the recollections, the reason, and the conciliatory spirit of the Majority of the people agst. their own errors; with a persevering hope of success, and an eventual acquiescence in disappointment unless indeed oppression should reach an extremity overruling all other considerations.[76]

Moreover, even to the extent Madison envisioned a role for the courts in curbing abuses emanating from the regime, he still believed the ultimate—and only reliable—recourse was the supremely majoritarian device of the ballot box. In his opening speech at the Virginia ratifying convention, he thus assured the people that they were secure against abuses by the new government because the legislative power would be held by representatives just like them, bound by the same laws, and replaceable at short intervals. "As long as this is the case," he observed, "we have no danger to apprehend."[77]

The fact that Madison did not contemplate a role for the courts in restraining majorities via the Bill of Rights is further evident in the fact that when he first previewed the speech in the letter to Jefferson, he did not mention the judiciary at all. It was Jefferson who brought this to Madison's attention: "In the arguments in favor of a declaration of rights, you omit one which has great weight with me, the legal check which it puts into the hands of the judiciary."[78] Jefferson's letter proceeds to specify that a Bill of Rights would be useful in restraining "the tyranny of the legislatures," and it was this threat—not the danger of a majority abusing minorities—to which Madison referred when adding the remark about the judiciary at his friend's behest.

It might be objected that this analysis of Madison's views on the judiciary and the Bill of Rights is glib: The fact that he did not empirically believe the courts were capable of withstanding majorities does not mean he would not have welcomed a role for them had he thought—as has turned out historically to be the case—that they could. After all, majoritarian or not, his concerns about abusive majorities are undeniable. Might Madison have thought it proper, at least in principle, for the judiciary to assume the leading role in determining the boundaries of rights, settling the meaning of the Constitution and protecting minorities against majorities? The answer, as we shall now see, is no.

Majorities, Constitutional Interpretation, and the Courts

Two assumptions undergird most contemporary interpretations of the constitutional order. The first is that constitutional interpretation is the province of the courts rather than the political branches. The second—and related—is that constitutional interpretation, and with it the courts, should be insulated from majorities: the Constitution, like the Bill of Rights, exists to tell majorities or their representatives in the elected branches what they cannot do. Madison saw neither the Constitution nor the courts in these terms. He wrote to Jefferson in 1810 that "in a Govt. whose vital principle is responsibility, it never will be allowed that the Legislative & Executive Depts. should be completely subjected to the Judiciary, in which that characteristic principle is so faintly seen."[79] Rather, Madison assigned the political branches, and ultimately the people themselves, a central place in constitutional interpretation: their sustained understanding of the Constitution held supremacy even over that of the courts. The key qualifier is "sustained." The judiciary and other constitutional strictures existed, on Madison's account, to impede impetuous interpretations, instead forcing majorities to cohere for a sustained period in order for their view of the Constitution to prevail. In this sense, the Constitution and the judiciary are devices of temporal republicanism, especially insofar as Madison believed the courts' authority was to arise from gradually accumulating precedents rather than sweeping and abstract constitutional doctrines that invalidate broad swaths of law.

To see Madison's views on constitutional interpretation both emerge and evolve, we shall encounter them at three phases of his career: first at Philadelphia, where he evinced concerns about an overly powerful national judiciary interfering with majoritarian institutions; then during his presidency, when he endorsed the constitutionality of a national bank on the grounds that the public had done so; and, finally, in his retirement, by which point he had grown comfortable with the idea of a robust national judiciary. Throughout, however, Madison hewed to a consistent belief that the authority of judges ultimately derived from and was subject to majorities.

The judiciary was not Madison's foremost concern at Philadelphia, but two episodes at the convention betray concern lest it grab power properly reserved to the elective branches. First, he raised doubts about a proposal to extend the judicial authority to cases arising under the Constitution in addition to those arising under federal law. Madison's reaction to this proposal to imbue the court with constitutional authority was that it should be restricted to cases "of a judicial nature" rather than being imparted "generally."[80] His concern was that the Court not be placed in a position to dispense constitutional judgments suddenly or at will—which would have undermined the interpretive authority of the other branches—as opposed to expounding the meaning of the document through gradually accumulating precedents rendered in the limiting circumstances of individual cases.[81] Second, the impropriety of the judiciary exercising final authority, even on constitutional matters, was among the reasons Madison advocated the creation of a Council of Revision comprised of judges and executive officers. The council would have reviewed and revised prospective legislation, with a supermajority required to overrule it. In addition to guarding against impetuous majorities, a council in which the judiciary participated would be able to express itself on constitutional matters before a bill became law—thus giving the legislature the option to overrule them on subsequent consideration and preventing the courts from annulling decisions of Congress after they had been enacted, a practice with which Madison was clearly uncomfortable. The alternative to a preenactment role for the judiciary was for it improperly to assume de facto supremacy based on the fact that it would always be the last in sequence to pronounce on constitutional questions. Not long after the convention finished its work, he warned:

> In the State Constitutions & indeed in the Fedl. one also, no provision is made for the case of a disagreement in expounding them; and as the Courts are generally the last in making their decision, it results to them, by refusing or not refusing to execute a law, to stamp it with its final character. This makes the Judiciary Dept. paramount in fact to the Legislature, which was never intended, and can never be proper.[82]

This frank admission of constitutional imprecision assumes what we have repeatedly seen Madison express: all three branches of government possess both the authority and the responsibility to weigh in on constitutional questions. Not only would the Council of Revision have involved Congress in constitutional debates, it would have made the legislature—the most immediately majoritarian branch—the last in sequence to pronounce on them, thereby, on Madison's reasoning, making its judgment appropriately supreme. Later in life, Madison reflected on this proposal, noting that it would have retained Congress' policy-making and constitutional supremacy while facilitating temperate consideration of constitutional disputes. The emphasis in the original underscores Madison's acute attention to the difference between a bill proposed by the legislature, which was open to judicial influence, and the finality of an act passed by it: "[He was reminded] of the attempts in the Convention to vest in the Judiciary Dept. a qualified negative on Legislative *bills*. Such a Controul, restricted to Constitutional points, besides giving greater stability & system to the rules of expounding the Instrument, would have precluded the question of a Judiciary annulment of Legislative Acts."[83]

The underlying idea was that the public played a central—indeed, ultimate—role in interpreting the Constitution. That assumption became more explicit during one of the most controversial episodes of Madison's political career: his 1815 decision to endorse the constitutionality of the national bank he had so bitterly opposed during the 1790s. His contemporaries later accused Madison of inconsistency, but he reacted to that accusation with what seems to have been genuine surprise.[84] Although there was no question that his views on the bank's constitutionality evolved, Madison denied that his standard for evaluating its compatibility with the Constitution had changed. The reason was that he believed majorities were entitled to settle the meaning of the Constitution so long as they were seasoned by time. Further constitutional disputation of the bank was "precluded in my judgment by repeated recognitions under varied circumstances of the validity of such an institution in acts of the legislative, executive, and judicial branches of the Government, accompanied by indications, in different modes, of a concurrence of the general will of the nation."[85]

Here the central role of temporal republicanism in Madison's theory of constitutional interpretation is evident. The Constitution's meaning depends on the people's settled understanding of the document, which is identifiable by their repeated expression over a considerable period of time. If the people's understanding at any given moment determined the meaning of the Constitution, there would be no difference between fundamental and ordinary or statutory law—a distinction Madison had drawn sharply in Federalist 53—and hence no Constitution to speak of. Time, according to Madison's understanding, is what preserves the authority of fundamental law while ensuring its ongoing compatibility with popular sovereignty. That is, the requirement of time ensures both that the statutory majority is heard on questions of policy and that the constitutive majority is heard on matters of fundamental law. The likelihood that such decisions would be based on reason was further enhanced because constitutional practice became "settled" based on the passive assent of the people, which registered their approval—or the absence of their disapproval—without the kind of direct engagement that Federalist 49 had warned should be reserved for "great and extraordi-

nary occasions" as opposed to frequently "disturbing the public tranquillity by interesting too strongly the public passions."[86] The veneration Madison recommended in that essay, in turn, imposes a sort of
compounding deceleration on the process of constitutional change:
The more the Constitution is venerated, the more pause the public is
given before contemplating change, so that the more time that
passes, the longer change takes. Veneration is voluntarily given, the
result of which is a passive mechanism by which the people implicitly consent to require gradually longer and longer periods of time
for the Constitution's meaning to change.

That was the theme to which he would return in his retirement.
In the interim, during the bulk of his political career, Madison remained remarkably silent on the judiciary even as controversy surrounding John Marshall's staunchly nationalist Supreme Court
mounted. There is scant evidence even of him having commented on
the flashpoint case that bore his name, *Marbury v. Madison*. That is to
say neither that he was unconcerned about the judiciary nor that he
maintained a principled aloofness from it, only that we have little
record in his own hand from which to extrapolate his views. However, the Marshall Court's decisions in two contentious cases—*Mc-
Culloch v. Maryland* in 1819 and *Cohens v. Virginia* in 1821[87]—drew
him into a correspondence that would ultimately include some of his
most detailed comments on the proper role of the judiciary in the
constitutional system.

The cases both sparked outrage, especially across the south, for
upholding national over state authority. In *McCulloch*, the court ruled
that the state of Maryland could not constitutionally tax the national
bank; in *Cohens*, it asserted a wide-ranging authority to review the
decisions of state courts. The voice of southern protest was Virginia
jurist Spencer Roane, who penned several newspaper missives on
the subject and sent them to Madison in an unsuccessful attempt to
draw him into the public dispute on the side of the states. Commentaries on this correspondence have correctly emphasized Madison's
refusal to join Roane in denouncing the Marshall Court. On the contrary, subject to significant limitations we shall presently encounter,
Madison appeared to endorse a robust judiciary, especially in cases
of federalism.

The difficult question is to what extent these views mark an
evolution from the positions he had taken at Philadelphia. David M.
O'Brien argues that during this stage of his thought, Madison shifted

toward a more expansive view of the court's role in settling constitutional disputes, reserving appeals to the majority for extreme cases alone.[88] Madison's comments to Roane do suggest that despite his earlier concern about the judiciary, Madison eventually made his peace with it. That was due in no small part to the fact that Marshall was an ally in the nationalism to which Madison had returned during his presidency. As Charles F. Hobson notes, whatever had happened in the interim, Madison and Marshall in the 1820s remained in sync with one another on the positions they had taken in the 1780s.[89] And, indeed, there is no question either that President Madison was more nationalist than Representative Madison had been in the 1790s or that the senior statesman Madison was more nationalist still. Moreover, Madison clearly found the judiciary of his retirement to be an ally where the judiciary of his early career had been a threat. He would likely say the evolution was caused less by any fundamental change in his views than by evolving threats to the constitutional order. In the 1790s, he turned to state government in the face of what he regarded as overreaching by such nationalist figures as Hamilton and Adams; as a senior statesman, he pushed back against the overreaching of states' rights partisans and nullifiers. Throughout, he retained his belief that national issues—including questions of constitutional interpretation—should be temperately decided by national majorities. In other words, whatever other evolution occurred in his views, he remained committed to temporal republicanism. The correspondence with Roane draws two boundaries around the court's authority that are relevant to that doctrine.

First, Madison insisted that such authority as the judiciary held in constitutional interpretation should accumulate gradually from the force of precedents in individual cases rather than from what he derided as "abstract" constitutional doctrines elucidated by the Supreme Court. This view echoed Madison's argument in Philadelphia that the judiciary should confine itself to deciding the particular dispute before it in a given case. Marshall had self-consciously gone beyond that point in both the cases that prompted the correspondence with Roane. Rather than merely ruling that a national bank was a valid exercise of congressional powers, for example, Marshall had articulated a broad-ranging doctrine of the necessary-and-proper clause that reached far beyond the immediate issue under dispute. Writing to Roane, Madison objected: "I have always supposed that the meaning of a law, and for a like reason, of a Constitution, so far as it depends on judicial interpretation, was to result from a course of particular decisions, [not] from a previous and abstract comment on the subject."[90] The judiciary's role in constitutional interpretation was not absolute: His comment pertained to the role of the judiciary only "so far" as the meaning of the Constitution was a matter for the courts to decide. To that limited extent, precedents were to accumulate gradually—"from a course of particular decisions"—rather than from abstract doctrines issued all at once, a position that evokes temporal republicanism and echoes the concerns he had raised at Philadelphia more than 30 years earlier. He wrote to Roane: "It could not but happen, and was foreseen at the birth of the Constitution, that difficulties and differences of opinion might occasionally raise in expounding terms & phrases necessarily used in such a charter; more especially those which divide legislation between the General & local Governments; and that it might require a regular course of practice to liquidate & settle the meaning of some of them."[91] Again, time—"a regular course of action"—is necessary to settle constitutional disputes. This commitment to constitutional gradualism was also why Madison indicated his preference that the process of accumulating precedents be slowed by the justices issuing their opinions seriatim in disputed cases—that is, one by one rather than Marshall's self-conscious practice of manufacturing a single position for the entire court. Such a practice, he wrote, would have strengthened the force of precedent where the decision was genuinely unanimous and weakened it—thereby slowing it—where the decision was disputed.[92] His objection to *Cohens* reiterated his concerns about the suddenness of the Court's decisions: "It is to be regretted that the Court is so much in the practice of mingling with their judgments pronounced, comments & reasonings of a scope beyond them."[93]

Nevertheless, even as he criticized the scope of Marshall's rulings, he endorsed the judiciary's authority to resolve constitutional disputes involving federalism, a move that surely disappointed Roane. However, and second, Madison endorsed the public's ultimate authority to interpret the Constitution. Observe in the following passage that it is not the authority of judges but ultimately public support of their decisions that legitimates judicial rulings: "Is it not a reasonable calculation also that the room for jarring opinions between the National & State tribunals will be narrowed by successive decisions *sanctioned by the Public concurrence*?"[94]

Madison further implied that even in cases where their authority was apparently highest, judges could be controlled via majoritarian processes.

> Such is the plastic faculty of Legislation, that notwithstanding the firm tenure which judges have on their offices, they can by various regulations be kept or reduced within the paths of duty; more especially with the aid of their amenability to the Legislative tribunal in the form of impeachment. It is not probable that the Supreme Court would long be indulged in a career of usurpation opposed to the decided opinions & policy of the Legislature.[95]

Notice the temporal overtones: the Court might momentarily usurp popular authority but would not be long indulged. The strong suggestion here is that judges can be impeached and removed—a process whose deliberate pace impedes impulsivity—for the content of their rulings, especially insofar as they represented usurpations of power properly belonging to the elective branches. However, popular interpretations of the Constitution must be deliberate, not impetuous, and time—"repetitions"—was once again the decisive factor: "In resorting to legal precedents as sanctions to power, the distinctions should ever be strictly attended to, between such as take place under transitory impressions, or without full examination & deliberation, and such as pass with solemnities and repetitions sufficient to imply a concurrence of the judgment & the will of those, who having granted the power, have the ultimate right to explain the grant."[96]

Later in the 1820s, during the tariff dispute, Madison repeated his belief that the people's settled understanding ultimately determined the Constitution's meaning. Once more, that interpretation needed the seasoning of time to be authoritative. If the people merely interpreted the Constitution to mean whatever the convenience of the moment dictated, there would be no difference between fundamental and statutory law. This was precisely why southern states that had lived under a tariff without protest virtually since the founding of the Union could not suddenly assert its unconstitutionality. He wrote in 1827: "A construction of the Constitution practised upon or acknowledged for a period, of nearly forty years, has received a national sanction not to be reversed, but by an evidence at least equivalent to the National will."[97] Reflecting on the tariff dispute during correspondence in 1830, Madison wrote: "That in a Con-

stitution, so new, and so complicated, there should be occasional difficulties & differences in the practical expositions of it, can surprise
no one; and this must continue to be the case, as happens to new
laws on complex subjects, until a course of practice of sufficient uniformity and duration to carry with it the public sanction shall settle
doubtful or contested meanings."[98]

According to this theory of constitutional evolution, the requirement of time ensures both that the statutory majority is heard
on questions of policy and that the constitutive majority is heard on
matters of fundamental law. Hence one key standard for constitutional interpretation is "the early, deliberate & continued practice
under the Constitution, as preferable to constructions adapted on the
spur of occasions, and subject to the vicissitudes of party or personal
ascendencies."[99] Similarly, he wrote in 1834 that constitutional
change should "be applied not in the paroxysms of party & popular
excitements: but with the more leisure & reflection," which would
occur if the people had to persist in a constitutional opinion for a period of years in order to prevail.[100]

Time therefore acts on the Constitution much like an anchor
does on a heavy ship in deep water: It is not actually immovably tied
to the bottom, but it makes drift require such force that it can occur
only gradually and in small increments. The result of all these observations, to employ the common metaphor, is that the Constitution
is indeed living, but its metabolism is exceedingly slow and grows
slower with time—a process on which Madison could dependably
rely because it drew its power from the natural conditions of republican political culture.

Time, then, is one criterion for legitimating constitutional
change. Recall that the bank's constitutionality had also been repeatedly upheld not just over time but also by all three branches of government. Hence the second criterion: the people must examine constitutionality from the multiple perspectives represented by each
branch of government. This was also an auxiliary effect of the system
of separation of powers, to which we now briefly turn.

Temporal Republicanism and the Separation of Powers

As has been seen, Madison believed any political system must be at-
tentive to the potential for abuse from its most powerful element—

in a republic, popular majorities. But a republic would also face the same danger as monarchies—indeed, all forms of government: that elected officials, once installed by the people, would turn on them and rule arbitrarily. This they could do if the same officials exercised all powers of the state—executive, legislative, and judicial, a combination Federalist 47 describes as "the very definition of tyranny."[101] The solution was a regime of separate powers that would prevent any one institution from exercising total authority. Tyranny would require the acquiescence of three distinct institutions of government, each of which, Madison famously explained in Federalist 51, is contrived to resist the encroachments of the others.

Still, setting this issue aside, the influence separation of powers exerts on Madison's democratic theory can be seen by asking, with James MacGregor Burns, whether this mechanism is duplicative.[102] After all, it was Madison himself who repeatedly described all three branches of government as emanating, in the final analysis, from the people. Witness, for instance, his 1831 claim that judicial precedents are authoritative if, over time, they carry "the sanction of those who, having made the law through their legislative organ, appear . . . to have determined its meaning through *their* judiciary organ."[103] All three branches—including, again, the judiciary—"deriv[e] their existence from the elective principle."[104] If, as Burns notes, the extensiveness of the republic already inhibits abusive majorities, why erect further barriers to majorities that—on Madison's own argument—survive only because they are devoted to justice and the general good? Unless there is some basis for the separation of powers in Madison's democratic theory, one may be compelled to conclude that whatever its other antityrannical virtues, it includes antimajoritarian features as well.

That basis does exist. One result of the separation of powers is to force the same popular majority to reconstitute itself and consider problems from a variety of different perspectives.[105] This was, Madison wrote, a result of "our complex system of polity": "The public will, as a source of authority, may be the Will of the People as composing one nation; or the will of the States in their distinct & independent capacities; or the federal will as viewed, for example, thro' the Presidential Electors, representing in a certain proportion both the Nation & the States."[106]

The requirement that these perspectives be combined ensures comprehensive consideration of issues. More immediate and parochial interests are likely to be felt most intensely in a congressional majority. The requirement of concurrence from the presidency introduces a broader, more national and longer-term perspective. Meanwhile, the potential for judicial review forces majorities to consider the more fundamental commitments of constitutionalism. That each of these majorities is drawn from the same fount does not make them duplicative, for in each case the same majority deliberates from a different perspective.

Equally important, separation of powers forces majorities to deliberate within—and persist across—the different periods of time each branch represents.[107] Recall that one purpose of the staggered terms in the Senate is to prevent sudden change in the regime, so that a majority whose ambitions are substantial enough to require change in the entire Senate would have to cohere across three election cycles. Separation of powers compounds this protection, adding the feature that the more dramatic a majority's desires, the longer it must cohere. In this sense, Beard perceives the system accurately: "A sharp differentiation is made in the terms of the several authorities, so that a complete renewal of the government at one stroke is impossible."[108] A majority seeking fundamental regime change might consequently have to persist in that belief for long enough to work a change in all three branches of government. One effect, therefore, of separation of powers is to require a majority to cohere for a period of time proportional to the gravity of the change it seeks.

Consider, then, what a majority might regard as the worst of all scenarios under the separation of powers: all three branches of government opposing its desires. History provides such an example: the wholesale transformation of the government's role represented by the New Deal. The Progressive critique of the founding was triggered by the Court's repeated opposition to economic reforms, which Beard and other critics treated as a roadblock to change. The Court was, in reality, a speed bump—and not, from history's perspective, a terribly steep one. It would be difficult to identify a persistent national majority in favor of dramatic economic reforms before 1932's election of Franklin Roosevelt.[109] Once that majority emerged, however, the constitutional system permitted dramatic change in reasonably rapid order. It took only until 1937's *West Coast Hotel v. Parrish* for the Supreme Court to yield to persistent majorities: five years to work what was, regardless of one's perspective on it, a nearly complete transformation of the nature of the national government.[110] Equally important, the change occurred through Madisonian means: ordinary political pressures, including those that produced the Court's famous "switch in time that saved nine."

Of course, five years seems like less time from the perspective of history than it would have to an aggrieved individual at the time, particularly against the backdrop of the Great Depression. Burns observes:

> One can view this drift and delay with a certain philosophical calm. In the end American government, like the belated hero in the horse opera, seems to come to the rescue. Delays may be hard, of course, on certain persons. A man whose working life stretched from 1900 to the mid-thirties might be a bit concerned in retrospect over the delay in federal social welfare programs. A twelve-year-old boy working in a textile mill during the 1920's, or even in the 1930's, might wonder, if he had a chance to wonder about such things, how a great nation like the United States had been unable to outlaw child labor despite general condemnation of it, while most of the civilized world had accomplished this primitive reform years earlier. A Negro in the 1960's might not be so detached toward states' rights and congressional obstruction as some of his fellow Americans. Still, most of us could reflect that progress has almost always come in the long run, even if the run has been longer for some than for others. And the slowness of change has meant, perhaps, less tension and disruption of the social fabric.[111]

Burns's complaint, of course, is fair, especially when viewed from the perspective of an individual who must defer his or her needs during the interim period necessitated by the slow pace of change. Still, Burns's description of the Madisonian order, and the outlook it reflects, is precisely correct. The reduced disruption Burns credits to the Madisonian system also means that change, once attained, rests on a more stable foundation. From Madison's perspective, there is no reliable alternative: change might be rushed, but it would not endure. It would appear, then, that despite Madison's desire to depend on no more than the natural dynamics of republican politics, tolerance of the constitutional system does in fact depend on a virtue: patience.

It is in this respect that temporal republicanism stands most starkly in conflict with the ethos of contemporary political life.

Chapter Five

Politics and Patience

The foregoing chapters have attempted to establish several features of Madison's democratic thought. The first is that he never entertained, much less endorsed, any alternative to majority rule. Majorities were the natural locus of political power in republican societies, and the American experience had repeatedly shown that persistent majorities inevitably prevailed. Attempts to erect barriers to them based on parchment alone were futile at best and dangerous at worst. This empirical belief acted as a linchpin for Madison's democratic theory, and it was matched by a deep normative commitment to majority rule, which he repeatedly identified as the "vital principle" of the Constitution. However, majorities might in some circumstances be tempted to behave impulsively, especially when their immediate appetites were at stake, and these impulses imperiled both the rights of minorities and the long-term interests of majorities themselves. Madison believed that these impulses inherently cooled with the passage of time. His democratic theory consequently relies on delaying mechanisms that compel majorities to cohere for an interval sufficient to dispel passions. This use of time to season majorities enhances the likelihood that they will behave reasonably and avoids the necessity of a trade-off between majority rule and minority rights.

This interpretation, which I have called "temporal republicanism," operates in several areas of Madison's thought. Among the reasons factious majorities are unlikely to prevail in extended republics is that the passion that animates them is unlikely to survive the delays inherent in communicating and acting across long distances. By establishing a common political lexicon in which appeals to the com-

munity can be made, the Bill of Rights helps to slow the pace of decision making and thereby increases the probability that majorities
will make decisions on the basis of reason rather than passion. Similarly, the separation of powers requires majorities to persist across
the lengths of time for which each branch of government serves. The
courts, likewise, could at best act as a speed bump, not a roadblock,
before popular majorities.

In exploring these mechanisms, it has also been seen, however,
that Madison believed majorities were entitled to rule even in those
cases in which their decisions were unwise or unjust. The best that
could be done was to establish conditions in which poor decisions
would be less likely. Consequently, Madison saw rights and justice—
two terms often cited in portrayals of him as antidemocratic—not as
substantive roadblocks to majority decisions but rather as procedural
mechanisms that compelled the majority to treat individuals pre-
dictably rather than arbitrarily. Individuals who object to the substance of majority decisions should, on Madisonian grounds, attempt
to persuade the majority rather than deny its legitimacy by appealing
to institutions like the courts. The process of doing so is slow and
might therefore be frustrating and even, from the point of view of aggrieved individuals, unfair. But such is also the pace at which majorities are likeliest to reach decisions that relieve those grievances.
There is, by Madison's reasoning, no reliable alternative. Burns is
correct to observe, of course, that the temporal perspective is hardly
comforting to an individual experiencing acute disappointment or
even injustice. But the fact that an individual in such circumstances
might be tempted to seek immediate yet ultimately, as will be seen,
ineffective redress is among the reasons that individuals are not permitted to judge their own causes. Ultimately, the Constitution must
be judged at the systemic rather than the individual level.

With these basic features of temporal republicanism in mind,
we may now consider several of the theory's implications, especially
for contemporary politics. We begin with the direction in which temporal republicanism suggests we should calibrate our expectations
of the speed at which the constitutional regime will produce results
that satisfy us—namely, downward.

Quantum Constitutionalism and the Law of Compounding Disappointment

Perhaps because of the prevalence of rights rhetoric, especially in Americans' understanding of the foundational purposes of the regime, we are accustomed to sharp disappointment when the Madisonian order fails to produce results in accordance with our expectations. Americans tend to see such moments as episodes of systemic failure. When Congress fails to pass a bill that seems to enjoy public support, this "gridlock" is taken as evidence that the political system is broken. Similarly, the impulse to transfer disputes to the judiciary results in part from the perception that the regime is supposed to protect rights above all else, so any instance in which it apparently fails to do so represents an injustice that calls for swift correction from the only branch that seems capable of acting with appropriate speed.

But temporal republicanism suggests that this episodic means of evaluating the regime—that is, according to its results at discrete moments in time—is mistaken. We should assess it over time instead. Hence a corollary to temporal republicanism, one I shall call "quantum constitutionalism": viewed at any given instant in time, the constitutional order cannot guarantee precise outcomes, only probabilities of them. These probabilities grow with time, so that the longer the period over which the constitutional order is viewed, the likelier it is that its results will accord with such values as majority rule and minority rights. A time-lapse photograph will thus yield a more accurate portrait of the regime than a snapshot, and the longer its exposure, the more illustrative it will become.

Consequently, the single moment at which a bill has not passed or an unjust decision has been rendered is, from Madison's point of view, uninformative. Any given day may well find Congress failing to respond to a majority view; a majority, likewise, may on a particular occasion oppress a minority. Such imperfections must be expected in part because even the most perfectly crafted parchment cannot dictate the outcomes of a regime whose true power rests with fallible majorities. But they are equally to be expected not in spite of parchment but because of it. The Constitution is specifically designed to require majorities to persist over time, so there is no reason to believe a majority would or, crucially, even should, prevail at a point arbitrarily chosen in time.

The Alien and Sedition Acts illustrate quantum constitutionalism at work in the case of rights. Consider a snapshot of the constitutional order taken on April 21, 1800. On that day, the newspaper
editor Thomas Cooper was convicted under the Sedition Act and
sentenced to six months in prison for publishing a handbill critical
of the Adams administration.[1] We need not take sides on that specific
case to observe that Madison believed prosecutions like Cooper's
represented a failure of a system he believed would protect minority
rights. Yet we have already heard Madison call the imbroglio surrounding the Alien and Sedition Acts a vindication rather than a failure of the constitutional system. The reason is that he evaluated the
Acts from a time-lapse perspective whose exposure stretched from
their enactment to their expiration. Madison never predicted that the
system would not produce days like April 21; he believed, on the
contrary, that such episodes were unavoidable and that snapshots of
them would therefore be unappealing. But the longer the film was
exposed, the likelier it became that the portrait would correct itself.
The Virginia Report of 1800 thus betrayed neither surprise nor irri-
tation that the Alien and Sedition Acts remained in operation a full
year after the Virginia resolutions first objected to them. The shutter
had to be held through the election of 1800—a political event, not a
judicial one—as well as the expiration of the Sedition Act and Jefferson's pardons of those convicted under it in order for an accurate
image of the Constitution to be captured. Note, then, the standard of
constitutional success as Madison, reflecting on the sedition controversy, expressed it: "Nor do I think that Congress, even seconded by
the Judicial Power, can, without some change in the character of the
nation, succeed in *durable* violations of the rights & authorities of the
States."

Quantum constitutionalism also suggests that discrete instances provide misleading portraits of whether the Madisonian
order defers to majority opinion as well. We have just seen an illustration of this point in the early twentieth-century controversy surrounding economic reforms. In that case, Beard and other Progressive critics faulted the system as antimajoritarian because the
judiciary obstructed majority opinion in favor of economic reforms.
Yet Madison would almost certainly have objected to the judicial rulings of that era, including *Lochner,* as judicial usurpations. In any
case, the Progressive mistake lay in both evaluating the system on
the basis of a snapshot and depressing the shutter prematurely. As

we have seen, persistent majorities in favor of national economic reforms did not emerge until 1932. A time-lapse image exposed from
that point through *West Coast Hotel* in 1937 would have showed the
system to be so rapidly adaptable to majority opinion—including a
dramatic adjustment of the Constitution's meaning—that it was arguably conservatives and not progressives who should have had the
greater quarrel with Madison.

From this quantum perspective, again, the fact that a majority
has not prevailed at any one moment does not mean the Constitution
does not respect majority will. It means, instead, that the majority
in question has not persisted for the interval the Constitution requires in order to assure that it is reasonable rather than impassioned
and settled rather than fluctuating.[2] The hand-wringing that accompanied the defeat of health care reform before its passage in 2010 is
an excellent case in point. It is true that majorities of Americans had
expressed themselves in favor of substantial health care reform at a
conceptual level for at least two decades, but there were few if any
points—and certainly no intervals—at which clear majorities had favored any specific reform proposal. In Madisonian terms, the failure
of health care reform in the case of the 1994 debate hardly merited
the subtitle Haynes Johnson and David Broder gave to their book-
length treatment of its collapse—*The System: The American Way of Politics at the Breaking Point.*[3] Regardless of one's views on the substantive issues at stake, majority support for any given proposal during
the period was transient at best. If the system to which Johnson and
Broder referred was the Madisonian one, it held up precisely as intended. The failure was political, not systemic; no party to the debate
convinced a majority of its views. To the extent individuals or interest groups wanted to pursue the issue further, Madison's counsel
would have been to reapply themselves to the task of building consensus. Few did, even as most funneled their energies into complain-
ing that the system was unresponsive, with the predictable result
that when the issue was resurrected in 2009, consensus remained elusive. Once reforms were finally enacted in 2010, even their supporters—their rhetorical fanfare notwithstanding—described them as an
incremental first step rather than the dramatic changes for which
they initially hoped.

Indeed, the perception that the system was rigged or otherwise
incapable of responding to public concerns arguably dampened the
enthusiasm for the very civic engagement that might have succeeded

in making it responsive. Here we arrive at another important corollary of temporal republicanism, one that derives from quantum constitutionalism and that we may call "the law of compounding disappointment." Excessive expectations for immediate results produce disappointment; the contemporary reaction to disappointment tends to be disengagement from majoritarian institutions; yet disengagement virtually assures political defeat, thereby perpetuating and progressively deepening the cycle. As we have seen in the case of the Alien and Sedition Acts, Madison believed frustrations with the constitutional system should be channeled toward rather than away from political institutions.[4] This was the case even, perhaps especially, when he viewed the frustrations as legitimate. In addition to the Alien and Sedition Acts, this was also the approach Madison counseled southern states to adopt during the nullification controversy, and it was the one that the "Memorial and Remonstrance" signaled he was willing to employ in the case of the religious assessment: "Should the event disappoint us, it will still leave us in full confidence that a fair appeal to the [people] will reverse the sentence against our liberties."[5] Madison's willingness to undertake the arduous task of convincing majorities of his views, even in a case in which he believed majorities exercised no rightful authority, is especially striking in comparison to the contemporary inclination to react to defeat by circumventing or rejecting majoritarian institutions, either by taking one's case to the courts or through a dejected assumption that defeat is the result of corrupt or dysfunctional institutions.[6] Yet Madison correctly perceived the peril of the contemporary approach: the farther we recede from majoritarian institutions, the likelier they are to disappoint us. According to the law of compounding disappointment, excessive expectations defeat themselves.

If this assessment of the contemporary ethos is correct, it may help us to understand a phenomenon that is otherwise so inexplicable in Madisonian terms that it could justly be called "the Madisonian paradox."[7] The phenomenon may be described as follows: Madison believed barriers to majority rule were futile because persistent majorities always prevail. Yet today, such barriers seem to have the endorsement of persistent majorities. A situation of which Madison could not have empirically conceived and which he refused constitutionally to endorse—widespread deference to the courts—has therefore acquired a sort of Madisonian legitimacy. How, on Madison's reasoning, could this be so? We might interpret deference to the courts as a form of constitutional maturity: Americans have learned the importance of fundamental law and hence yield, even in defeat, to the institution they task with safeguarding the Constitution. It is conceivable—questionable, but conceivable—that Madison himself might endorse a form of judicial supremacy in constitutional interpretation if the meaning of the Constitution and the rights it asserts admitted of the precision that he associated with judicial interpretation. But as we know, and as ongoing disputes have repeatedly proved, they do not. Moreover, Americans' deference to the judiciary is uneasy at best. Both conservatives and progressives endorse judicial supremacy when it suits their goals and decry it when their oxen are gored. Rather than being a sign of maturity, the courts may simply have supplanted the state legislatures of Madison's time as a seductive arena for instant results. Judicial deference is, in an important sense, a creed that allows its adherents both to have and eat their political cake: achieve instant results when they can, rail against the system when they fail, but in neither case undertake the actual work of building consensus. Put otherwise, majorities may be less committed to majority rule per se than to the most convenient avenue for promoting their immediate preferences.

One consequence of the resort to the courts has been the erosion of the skills of civic engagement that are central to the successful operation of the Madisonian regime. These skills include accepting defeat graciously and reacting to it industriously—that is, by seeking to change the community's mind, which in turn presumes the skills of persuasion, openness to persuasion, empathy, and reasonableness. The polarization produced by rights cases suggests an alarming atrophy of these capacities. By contrast, Madison believed that productive majority deliberation was the only reliable guarantor for rights. Rights, he assumed, were inherently fragile as long as they lacked public support, a belief borne out by public reactions to rights discovered and imposed by the courts today. As Gerald Rosenberg has shown, attempts to impose change through the courts have generally been ineffective and have often produced backlashes that resulted in the rights they sought to establish being even further curtailed.[8] Partisans of the "rights revolution" have tended to suggest there is a certain indignity in forcing individuals into the public square to plead for what supporters of individual rights assert should naturally be theirs.[9] The question Madison forces us to confront, however, is not whether it should be necessary to plead for rights—although we have seen evidence to suggest he did indeed believe argumentation on the subject was both unavoidable and appropriate—but rather on what basis they are apt to be left more secure. Referring the issue to majorities, and thus drawing the debate into the public square, has the effect also of drawing individuals out of their otherwise atomized modern-day realms, thereby humanizing, so to speak, their grievances. Madison's assumption is that Americans will respond to such grievances reasonably—which is, of course, open to debate. But Madison's reply would likely be that if the population of a republic is not capable of behaving reasonably even in circumstances that dissipate passions, rights are a lost cause regardless.

Choosing the path of majority deliberation rather than the potential for instant gratification through the courts requires time. In Madison's era, empirical circumstance imposed that restraint. The naturally slow tempo of communication and transportation limited majorities' options. Today, of course, this is no longer the case—which means that for Madison's system to operate as intended, a virtue must intervene: patience. Patience, we shall see by way of bringing the present study to conclusion, has now replaced Madison's assumption about the inevitability of majority rule as the linchpin of his system. It is the central constitutional virtue—and it is, by all signs, a lost one.

The Lost Virtue

As William E. Scheuerman's perceptive study *Liberal Democracy and the Social Acceleration of Time* both documents and explores, a—perhaps the—dominant fact of contemporary political life is speed.[10] We need hardly recount the technological reasons that this is so. Madison himself saw the pace of politics quickening at the hands of technology. In 1833, shortly before his death, he reflected with some satisfaction that the country was able to operate on a larger and larger scale:

> It is true that the sphere of action has been and will be not a little enlarged by the territories embraced by the Union. But it will not be denied, that the improvements already made in internal navigation by canals & steamboats, and in turnpikes & railroads, have virtually brought the most distant parts of

the Union, in the present extent, much closer together than they were at the date of the Federal Constitution. It is not too much to say, that the facility and quickness of intercommunication throughout the Union is greater now than it formerly was between the remote parts of the State of Virginia.[11]

In fact, Madison had noted the significance of improvements in communication as early as 1791: "Whatever facilitates a general intercourse of sentiments, as good roads, domestic commerce, a free press, and particularly a circulation of newspapers through the entire body of the people, and Representatives going from, and returning among every part of them, is equivalent to a contraction of territorial limits, and is favorable to liberty, where these may be too extensive."[12]

Both passages clearly celebrate the projection of republican government across a wider territory. But the careful reader of Madison will also observe that, in the terms of the extended republic thesis, "a contraction of territorial limits" is not an entirely welcome development. It is unsurprising, then, that the acceleration of these improvements in communication to an infinite—indeed, now instant—degree has had the effect of resurrecting many of the factious dynamics Madison feared. Although the republic may have become more diverse by dint of growing more extended, majority factions that do exist can also "discover their own strength" readily, communicate their views instantly, and, most important, demand and therefore expect results before the seasoning process that was so crucial to Madison's thought can take hold.

Not only is it now possible for results to be delivered rapidly, but speed is considered to be a positive virtue. It is, indeed, the very hallmark of the effective modern leader. Today's political ethos, reflecting the new activist purposes of the regime, measures success not by governing but rather by policy making—a standard that is so ingrained that it is necessary to specify that these are not the same thing. Whereas governing calibrates the extent of policy making to public needs, the more or less permanent assumption of the policy-making ethos is that the current state of affairs, whatever it may be, is, to varying degrees, inadequate. The drive for perfection and "rational" results, even from systems of infinite complexity such as a modern economy, makes satisfaction a vice and change a constant need. Political leaders are thus judged by the volume of policy making rather than outcomes. In congressional campaigns, for example, it is taken to be self-evident that a legislator who has not written or sponsored a considerable volume of bills has not done his or her job.[13] Mutability and multiplicity of lawmaking—which Madison specifically hoped the Constitution would halt—are thereby encouraged. Whereas Madison believed decisions should take longer to make as their gravity increased, the contemporary ethos holds the opposite: the more urgent change is assumed to be, the more quickly it must be delivered.

This standard exerts particular pressure on presidents, whose legacies in history depend not only on the extent to which they cause affairs to be different from what they otherwise would have been, but also on the speed at which they do so.[14] Such is the implicit demand of the "first 100 days" test attached to each presidential term, a length of time that originated with the crisis Franklin Roosevelt confronted at his 1933 inauguration but that now persists regardless of whether any such crisis exists—including the second terms of presidents who are reelected precisely because the country is satisfied. The standard may now be escalating. Dawn had literally not yet broken over President Obama's hundredth day in office when, at 4:16 A.M. on April 29, 2009, the influential news site Politico.com posted an article entitled "10 Decisions for Obama's Next 100 Days."[15] On the basis of these observations, the standard of presidential success, but also of the successful application of political power of any sort, may be expressed as follows: Success equals change divided by time ($s = c/t$). The more change a political actor can deliver in a shorter period of time, the more successful he or she is assumed to be.

The application of this formula is problematic for several reasons, including the fact that it inherently classifies prudence as failure, at least insofar as prudence values inaction when change is not specifically warranted and gradualism when it is. Change is not always necessary; sometimes, Madison might even say "usually," mere governance is. The chief flaw of the speed standard, however, is that it places stresses on the constitutional system that it was not designed to bear and was, on the contrary, specifically engineered to avert. The result, we have seen, is a simultaneous and apparently endless escalation of both expectations and disappointment.

Madison thus occupies an awkward position. A foundational

assumption of his order—the leisurely pace of politics and its atten-
dant quality of patience—has been transformed from an empirical
reality into a virtue. Put otherwise, one of the most important features of his democratic thought began as the very kind of empirical
reality he regarded as the surest basis for enduring institutions, yet
now depends on exactly the kind of foundation of which he was
most skeptical: a virtue. Madison knew, toward his life's end, that
the American regime would have to rely increasingly on "moral
causes" as time progressed and the once-unifying memories of past
emergencies faded. The memory of the Revolution, he thought,
might help to inspire the necessary virtue:

> Still the increasing self-confidence felt by the Members of the
> Union, the decreasing influence of apprehensions from
> without, and the natural aspirations of talented ambition for
> new theatres multiplying, the chances of elevation in the
> lottery of political life, may require the co-operation of
> whatever moral causes may aid in preserving the equilibrium
> contemplated by the Theory of our compound Government.
> Among these causes may justly be placed appeals to the love
> and pride of country; & few could be made in a form more
> touching, than a well-executed picture of the Magical effect of
> our National Emblem, in converting the furious passions of a
> tumultuous soldiery into an enthusiastic respect for the free &
> united people whom it represented.[16]

Temporal republicanism suggests that an appeal to another
"moral cause" may now be necessary to preserve the Madisonian
order: patience. If time is to act as the "sovereign physician of our
passions," in Montaigne's words, patience must act as its nurse. This
study therefore concludes where it began: in Madison's childhood
commonplace book, where, just before transcribing Montaigne's
dictum about time and passions, the future founder recorded an
aphorism from the memoirs of Cardinal DeRetz: "Patience," DeRetz
counseled and Madison transcribed, "works greater effects than activity."[17]

Notes

Preface

1. McDonald, *Novus Ordo Seclorum*, 208–209.

Introduction

1. Madison, *Papers of James Madison*, ed. Hutchinson and Rachal, 1:16 (hereafter *PJM*). The precise date of the notes cannot be conclusively ascertained. The first heading in the book reads "December 24, 1759," when Madison was eight years old, but no subsequent entry is dated. The initial entries are a lengthy series of aphorisms and other observations from the memoirs of Cardinal DeRetz. The entries on Montaigne immediately follow these. The editors note that the Latin translations included in these early entries, as well as the fact that Madison also recorded some of Montaigne's reflections on romance, suggest that they date to the time of his study with the Scottish tutor Donald Robertson. See *PJM*, 1:4–6. Madison's autobiographical reflections late in life indicate that this study commenced around the age of 12. For the quotation from Montaigne, see his essay "On Diversion," in *Complete Essays*.

2. The progressive historian Charles Beard pioneered the aristocratic view of Madison, while Lance Banning typifies the redemptive strain. See Beard, *Economic Interpretation*, and Banning, *Sacred Fire*.

3. Willmoore Kendall observes of Madison and Hamilton: "We err greatly when we confuse their animus against the popular majority bent on injustice with an animus against the popular majority, the majority of the people, as such." "Two Majorities," 334. The contemporary assumption that justice cannot be objectively defined obscures this distinction; see Carey, "Majority Rule."

4. Madison to John G. Jackson, December 27, 1821, in *Writings of James Madison*, ed. Hunt (hereafter *WJM*), 9:70–77. I use Hunt's edition for those of Madison's writings that are not yet published in the University of Virginia's Papers series.

5. Virginia Report of 1800, *PJM*, 17:310.

6. Madison to Edmund Randolph, June 11, 1782, *PJM*, 4:333–334.

7. Madison to the Marquis de Lafayette, November 25, 1820, *WJM*, 9:35–38.

8. Madison's unaddressed 1833 letter on "Majority Governments," *WJM*, 9:520.

9. Tocqueville, *Democracy in America*, 501–506.

10. Federalist 63:327.

11. Madison in Convention, June 5, 1787, *PJM*, 10:26. All references to the convention are to Madison's notes unless specified otherwise. For simplicity, rather than referring to a separate volume of Madison's notes, I cite them as they appear in his published papers.

12. Madison to Judge Spencer Roane, May 6, 1821, *WJM*, 9:59.

13. See Federalist 10:43 and 42:219, among others.

14. Federalist 63:326.

15. Truman, *Governmental Process.*

16. Alan Gibson makes a compelling case for discarding, or at least transcending, this dichotomy. See Gibson, *Understanding the Founding*, 156. Many analyses of republicanism during the Founding era refer to it as a broader doctrine including public-spiritedness and civic virtue in addition to majority rule. Rather than entering the long-standing debate over civic republicanism and the Founding, the present study is concerned with the dimension of majority rule alone.

17. Banning, *Sacred Fire*, 10.

18. It is less clear precisely how many Americans actually believed a choice would be necessary. The number may well have been growing, but to judge from the debates in Philadelphia, it was not large enough to register with the overwhelming number of delegates to the convention. The closest any delegate came to suggesting that majority rule might have to be sacrificed to individual rights was Alexander Hamilton's speech of June 18, 1787, which is notable chiefly for having been totally ignored by his colleagues. I am aware of no substantive debate in which the delegates actually contemplated a material choice between majority rule and individual rights. In fairness, Hamilton believed his own proposal to be republican, and it complies with the criteria Madison elucidated for republicanism in Federalist 39.

19. Schumpeter, *Capitalism, Socialism*, 242 (emphasis in original).

20. Beard, *Supreme Court.*

21. "Memorial and Remonstrance," *PJM*, 8:298–304.

22. Jefferson, First Inaugural, March 4, 1801, in Jefferson, *Papers*, 33:134; emphasis added.

23. Scheuerman, *Liberal Democracy*, xiii.

Chapter 1: Madison on Majorities

1. *WJM*, 1:351.

2. Ratner, Soltow, and Sylla, *Evolution of the American Economy*, 86–87. See also Ferguson, *The Power of the Purse.*

3. Abrahamson, *American Home Front*, 30.

4. Address of Congress to the States, April 25, 1783, *PJM*, 6:487–494.

5. *PJM*, 11:79.

6. For a catalog of legislative escapades during the period, see McDonald, *E Pluribus Unum*, 87–100. See also Corwin, "Progress of Constitutional Theory."

7. Rossiter, *1787*, 43–44.

8. Ibid., 46.

9. Fiske, *Critical Period*, esp. chap. 4, and Wood, *Creation of the American Republic*, 393–396.

10. *PJM*, 9:355.

11. "Vices," *PJM*, 9:349, emphasis added.

12. *PJM*, 9:353.

13. *PJM*, 9:355–356.

14. "Notes for Speech Opposing Paper Money," *PJM*, 9:158–159.

15. See Madison to Joseph Jones, November 14, 1780, *PJM*, 2:172–174, and Madison to Ambrose Madison, August 7, 1786, *PJM*, 9:89.

16. For the Virginia Plan, see *PJM*, 10:15–17. Madison outlined its basic features in a letter to Virginia governor Edmund Randolph on April 8, 1787, nearly two months before Randolph introduced the plan in Philadelphia. See *PJM*, 9:368–371.

17. Adair, *Fame and the Founding Fathers*.

18. Madison in Convention, May 31, 1787, *PJM*, 10:19, emphasis added.

19. *PJM*, 10:39–40.

20. Madison in Convention, July 14, 1787, *PJM*, 10:100–102.

21. *PJM*, 10:86–87.

22. Madison in Convention, July 5, 1787, *PJM*, 10:92–93. Yates's notes of the convention record Madison even more starkly: the smaller states were asking "two thirds of the inhabitants of the union . . . to please the remaining one third by sacrificing their essential rights." See editor's note, *PJM*, 10:94. Note that in Madison's version, majority rule is connected with justice, while in Yates's, majorities have a right to rule. In neither case are justice or rights attached to minorities.

23. Federalist 62:320.

24. Madison in Convention, July 21, 1787, *PJM*, 10:110–111.

25. Smith, *Spirit of American Government*, 332.

26. Madison in Convention, July 25, 1787, *PJM*, 10:115–117. In this speech, as in other contexts, Madison also opposed election of the president by the legislature—the very mechanism the Virginia Plan had proposed. In his preconvention comments on a draft constitution for Kentucky, Madison pronounced himself undecided on whether a legislature should choose an executive; after the convention, he called such an approach "improper." The sequence strongly suggests it was during the convention itself that Madison reached the conclusions about separation of powers later adduced in Federalist 51. For his early comments on the Kentucky constitution, see Madison to Caleb Wallace, August 23, 1785, *PJM*, 8:350–357. For his postconvention comments, see "Observations on

Jefferson's Draft of a Constitution for Virginia," ca. October 15, 1788, *PJM*, 11:285–293. The latter document provides further evidence of Madison's majoritarianism: he opposed term limits on the executive because they "fetter[ed] the judgment and inclination of the Community." See *PJM*, 11:287.

27. *PJM*, 10:23–24.

28. Federalist 40:203.

29. Federalist 51:271.

30. Federalist 58:305. To be sure, Madison spoke approvingly of supermajorities in other situations, most clearly in his comments on Jefferson's draft of a constitution for Virginia, in which he suggested that supermajorities should be required to override an adverse recommendation of a Council of Revision comprising the executive and judicial branches (*PJM*, 11:285–293). However, the criticism with which we are dealing at present is the relationship of a popular majority to a popular minority. Madison disapproved of blocking popular majorities by giving legislative minorities a veto over public acts. It is true that such a minority could exercise a veto under this suggestion, but only after a decision of the executive or judicial members of the Council of Revision, each of which, on Madison's view, emanated ultimately from popular majorities. He may have been mistaken in assuming the judicial branch in particular represented majorities; perhaps Madison's proposal would have empowered minorities in its practical operation. The relevant point, however, is that Madison did not assume a Council of Revision would represent any fixed popular minority—or, indeed, any particular segment of the populace at all—so empowering minorities was, at the very least, not his deliberate intent. For a thoughtful discussion and contrary interpretation, see Kerner, *James Madison*, 239–240.

31. Hartz, *Liberal Tradition*, 129, 130.

32. For Madison's acknowledgment of the honor, see his letter to the French interior minister in April 1793, *PJM*, 15:4.

33. As will be seen in Chapter 3, this model of representation—the highborn leading the common—was decidedly not what Madison meant when he spoke in Federalist 10 of "fit characters" "refining and enlarging" public opinion.

34. On this point, see McWilliams, "Democracy and the Citizen." This is also substantially the interpretation of "civic republican" commentators who see the Constitution as a departure from the republican ideals of the Revolutionary era. See, for example, Wood, *Creation of the American Republic*.

35. By "local," I mean simply "not fully national"—i.e., state-level or regional, but less than national.

36. Henry's speech in the Virginia ratifying convention, June 24, 1788, Elliot, *Debates*, 3:589–590. See also Einhorn, "Patrick Henry's Case against the Constitution."

37. *WJM*, 6:94.

38. Zvesper, "Madisonian Systems."

39. There are other theoretical reasons to regard Congress as the more majoritarian branch. The presidency is a winner-take-all institution in which the preferences of voters on the losing side can be more easily discarded than in

Congress, in which shifting coalitions allow realignments on multiple issues. The presidency is also a blunt instrument: policy rests ultimately in the hands of a single individual whose judgment may or may not accommodate minority views, whereas Congress is a more supple institution in which subtle accommodations can be made. More important is the role of deliberation. Most voters do not cast ballots with fixed preferences on all policies in mind. Rather, voters fully expect issues to arise of which we were not aware on Election Day, and we expect views on these and other issues to develop and evolve in response to argumentation and deliberation. It is in the inherent nature and institutional design of a legislature to accommodate and respond to these changes, whereas the concentration of executive authority in a single individual does not. This is not to say presidents do not respond to minority views, only that an individual does not realign in the same subtle and complex ways a legislature does. On the deliberative role of Congress, see Kendall, "Two Majorities," and Carey, "Future of Conservatism."

40. Federalist 52:273. Cf. *American Government and Majority Rule: A Study in American Political Development* (Princeton: Princeton University Press, 1916), iii.

41. Patrick Henry retaliated for Madison's victory in the Virginia ratifying convention by scheming to deny him election to the Senate, but there is no indication Madison ever aspired to any position other than the House. In pursuit of that goal, he engaged in a fierce campaign against his friend James Monroe, going so far as to violate his long-held dictum against delivering speeches on the stump. For accounts of the campaign, see Ketcham, *James Madison,* and Irving Brant, *Fourth President.*

42. See the petition Madison drafted to the Virginia General Assembly on this topic; *PJM,* 16:95–103.

43. See, for example, Madison's speech in Congress, December 7, 1791, *PJM,* 14:142–143.

44. Virginia Report, *PJM,* 17:324.

45. Madison in the House of Representatives, November 19, 1792, *PJM,* 14:413–414.

46. See editor's note, *PJM,* 15:461. For the motion about which Madison raised questions, see United States Congress, House, *Annals of Congress,* 1163.

47. Madison in the House of Representatives, March 1, 1793, *PJM,* 14: 456–468.

48. Burns, in *Deadlock of Democracy,* regarded separation of powers as undemocratic because, among other reasons, it prevented presidents from acting on their popular mandates. Madison's writings substantially predate the onset of the plebiscitary presidency. As we have seen, although Madison did believe the president should be directly elected by the people, he simply did not see the executive as a policy-making branch. The tone of his Helvidius essays suggests that he believed he was expressing a truism in stating this fact.

49. For the complete exchange between Hamilton and Madison, writing as Pacificus and Helvidius, see Frisch, *Pacificus–Helvidius Debates.* The argument appears in Helvidius Number I. The emphasis is mine.

50. See Helvidius Number V.

51. See Helvidius Number I.

52. Madison to Jefferson, September 3, 1802, in Madison, *Papers of James Madison*, Secretary of State Series, ed. Robert J. Brugger et al. (hereafter *PJM-SS*), 3:537–538.

53. Madison to Robert C. Latimer, January 11, 1803, *PJM-SS*, 4:250.

54. Madison to James Monroe, March 1, 1803, *PJM-SS*, 4:361–362.

55. Madison to Jefferson, March 27, 1809. In Madison, *Papers of James Madison*, Presidential Series, ed. Robert Allen Rutland et al. (hereafter *PJM-PS*), 1:82.

56. Siemers, *Presidents and Political Thought*, 94–95.

57. *PJM-PS*, 1:327–328.

58. Ibid., 2:595–596.

59. See Madison to Jefferson, August 16, 1809, *PJM-PS*, 1:327–328, and Madison to Jefferson, October 19, 1810, *PJM-PS*, 2:585–586.

60. *PJM-PS*, 4:437.

61. For further evidence of Madison's majoritarian commitments, see his November 30, 1812, letter to Jonas Galusha (*PJM-PS* 5:472), which alludes to northeastern states' opposition to the war but says that they are nonetheless bound by the decision of a national majority.

62. Madison also vetoed a bill that would have empowered him to require Supreme Court justices to hear cases in district court, explaining in his veto message that it "introduce[d] an unsuitable relation of Members of the Judiciary Department, to a discretionary authority of the Executive Department." *PJM-PS*, 4:285–286. Presidents, it seems, are no longer in the habit of denying themselves discretionary authority.

63. Madison to the chairman of the Republican Society of Hancock County, Massachusetts, March 15, 1809. *PJM-PS*, 1:53.

64. Madison to Vermont Governor Jonas Galusha, November 30, 1812. *PJM-PS*, 5:472.

65. "Majority Governments," 1833, *WJM*, 9:572. Cf. Alexander Hamilton, Federalist 22:106: "The fundamental maxim of republican government . . . requires that the sense of the majority should prevail."

66. Madison's 1830 letter to Edward Everett, *WJM*, 9:383–403, at 399.

67. *WJM*, 9:597.

68. Burns and other progressives have also criticized the supermajority requirement for constitutional amendments. Martin Diamond, in "Democracy and *The Federalist*," correctly notes that the requirement is actually that simple majorities in three-quarters of the states ratify an amendment. Its effect is thus to ensure that a simple majority is nationally distributed. As will also be seen, Madison believed the entire constitutional edifice to rest on the sustained tolerance of simple majorities.

69. Madison appended a footnote to "Notes on Nullifcation" (*WJM*, 9:589) asserting that the right to nullification that Jefferson adduced in the Kentucky Resolutions of 1798 was a "natural right, which all admit to be a remedy against

insupportable oppression," as opposed to a political or civil right guaranteed under the forms of the Constitution. The natural right, in other words, was to revolution.

70. Madison's formulation is consistent with, and even remarkably similar to, Willmoore Kendall's understanding of Locke's Second Treatise—that is, individuals give over all rights to majorities upon entering civil society, with no other recourse but the "appeal to Heaven" implicit in revolt. See Kendall, *John Locke and the Doctrine of Majority-Rule*. Cf. also Smith, *Spirit of American Government*, 296: "All governments must belong to one or the other of two classes according as the ultimate basis of political power is the many or the few. There is, in fact, no middle ground. We must either recognize the many as supreme, with no checks upon their authority except such as are implied in their own intelligence, sense of justice and spirit of fair play, or we must accept the view that the ultimate authority is in the hands of the few. Every scheme under which the power of the majority is limited means in its practical operation the subordination of the majority to the minority." The fact that the first two sentences of this quotation so precisely mirror Madison is proof of how profoundly Smith misconstrued him.

71. *WJM*, 9:523.

72. Calhoun, *Union and Liberty*, 240. For a comparison of Madison's and Calhoun's views of popular majorities, see Ford, "Inventing the Concurrent Majority."

73. Calhoun referred to the analysis of Madison's Federalist 39 but cited the entire *Federalist*, imputing it to both Hamilton and Madison. For his critique of Federalist 39, see *Union and Liberty*, 108–109.

74. The contrast between Madison and Calhoun is sharpened by the latter's belief that, as James Read writes, "a slow, deliberate, long-in-forming majority was precisely the greatest danger," apparently because only venal interests would be strong enough to overcome the barriers of time. Read, *Majority Rule Versus Consensus*, 49.

75. Beard, *The Supreme Court and the Constitution*, 165.

76. See Madison's speeches on July 26 and August 7, *PJM*, 10:117–118 and 138–139, respectively.

77. "Observations on Jefferson's Draft of a Constitution for Virginia," *PJM*, 11:287. Madison commented on Jefferson's draft in response to a correspondent who asked how it might be adapted for Kentucky.

78. Madison's speech of July 26, *PJM*, 10:117–118. His point was that a landholding requirement would not achieve its stated objective of protecting wealth. Nor should we necessarily equate a property requirement with venality. Blackstone (*Commentaries*, 165) identified the requirement as ensuring voters had a will of their own and therefore were not merely amplifying the views of feudal aristocrats.

79. Bernard Bailyn, *Origins of American Politics*, 87.

80. Madison's speech of August 10, *PJM*, 10:143. What distinguished this

proposal from Madison's comments on Kentucky was that the property qualification in the latter case would have been fixed in the Constitution rather than
being left to legislative discretion.

81. *PJM*, 11:287.

82. *PJM*, 14:197–198. The apparent target of this remark was either John
Adams or Alexander Hamilton, both of whom Madison believed actively favored unequal distribution of wealth so that American society could be "balanced," as Great Britain's was. It would be absurd, Madison wrote, to inflate distinctions in wealth artificially merely to ensure the existence of mutually
contending interests.

83. Madison to Francis Corbin, November 26, 1820, *WJM*, 9:40–41; emphasis added.

84. *WJM*, 9:359.

85. We must take note of one important problem at this point. There can
be no denying that the three-fifths clause expanded Southern representation
without giving slaves the right to vote. Madison's support for the compromise—
versions of which he articulated in separate contexts in both the Articles Congress and the Virginia Constitutional Convention of 1829—must be acknowledged as an exception to what is otherwise an overall trend toward expanding
suffrage. In weighing this position against the evidence otherwise supporting
a majoritarian interpretation of Madison, one can only observe that it arises from
the appalling nature of slavery as an institution, for which he, among many
other Founders, must be accountable. Once one has established that human beings are property, the conclusion that they should not vote follows. Slavery itself
creates the problem, not the three-fifths compromise per se. All the contemporary commentator can offer is perspective, not rehabilitation, on that point. To
say Madison is a majoritarian is to say he believed the views of a majority of voters should prevail. The reader must judge to what extent our understanding of
him as majoritarian is impaired by his exclusion of slaves and women from that
group, especially while using a portion of the slave population to inflate the political representation of the South. He was far from alone on this score; if these
positions preclude considering those who held them as supporters of majority
rule, it seems impossible to come to an accurate understanding of how the
Founders understood themselves.

86. Hume, *Essays*, 32–33. For interpretations of Madison emphasizing
Hume's influence, see, among others, Adair, *Fame and the Founding Fathers;* Roy
Branson, "James Madison and the Scottish Enlightenment"; Morgan, "Safety in
Numbers"; Werner, "David Hume and America," and Wills, *Explaining America.*

87. See Federalist 49:262: "If it be true that all government is based on
opinion."

88. *PJM*, 14:191–192.

89. Ibid., 14:201–202.

90. Ibid., 14:161.

91. *WJM*, 9:359.

92. Garry Wills, citing Johnson's *Dictionary* as well as Hume's *History of England*, defines the term as "ethos." See Wills, *Explaining America*, 281.

93. Madison to Jefferson, May 9, 1789, *PJM*, 12:142–143.

94. Madison to Randolph, May 11, 1789, *PJM*, 12:155–156.

95. Madison in Convention, June 6, 1787, *PJM*, 10:32–34.

96. Madison to Spencer Roane, May 6, 1821, *WJM*, 9:58, emphasis added. For Madison's opposition to the Missouri Compromise, see Madison to Robert Walsh, November 27, 1819, *WJM*, 9:6–10.

97. Madison in Convention, June 12, 1787, *PJM*, 10:50–51.

98. Madison in Convention, June 4, 1787, *PJM*, 10:24.

99. Federalist 48:260. Cf. Hamilton in Federalist 25:126: Pennsylvania and Massachusetts prohibited standing armies but routinely violated the rule in situations of danger. "It teaches us . . . how unequal are parchment provisions, to a struggle with public necessity."

100. Marvin Meyers summarized Madison's view as a dislike "of absolute prohibitions that would have to yield to political necessity." Meyers, *The Mind of the Founder*, xxxvii.

101. Federalist 41:209.

102. "Observations on Jefferson's Draft of a Constitution for Virginia," *PJM*, 11:293.

103. Madison to Caleb Wallace, August 23, 1785, *PJM*, 8:350–357.

104. In other words, two-thirds of Congress must pass an amendment to refer it to the states, or two-thirds of state legislatures must agree to call a convention. Diamond, in "Democracy and *The Federalist*," argues that this requirement and its ratification counterpart cannot accurately be described as supermajority rules.

105. See Elliot, *Debates*, 2:178 for Massachusetts, 2:412–413 for New York, and 3:654–655 for Virginia.

106. Federalist 49:262.

107. This raises the intriguing question of whether Madison's democratic theory was better suited to a period of founding than to a stable republic.

108. Madison in Congress, August 15, 1789. See Veit, Bowling, and Bickford, *Creating the Bill of Rights*, 167. In the same speech, Madison denied the authority of "detached bodies"—i.e., representative institutions—to "contravene an act [the Constitution] established by the whole people," thereby placing his argument for constitutionalism on majoritarian grounds. In other words, a legislature that contravened the Constitution betrayed the will of the majority.

109. Adair, *Fame and the Founding Fathers*, 151.

110. Meyers, *Mind of the Founder*, xliii–xliv.

111. For roughly corresponding analyses of the convention, see Kramer, "Madison's Audience," and Wolfe, "On Understanding the Constitutional Convention."

112. Madison, *Notes*, 57.

113. Hamilton, like Adams, disputed the characterization of a president for life as monarchical rather than republican.

114. On Hume's reasoning, sustained submission to forceful rule could be taken as evidence of acquiescence, but the converse—revolution—was an outcome Madison was obviously keen to avoid.

115. Address of Congress to the States, April 25, 1783, *PJM*, 6:487–494.

116. Madison to Pendleton, February 24, 1787, *PJM*, 9:294–295.

117. Madison to Randolph, February 25, 1787, *PJM*, 9:299, emphasis added.

118. This was among the scenarios that the separation of powers was designed to prevent.

119. Madison to Jefferson, May 11, 1789, *PJM*, 12:155–156.

120. "A Candid State of Parties," September 22, 1792, *PJM*, 14:370–372, emphasis added.

Chapter 2: Time and Tranquility

1. *PJM*, 17:161. After Jefferson's death, Madison allowed that his longtime compatriot had a tendency "of expressing in strong and round terms, impressions of the moment." Madison to Nicholas Trist, May 15, 1832, *WJM*, 9:479. His use of the word *philosophy* as a synonym for *temperate* or *sober* in the toast's context is evident from his use of it when doubting a rumor that, after his wife's death, Jefferson "swooned" in the presence of his children: "I conceive very readily the affliction & anguish which our friend at Monticello must experience at his irreparable loss. But his philosophic temper renders the circulating rumor . . . altogether incredible." Madison to Randolph, September 30, 1782, *PJM*, 5:170–171. Richard K. Matthews also cites Madison's critiques of Adams, but disapprovingly. His complaint is that Madison elevated what Matthews takes to be the cold and joyless quality of reason over matters of the heart. On the basis of this assessment, he casts Madison in the role of Max Weber's antiseptic bureaucrat. It would have been both more accurate and more charitable to have associated him with the stoic tradition that was en vogue among a wide range of Madison's contemporaries. See Matthews, *If Men Were Angels*, 6, 7.

2. Madison to Jefferson, February 11, 1783, *PJM*, 6:220–221.

3. Madison to Jefferson, February 18, 1798, *PJM*, 17:83. Cf. Madison to Jefferson, June 3, 1798: "It is said, and there are circumstances which make me believe it, that the hotheaded proceedings of Mr. A are not well relished in the cool climate of Mount Vernon." *PJM*, 17:141–142.

4. Madison to J. K. Paulding, April 1831, *WJM*, 9:454. Paulding, a historian, had asked Madison for biographical reflections on several founding fathers, including Adams.

5. Aristotle, *Nicomachean Ethics*, 1139a11. Aristotle's understanding of prudence as "a state grasping the truth, involving reason, concerned with action about things that are good or bad for a human being" (1140b5) also applies, although Madison more often used *reason* in the instrumental sense of choosing the means likeliest to achieve a given end.

6. Federalist 37:179. Madison similarly wrote that one problem with religious assessments was their propensity to invite passionate beliefs into the political realm and thereby "destroy that moderation and harmony" that enabled a diversity of sects to prevail in the United States without extracting the blood other societies had shed over religion. "Memorial and Remonstrance," *PJM*, 8:298–304. Hints of that dangerous kind of zeal were, to Madison's chagrin, already appearing. The bill for religious assessments that provoked the "Memorial and Remonstrance" had "produced some fermentation below the mountains & a violent one beyond them. The contest at the next Session on this question will be a warm & precarious one," with *warmth* denoting the metaphor of heat that Madison often applied to the passions. Madison to Jefferson, April 27, 1785, *PJM*, 8:265–270. The contrary—coolness—referred to reason, as in another remark about the assessments bill: "The Episcopal people are generally for it, tho' I think the zeal of some of them has cooled." Madison to Monroe, April 12, 1785, *PJM*, 8:260–261.

7. Madison to Jefferson, August 10, 1788, *PJM*, 11:225–227.

8. Madison to Benjamin Rush, March 7, 1790, *PJM*, 13:93–94. Note that Madison refers here to the criterion of *truth*, not to whether the majority should rule. Nothing in this passage questions the legitimacy of majority rule, only the accuracy of some majority opinions.

9. *PJM*, 9:348–357. Notice that the interest is only "apparent."

10. Madison in Convention, June 26, *PJM*, 10:76–77.

11. Madison in Virginia Ratifying Convention, June 18, 1788, *PJM*, 11:155–156.

12. Federalist 10:43.

13. Federalist 49:262.

14. Federalist 57:298 ("the caprice and wickedness of men").

15. Madison in Convention, June 26, 1787, *PJM*, 10:76–77.

16. Federalist 55:288.

17. *PJM*, 13:216–219. Note that on this assumption, a longer debate is likelier to lead to a reasoned conclusion.

18. *PJM*, 13:383.

19. "Political Reflections," February 23, 1799, *PJM*, 17:237–243.

20. Madison to the Republican Committee of Talbot County, Maryland, March 21, 1809. *PJM-PS*, 1:69–70.

21. Madison to David Humphreys, March 23, 1813, *WJM*, 8:239–241.

22. Federalist 41:207.

23. "A Candid State of Parties," *PJM*, 14:370–372. Decades later, while Madison questioned the constitutionality of the Missouri Compromise, he comforted President Monroe with the observation that "there can be no room, with the cool and candid, for blame in a conciliatory course, the demand for which was deemed urgent, and the course itself deemed not irreconcilable with the Constitution." Madison to Monroe, February 23, 1820, *WJM*, 9:23–26.

24. Madison to Pendleton, November 11, 1780, *PJM*, 2:165. For accounts of this dispute, see Jack Rakove, *Beginnings of National Politics*, 243–275, and

Henderson, "Congressional Factionalism." Rakove, noting that the Lee faction took to the press to whip up public animosity toward Franklin, describes this episode—some of which took place before Madison took his seat in 1780—as the first time public pressure was immediately brought to bear on Congress. Henderson notes that voting blocs for and against Franklin were rigid, which also suggests that minds were closed and hence not subject to the faculty of reason.

25. Federalist 49:264.

26. *PJM*, 11:237–238.

27. Federalist 55:288.

28. Federalist 10:45–46.

29. Federalist 63:325. The sentence continues, "or in an assembly so durably invested with public trust, that the pride and consequence of its members may be sensibly incorporated with the reputation and prosperity of the community." This, for Madison, was the Senate, which I discuss below. For now, though, the relevant observation is that the key word in this passage is "durably." The unique quality of the Senate lay in the fact that it could resist public passions because they would dissipate over the course of a six-year term.

30. Madison to Jefferson, June 10, 1798, *PJM*, 17:150–151. This was related to Madison's long-standing assumption that psychological controls collapsed in group settings. He had warned in Federalist 10 that moral or religious motives "lose their efficacy in proportion to the number combined together" (45–46) and in Federalist 63 that character could only be counted upon as a restraint in groups "so small, that a sensible degree of the praise and blame of public measures may be the portion of each individual" (63:325).

31. Madison to Jefferson, May 13, 1798, *PJM*, 17:130–131.

32. Eugene Miller, in "What Publius Says about Interest," makes an intriguing argument that Publius uses the terms "interest" and "interests" in several senses, not all of which carry a negative connotation. However, there are several instances in *The Federalist* in which the word does carry the same connotation as Samuel Johnson's definition of *interested:* "having regard to private profit." These are the instances on which I focus here. See *Johnson's Dictionary*, 185.

33. Federalist 10:42.

34. Federalist 10:44.

35. Smith, *Theory of Moral Sentiments*. Garry Wills, in *James Madison*, also notes that the use of neutral arbitrators to resolve business disputes was common practice in Virginia (33). On the importance of impartiality in Madison's Federalist 10, see Carey, "Majority Rule." Early in his congressional career, Madison advocated an impartial tribunal to assess the states' competing claims to national relief of their Revolutionary debts, arguing that members of Congress were inappropriate for the task because they were sworn to be advocates for their states rather than neutral judges of the national welfare (*PJM*, 6:399–402). This was the complaint he lodged against members of the Articles Congress in Federalist 46: They had "but too frequently displayed the character, rather of partisans of their respective states, than of impartial guardians of a common in-

terest" (245). Similarly, Madison's "Detached Memoranda" contains his thoughts on bank reform, including the importance of appointing directors who are "impartial Judges." "Detached Memoranda," in *Writings*, 754.

36. Federalist 10:48.

37. "Majority Governments," 1833, *WJM*, 9:520.

38. See Madison to Jefferson, August 12, 1786, *PJM*, 9:93–99, and Federalist 10:48.

39. Madison to John Cartwright, 1824 (precise date unknown), *PJM*, 9:180–181.

40. *WJM*, 9:61.

41. Madison to Edmund Randolph, June 11, 1782, *PJM*, 4:333–334.

42. Madison to Caleb Wallace, August 23, 1785, *PJM*, 8:350–357, emphasis added.

43. Madison in Convention, June 26, 1787, *PJM*, 10:76–77, emphasis added.

44. Madison to Jefferson, October 17, 1788, *PJM*, 11:295–300, emphasis added.

45. Federalist 62:322, emphasis added.

46. *PJM*, 14:159.

47. Madison to Adams, May 22, 1817, *WJM*, 9:390–391.

48. Madison to John Cartwright, 1824, *WJM* 9:181–183.

49. Madison to Monroe, May 18, 1822, *WJM*, 9:94–97.

50. As we proceed, it bears repeating that, unlike Calhoun, Madison did not regard all majorities as abusive; nor, to use Hartz's phrase, was he seized by a "neurotic terror" of them (Hartz, *Liberal Tradition*, 130). Abusive majorities were one problem to be worked out as the constitutional system was shaped. The primary problem was still the inability of national majorities to act on national issues.

51. Federalist 63:327.

52. This confidence is evident, among other places, in Madison's November 25, 1820, letter to Lafayette (*WJM*, 9:35–38).

53. Kendall, "Two Majorities"; Carey, "Majority Rule"; and Kramnick, "Great National Discussion." Fit characters may play a more important role in developing reasoned ideas than in blocking impassioned ones.

54. Madison does depend on "fit characters" to hold out until passions dissipate.

55. "Democracy and the Federalist."

56. Sheehan, *James Madison*.

57. Rosen, *American Compact*, 68–70.

58. Quoted in McCoy, *Last of the Fathers*, 121. Indeed, the very reason religious motives could not be depended on to restrain leaders was that such motives would have to be strongly felt to be effective, whereas "enthusiasm is only a temporary state of religion." "Vices," *PJM*, 9:348–357.

59. Hume, *Essays*, 54–63.

60. Adair, *Fame and the Founding Fathers*, 150.

61. Hume's analysis appears in "Of Parties in General," 59–61; italics in

the original. The quoted passages from Madison's analysis may be found in Federalist 10:43–44. My analysis parallels but exceeds Adair's. Madison believed economic disputes could draw forth the passions. The constant to-and-fro of state legislation on debts and paper money reflected precisely this dynamic. Disputes based on property did not dissipate as quickly as those based on abstract principles and hence required special attention.

62. Madison to Monroe, May 18, 1822, *WJM*, 9:94–97.

63. Madison to Thomas Lehre, August 2, 1828, *WJM*, 9:314–316.

64. Madison to Jefferson, August 23, 1788, *PJM*, 11:238–239.

65. Madison in Convention, June 26, 1787, *PJM*, 10:76–77; emphasis added.

66. Madison in Convention, June 7, 1787, *PJM*, 10:39–40.

67. Federalist 62:322.

68. *PJM*, 10:15–17. The Virginia Plan also said that House members were not to be eligible again, but the purpose of this could not have been to insulate them from public opinion because the plan also said they were to be subject to recall and that they could return to Congress after an unspecified hiatus. Neither specification is present in Madison's preconvention letter outlining the Virginia Plan to Randolph, which suggests they may have been inserted to placate the concerns of others. In either case, however, the case for ineligibility at the time was generally to prevent representatives from becoming an entrenched political class and growing distant from their constituents—that is, to tie them more closely to the people.

69. "Public Opinion," *National Gazette, PJM*, 14:161.

70. "Observations on the Draught of a Constitution for Virginia," ca. October 15, 1788, *PJM*, 11:285.

71. Madison in Convention, June 26, 1787, *PJM*, 10:76–77.

72. Federalist 63:327, emphasis added.

73. The fact that the Senate enables a majority to regain its senses also helps to illustrate why Madison championed it even though he remained a House supremacist. The Senate was a braking mechanism, but the House remained the main engine, a dynamic made clear in his description of the Virginia Senate as "a useful bitt [sic] in the mouth of the house of Delegates." See Madison to Caleb Wallace, August 20, 1785, *PJM*, 8:350–357.

74. Madison to Jefferson, August 12, 1786, *PJM*, 9:93–99.

75. Madison to George Nicholas, May 17, 1788, *PJM*, 11:44–51.

76. This analysis applies indirectly to appointment of senators by state legislatures, but even more clearly to the direct popular election that Madison preferred. Cf. H. B. Mayo's description of an upper house that "can exercise only a delaying power over legislation. The effect is to introduce a short time lag, in which the majority support of representatives and public can crystalize while being put on the defensive." Mayo, *Introduction to Democratic Theory*, 168–169.

77. I have borrowed Martin Diamond's metaphor but applied it to a different set of concerns. Diamond argued that a commercial republic diverted popular energies from hotly contested and irreconcilable disputes like religion to commercial issues on which broad consensus was possible. Hence the viability

of constitutional barriers "depend[ed] upon a prior weakening of the force applied against them." See Diamond, "Democracy and *The Federalist*," 65–66. My analysis is compatible with Diamond's interpretation.

78. This is the heart of Matthews's critique in *If Men Were Angels.*

79. "Universal Peace," January 31, 1792, *PJM*, 14:207–208.

80. Bryce, *Modern Democracies*, 2:11.

81. McCoy, *Last of the Fathers*, 42.

82. "Vices," *PJM*, 9:348–357.

83. Federalist 10:45.

84. Federalist 42:219. Madison told the Virginia Constitutional Convention of 1829 that "as to the permanent interest of individuals in the aggregate interests of the community, and in the proverbial maxim, that honesty is the best policy, present temptation is often found to be an overmatch for those considerations." *WJM*, 9:361.

85. Federalist 50:265.

86. Madison to Monroe, October 5, 1786, *PJM*, 9:140–142.

87. See, for example, Liebman and Garrett, "Madisonian Equal Protection," 873n165. Ford quotes this passage, as does, among others, Ketcham, *James Madison*, 181.

88. McGinnis, "Once and Future Property-Based Vision," 75n108.

89. Kloppenberg, *Virtues of Liberalism*, 178.

90. Ketcham, *James Madison*, 181.

91. In separate correspondence, Madison made clear to the Marquis de Lafayette that he viewed the free navigation of the Mississippi as a nationwide issue because, among other reasons, it affected the value of the nationally owned lands to the west and because the American states, unlike European countries, comprised a single people whose complex interdependence made it folly to speak of the Atlantic and Western states as having different interests. Madison to the Marquis de Layfayette, March 20, 1785, *PJM*, 8:250–254.

92. Their interests were the same because Madison believed the Western and Eastern states would both benefit from maintaining an open river. Drew McCoy also notes that free navigation of the Mississippi was central to Madison's national vision of an agricultural society. McCoy, *Elusive Republic*, 124.

93. Madison to Monroe, August 7, 1785, *PJM*, 8:333–336.

94. Gargarella, *Scepter of Reason.*

95. Rives, *History*, 2:217, emphasis added.

96. See Liebman and Garrett, "Madisonian Equal Protection," 873. Liebman and Garrett correctly interpret the passage as a rejection of the assumption "that the majority view is necessarily consistent with the public good." However, the passage clearly states that the majority's ultimate good *is* the public good. The relevant issue is a majority's inability to perceive its own good accurately.

97. "Public Opinion," ca. December 1791 to March 1792, *PJM*, 14:170.

98. Madison in Convention, June 26, 1787, *PJM*, 10:76–77.

99. Madison to Jefferson, Sept. 22, 1788, *PJM*, 11:257–259.

100. Madison to Monroe, May 14, 1796, *PJM*, 16:356–358. Cf. also a letter to Jefferson endorsing his correspondent's call for a congressional adjournment to ascertain the sense of the public on an Adams administration request for military funds: "The expedient is the more desirable as it will be utterly impossible to call for the sense of the people generally before the season will be over, especially as the Towns &c. where there can be most despatch in such an operation are on the wrong side; and it is to be feared that a partial expression of the public voice, may be misconstrued or miscalled, an evidence in favor of the war party." *PJM*, 16:104–105.

101. Speech in Congress, *PJM*, 13:387.

102. Madison to Jefferson, April 22, 1798, *PJM*, 17:118–119.

103. Jefferson to Madison, September 6, 1789, *PJM*, 12:382–387.

104. Madison to Caleb Wallace, August 23, 1785, *PJM*, 8:350–357.

105. Madison to Jefferson, February 4, 1790, *PJM*, 9:18–21.

106. Burke's views on the respect as a result of posterity evoked strident opposition from Joseph Priestley, who argued for a time limit on public debts. It was to this exchange that Madison referred. See Madison to Jefferson, May 1, 1791, *PJM*, 14:18.

107. Federalist 63:326.

108. Federalist 37:182. This was also the partial basis of Madison's critique of Robert Owen's utopian New Harmony Colony, which is reprinted in Meyers, *Mind of the Founder*, 453–455. On that critique, and for Madison's views on these themes more broadly, see Ralph Ketcham, "James Madison and the Nature of Man."

109. See the editor's notes in the *PJM*, manuscript of this letter.

110. See, for example, Federalist 49.

111. For Madison's prudence and gradualism, see also his commentaries on Fanny Wright's plan for a series of utopian communities for emancipated slaves and Robert Owen's similarly utopian New Harmony experiment. He gently suggested to Wright that her plan might "be better commenced on a scale smaller than that assumed in [her] prospectus." *WJM*, 9:228. He wrote of Owen's plan that it failed to take account of human frailty, which thus led its author to overly ambitious rather than appropriately circumspect ambitions. Here again he sounds more Burkean than Jeffersonian—or, perhaps more accurately, like a mean between the two: "With this knowledge of the impossibility of banishing evil altogether from human society, we must console ourselves with the belief that it is overbalanced by the good mixed with it, and direct our efforts to an increase of the good proportion of the mixture."

112. Hartz, *Liberal Tradition*, 83; Dahl, *Preface*; and Matthews, *If Men Were Angels*, 35. For a compendium of pessimistic interpretations and a thoughtful refutation of them, see Kobylka and Carter, "Madison." For the Calvinist influence on Madison, see Sheldon, *Political Philosophy*.

113. Federalist 55:291. Cf. Hamilton, Federalist 76:395: "The supposition of universal venality in human nature, is little less an error in political reasoning, than that of universal rectitude."

114. Wood, *Creation of the American Republic,* 611–612.

115. Diamond, "Democracy and *The Federalist*"; and Will, *Statecraft as Soulcraft.*

116. Madison never actually favored the proliferation of interests; he observed that a multiplicity of them already existed. His point in Federalist 10 was not that interests would neutralize one another in any active sense, but rather that there would be so many that no one faction would constitute a majority. This, like his view of time, is a passive mechanism.

117. Federalist 10:44.

118. It is for this reason that Madison did not need to specify how the public good would be represented or provided for in the constitutional order. He assumed the public good would be naturally evident and attainable, barring the influence of obscuring forces. Consequently, his concerns pertained to mitigating those forces. On Madison's reasoning, one could not infer from the absence of an explicit discussion of the public good that he did not believe it to be important. For a contrary view, see Erler, "The Problem of the Public Good."

119. *PJM,* 11:158–165. With respect to Madison's Aristotelian model of prudence, note that the people need only "intelligence," while leaders need "wisdom."

120. Madison to LaFayette, November 25, 1820, *WJM,* 9:35–38.

Chapter 3: Time and the Tenth Federalist

1. For an account and analysis of the incident, see Farley Grubb, "U.S. Constitution and Monetary Powers." The precise circumstances of the episode remain obscure. I reconstructed the narrative from Madison's account and from sources cited by Grubb.

2. Madison to Jefferson, July 18, 1787, *PJM,* 10:106–107.

3. Note, however, that Madison's sympathies lay plainly with the "poorer Citizens," not the wealthy bankers (*PJM,* 10:106–107).

4. Madison to Jefferson, October 24, 1787, *PJM,* 10:206–219.

5. Federalist 10:42.

6. Federalist 10:45.

7. *PJM,* 10:33.

8. Federalist 39:194.

9. This evidence alone does not convict Madison of low venality, nor should disputes over property be equated with class conflict. Disparities in wealth were far less extreme in Madison's time, and disputes between creditors and debtors or between planters and merchants were not proxies for class conflict. There were, for example, rich debtors and poor planters in plentiful supply in Madison's America. Moreover, to the extent he was concerned about property rights—and that extent was certainly substantial—he stood in a long line of political theorists who understood those rights as essential to personal autonomy. The present-day mind is often disposed to assign tawdry motives to assertions

of property rights—an attitude perhaps aggravated by the tendency of contemporary liberal theory to demote property rights to second-class status among liberties—but their normative dimensions in Madison's time must not be overlooked if we are to understand him on his own terms.

10. I do not mean to suggest Madison never used *justice* in a substantive sense. In 1790, for example, Congress debated the status of paper securities that individuals received in compensation for property impressed during the Revolution. Because the long-term value of these securities was unclear, while their holders' needs were immediate, many resold the debts to speculators. The question in Congress was whether the original holders of securities were entitled to some compensation despite having sold them. Madison once more framed the question as one of justice, a measure of which he admitted lay on both sides—apparently a reference to substantive justice. Those whose property was originally impressed in exchange for paper securities had resold them only because circumstances presented them with an onerous choice between doing so and receiving nothing at all. On the other hand, the speculators whom Madison otherwise despised had made investments on the basis of promises of future payment, so refusing to honor their securities would diminish the predictability on which public credit was built. Given the merit of both claims, Madison called for a compromise based "on the great and fundamental principles of justice" under which compensation would be balanced between original and secondary holders of securities (*PJM*, 13:47–56). That would appear to be a case of substantive justice. Significantly, a congressional colleague of Madison's accused him of seeking to "strip one class of citizens, who have acquired property by the known and established rules of law, under the specious pretense of doing justice to another" (Banning, *Sacred Fire*, 316). Nevertheless, Madison typically used words other than *unjust* to describe substantive outcomes to which he objected.

11. Federalist 10 pertains only to these situations. The fact that the essay encompassed some of Madison's most original and theoretically significant thought may have led subsequent commentators to exaggerate its importance in understanding the routine operations of government. Madison did indeed see the extended republic theory as important to a viable republican system, but the essay was not meant to address all political situations. In many, perhaps most, cases, Madison envisioned elected officials making choices on issues and from alternatives presented to them by the ordinary dynamics of statecraft, such as trade, revenue, or the structure of government. These issues had to be resolved in a manner tolerable to majorities, but Federalist 10 applied to a different case.

12. Madison to Jefferson, October 17, 1788, *PJM*, 11:295–300. See also Madison to Andrew Stevenson, November 27, 1830, *WJM*, 11:426: the Constitution reflects "not only an apprehension of abuse from ambition or corruption in those administering the Government, but of oppression or injustice from the separate interests or views of the constituent bodies themselves, taking effect through the administration of the Government."

13. Federalist 51:271.

14. Federalist 44:232.

15. Madison to Caleb Wallace, August 23, 1785, *PJM*, 8:350–357.

16. Madison's reflections on slavery are sparse. The abolitionist impulse to restrict the importation of slaves would certainly be a precursor to the rights of process and participation. However, there is little basis for explaining his motives in this case. Restrictions on importation could certainly have served the interests of those involved in the domestic slave trade. Rather than attempting to divine motives that he did not elucidate, I wish merely to acknowledge the statement. Whether Madison would have placed it in the categories of process or participation is unclear. I do not believe his inclusion of the ban on slave importation contradicts my analysis as a whole.

17. "Vices," *PJM*, 9:353.

18. Ibid.

19. Federalist 62:324.

20. The literary allusion to Rawls ("justice as fairness") is unavoidable, but I do not mean to associate Madison with him.

21. See *PJM*, 10:86–87 and 92–93.

22. *PJM*, 11:90–98, emphasis added.

23. See *PJM*, 11:99n4.

24. Madison to Jefferson, March 18, 1786, *PJM*, 8:500–504.

25. Federalist 44:231.

26. Madison to Jefferson, August 12, 1786, *PJM*, 8:93–99.

27. Madison to Edmund Randolph, April 2, 1787, *PJM*, 9:361–362. He referred specifically in this letter to Rhode Island, widely regarded to be the most promiscuous of the states, but Madison used equally strong language in describing paper in other contexts as well.

28. Holton, *Unruly Americans*. Although my interpretation of Madison's motives is far different from Holton's, he nonetheless makes a compelling argument that poor farmers were trapped in an impossible position—to which one can only reply that everyone was. From Madison's point of view, issuing more paper was no more a solution to these genuine problems than it would be to solve the problem of compounding gambling losses by placing ever-larger bets.

29. Madison to Jefferson, March 19, 1787, *PJM*, 9:317–322.

30. Notes for speech on paper money, *PJM*, 9:158–159.

31. Madison wrote his father, James Madison Sr., about an assize bill: "An interposition of the law in private contracts is not to be vindicated on any legislative principle within my knowledge and seems obnoxious to the strongest objections which prevailed against paper money." See *PJM*, 9:205–206. Similarly, he argued in the Articles Congress that paper was "unjust" in part because it "affects property without trial by jury." *PJM*, 9:158–159.

32. Federalist 44:231.

33. John Locke, *Two Treatises of Government*.

34. "Property," *National Gazette*, March 29, 1792, *WJM*, 6:101, emphasis in original.

35. On the issue of the community's authority to regulate property, see Kendall, *John Locke and the Doctrine of Majority-Rule*, and Tully, *Discourse on Prop-*

erty. More generally, my interpretation of Madison—that he was in all cases a majoritarian—parallels theirs of Locke.

36. Madison's presidential years also illustrate this focus on rule-based predictability. In 1816, he wrote to his treasury secretary, Alexander J. Dallas, concerning an economic crisis precipitated by the refusal of local banks to honor paper notes they had issued by exchanging them for specie. Madison suggested that the treasury, which held several of the notes, file lawsuits to establish the date from which banks owed it interest. Because the notes bore interest and were therefore valuable, the treasury could issue them as payments in place of specie, "& so far injustice to the several classes of creditors might be lessened, whilst a check would be given to the unjust career of the Banks." In the present context, the details of the episode matter less than the fact that creditors faced "injustice" and the banks' behavior was "unjust" on the basis of the extent to which agreements previously made were honored—in other words, whether agreed-upon rules were followed (*WJM*, 8:359–362). For a fuller account of the banking disputes and currency crisis, see Wainwright, *History of the Philadelphia National Bank*.

37. Cf. Hamilton, Federalist 85:456: "Many of those who form the majority on one question, may become the minority on a second, and an association dissimilar to either, may constitute the majority on a third."

38. "Detached Memorandum," 757–758. See also Madison to Jefferson, June 19, 1786, *PJM*, 9:76–81. There, Madison responded to Jefferson's observations about the wretchedness of European poverty by saying the "misery of the lower classes" could only be abated by political freedom as well as "laws [that] favor a subdivision of property"—an apparent reference to prohibiting entails.

39. He also argued that paper money was potentially unjust to both creditors (if it was legal tender) and debtors (if it was not). See "Notes for Speech Opposing Paper Money," ca. November 1, 1786, *PJM*, 9:158–160.

40. "Detached Memorandum," 761, emphasis added.

41. Ibid., 762, emphasis added.

42. Madison to Jefferson, December 31, 1824, *WJM*, 9:213–214. The letter goes on to compare irrevocable charters for religious institutions with irrevocable entails on individual estates, underscoring the fact that his logic applies equally to all forms and owners of property.

43. On state assessments to support established churches, see Levy, *Original Intent*, 188–192. For state constitutions requiring officeholders to espouse "the Protestant religion," see Lutz, *Colonial Origins*.

44. I grant that Madison's *National Gazette* essay "On Property" follows Locke in extending the right of property to property in one's rights and conscience, but that is plainly not what he meant by property in the writings currently under consideration. His reply to Jefferson's "earth belongs to the living" letter (*WJM*, 515) offers a more straightforward Lockean account of property in the economic sense.

45. See in particular Madison's assessment of "preventive justice" at *PJM*, 17:318.

46. I reiterate the crucial point that while the Constitution does require supermajorities in certain situations, the Constitution itself was ratified by simple and sometimes narrow majorities in each state.

47. Federalist 10:43.

48. Federalist 10:46.

49. "Vices," *PJM*, 9:348–357.

50. Madison to Caleb Wallace, August 23, 1785, *PJM*, 8:350–357.

51. Federalist 14:67.

52. Madison to Andrew Stevenson, November 27, 1830, *WJM*, 9:411–424.

53. For example, he said in the First Congress that holders of public debt should be paid what they were due—a case Madison often associated with property rights—because "the public good is most essentially promoted by an equal attention to the interest of all." *PJM*, 13:387. The best case for protecting the right of property, he said in Philadelphia, was that doing so served the public purpose of encouraging industry. *PJM*, 9:138–140.

54. Madison to Jefferson, March 18, 1786, *PJM*, 8:500–504.

55. Federalist 10:47.

56. Federalist 10:44.

57. Federalist 10:47.

58. Federalist 10:45.

59. The multiplicity and diversity of religious sects was the primary reason Madison did not fear the ascendance of any one of them. However, the analysis of Federalist 10 also suggests an underlying belief that religious zeal was short-lived, at least in the political realm. On this issue, see Arkin, "Intractable Principle."

60. Federalist 10:44.

61. Federalist 10:45. Madison solves the problem of faction, but this lament is one of the factors that compels him to do so without relying on institutional mechanics.

62. Federalist 10:44.

63. It appeared first in his thought in his preconvention research memorandum "Vices" (Madison's numbered point 11); again in a letter to Washington framing the choices to be faced in Philadelphia (Madison to Washington, April 16, 1787, *PJM*, 9:382–387); in a June 6 address to the Philadelphia Convention (*PJM*, 10:32–34); in postconvention correspondence summarizing the proposed constitution for Jefferson (Madison to Jefferson, October 24, 1787, *PJM*, 10:206–219); most famously in Federalist 10, with a reprise in Federalist 51; and finally, in a handful of retirement letters mostly directed against the doctrine of nullification (see 1833's "Majority Governments").

64. "Vices," Madison's numbered point 11.

65. Federalist 10:42.

66. Federalist 10:44. Again, we refer here to a majority pressuring the regime. A majority need not form for most of the business of government to be conducted.

67. Federalist 51:271.

68. Federalist 10:44.

69. Federalist 51:271.

70. Ibid. The context is Madison's claim that a majority could "seldom take place" on a basis other than the public good. However, the converse clearly applies as well: majorities that are based on the common good can form.

71. Dahl, *Preface*, 29–30.

72. Moral or not, it is certainly objective.

73. Federalist 51:271.

74. Madison in Convention, June 26, 1787, *PJM*, 10:76–77, emphasis added.

75. Madison to Jefferson, October 17, 1788, *PJM*, 11:295–300.

76. "Majority Governments," 1833, *WJM*, 9:520.

77. "Detached Memorandum," 758.

78. On the rapid spread of opinion in small societies, see Gibson, "Veneration and Vigilance," and Gabrielson, "James Madison's Psychology of Public Opinion."

79. Madison to Adams, May 22, 1817, *WJM*, 9:390–391.

80. Scheuerman similarly emphasizes the temporal analysis of the extended republic thesis. See Scheuerman, *Liberal Democracy*, 44.

81. Federalist 10:45.

82. Federalist 10:48.

83. Wood, *Creation of the American Republic*, 562.

84. Lee, "Representation, Virtue, and Political Jealousy."

85. Brutus III, in Storing, *Anti-Federalist*, 125.

86. "The Address and Reasons of Dissent of the Minority of the Convention of Pennsylvania to Their Consitituents," Storing, *Anti-Federalist*, 214. We have also already encountered Patrick Henry's fears of a Congress composed of the highborn. A subtext in these Anti-Federalist complaints was not merely the inadequacy of representatives but also the atrophy of public participation in affairs that were so seemingly removed from the community.

87. Federal Farmer VII, Storing, *Anti-Federalist*, 74. Madison's most direct rebuttal to these critiques may be found in Federalist 57, which notes that representatives will be chosen by "the great body of the people of the United States," not a favored or aristocratic class. We are nonetheless concerned chiefly in this section with the extent to which Madison's idea of representation did directly conflict with that of his adversaries. These debates have an important subtext: whether republicanism demanded a robust participatory ethic, or whether it was merely necessary for leaders to be ultimately accountable to the people. Madison's criterion was the latter. Contemporary commentators like Wilson Carey McWilliams and Gordon Wood have emphasized the importance of the former in Anti-Federalist thought. To the extent citizen participation is an important feature of politics or a worthy goal of the regime, Madison is justly open to criticism. His view of the state seems to be more or less instrumental.

88. Federalist 10:46.

89. Madison speaking in the Articles Congress, January 28, 1783, *PJM*, 6:141–149.

90. Federalist 63:327.

91. Rakove, "Madisonian Moment," 475.

92. Edmund Burke, "Speech to the Electors of Bristol," in *Selected Works*, 4:16. I use Burke for comparison, not to link him with Madison directly.

93. Madison to Jefferson, February 18, 1798, *PJM*, 17:83.

94. Madison in Convention, June 26, 1787, *PJM*, 10:76–77.

95. Madison to Washington, April 16, 1787, *PJM*, 9:382–387.

96. Madison to Washington, *PJM*, 9:382–387.

97. This example must be considered before the judicial doctrine of incorporation gave the federal courts jurisdiction over such cases by applying the Bill of Rights to the states via the Fourteenth Amendment.

98. Michael Zuckert emphasizes the negative character of the veto, suggesting the fact that Congress could block legislation but not enact it mitigates its antimajoritarian dimensions. The distinction is valid, but because the power to block can be as substantively important as the power to enact, it cannot fully rehabilitate Madison on this point. "Arming the general government with a negative power to help secure rights and the steady dispensation of justice within the States, rather than with positive power to provide those things directly itself, helps to prevent the 'due independence' which the extent of the extended republic supplies from turning into a source of danger." Zuckert, "Federalism and the Founding," 196.

99. Jefferson to Madison, June 20, 1787, *PJM*, 11:480–481.

100. Wills, *James Madison*, 27–28.

101. Zuckert, "Federalism and the Founding," esp. 189–190. Zuckert is not a critic of the veto.

102. Haworth articulates this suggestion in "Community and Federalism in the American Political Tradition."

103. For illustrations, see Madison's handling of the Vermont land dispute during the Articles Congress, during which he sought congressional resolution of Vermont's claim to independence from New York and New Hampshire, in large part out of fear that Vermont would jeopardize the Revolution by making its own peace with Britain (*PJM*, 2:86–87, 113); and his political testament, "Advice to My Country," which emphasized the maintenance of the union as the key to the United States' future (*WJM*, 9:611–612). The process by which Madison proposed that the Vermont dispute be settled bears a strong resemblance to how he would eventually see the negative working: an issue with national implications being decided by national majorities, which, while having a stake in the outcome and thus authority to render judgment, were less intensely interested and therefore more reasoned than local majorities in Vermont, New York, and New Hampshire. See also the justification of the national power to quell domestic violence: "In cases where it may be doubtful on which side justice lies, what better umpires could be desired by two violent factions, flying to arms and tearing a state to pieces, than the representatives of confederate states, not heated by the local flame?" Federalist 43:227. Again, Madison's point is not that the confederation would have no interest in a domestic dispute (its interest would be

to contain it), but rather that its interest would be diffuse compared to that of the direct parties.

104. Federalist 46:242–248.

105. Madison in Convention, June 8, 1787, *PJM*, 10:41.

Chapter 4: Constitutional Metabolism

1. Mayo, *Introduction to Democratic Theory*.

2. Dworkin, *Taking Rights Seriously*, 271. Dworkin makes the remark in connection with freedom of speech specifically, but his general claim is that all rights are by definition exempt from questions of social utility; or, conversely, that when we say something can be balanced against the general good, as Dworkin plainly believes many things can and should be, we do not mean to describe it as a right per se. I use his point as contrast; Dworkin does not associate this view with Madison.

3. Robert W. T. Martin similarly regards the "Memorial and Remonstrance" as affirming Madison's commitment to popular government. See Martin, "James Madison and Popular Government."

4. It is significant, however, that Madison tended to describe these as the rights of "minorities"—that is, in the plural. He generally assumed that rights were issues to be resolved in community contexts rather than the atomized "individual versus majority" dynamic in which they tend to be construed today.

5. Martin, "James Madison and Popular Government."

6. "Memorial and Remonstrance," *PJM*, 8:299.

7. Paine, *Rights of Man*. Paine's mode of argument continues to dominate many liberal interpretations of social contract theory today. See, for example, Louis Henkin: "Individual rights, then, are 'natural,' inherent. They cannot be taken away, or even suspended. . . . They do not derive from any constitution; they antecede all constitutions." The rights individuals retain upon establishing the social contract are "determined also by what they agreed to give up in creating a political society and establishing a government. Individuals pooled some of their autonomy when they formed 'the people,' subjecting themselves to majority rule; the people also gave up some of their autonomy to their government, retaining the rest as individual rights and freedoms under government. . . . The authority granted to government was not particularized either, but its scope is defined by the purposes for which governments were formed, purposes commonly understood." Henkin, *Age of Rights*, 86–87. If Madison espoused this view, he could have dismissed religious assessments merely on the grounds that regardless of the question of their utility, the social compact was not formed for that purpose, in which case the "Memorial and Remonstrance" would have been a much shorter document. The fact that he felt compelled to answer the question of whether the proposed assessment served a public purpose says a great deal about his view of rights.

8. Locke, *Letter Concerning Toleration.* My analysis here generally corresponds with that of Munoz, "James Madison's Principle of Religious Liberty."

9. "Memorial and Remonstrance," *WJM*, 8:299.

10. On the structure of "Memorial and Remonstrance," see Munoz.

11. *PJM*, 8:304.

12. Although Madison's position on state involvement in religion was absolutist on almost all occasions, an exchange of memos with Jefferson in 1803 nonetheless contains an intriguing suggestion that he might have been willing to relax his stridency if a public purpose could reasonably be served. The memos concern Jefferson's draft of a message to Congress summarizing a treaty with the Kaskaskia Indians under which the U.S. government would pay a Roman Catholic priest to provide educational and religious services to the tribe. We know from Madison's later opposition to the use of public funds to pay for clergy in Congress and the military—as well as the treaty's similarity to the religious instruction he opposed in "Memorial and Remonstrance"—that he would have regarded the measure as violating the principle of religious liberty. Yet not only did Madison raise no objection, he also advised Jefferson to omit specific mention of the measure from his message to Congress because "the jealousy of some may see in it a principle, not according with the exemption of Religion from Civil power &c." It is possible, if not probable, that Madison's advice was political in nature. Nevertheless, it seems equally plausible that he relaxed his usual strictness because the funding could serve a public function with a diplomatic, rather than religious, purpose. See Madison's memo of October 1, 1803, *PJM-SS*, 5:479–481. Similarly, the "Detached Memorandum" admits that chaplains might be more justifiable in the navy than in the army because sailors at sea form a contained society that might have no other religious influence. (Madison nonetheless comes down against naval chaplains, stating that he prefers principled to prudential reasoning on the issue.) See "Detached Memorandum," 762–764.

13. "Memorial and Remonstrance," *PJM*, 8:300.

14. "Speech Introducing Proposed Constitutional Amendments," *WJM*, 442. The provision applying to the national government would have protected the "full and equal" rights of conscience. I do not mean to attach any significance to this distinction. The right of conscience arose for Madison in a social context—that is, via reciprocity.

15. "Detached Memorandum," 762–764.

16. *WJM*, 9:100–101. Madison noted that while he sometimes felt compelled as president to follow this practice, his own proclamations always used the recommendatory form.

17. Madison did believe in something like individual autonomy in cases involving conscience. My concern here is to understand the reasoning by which he reached that conclusion.

18. "Memorial and Remonstrance," *PJM*, 8:299.

19. On Madison's reasoning, a legislature would be the proper forum for

such a discussion because defining the precise boundaries of the right of conscience requires prudential judgment. In an 1832 letter, Madison attributed his own absolutism on freedom of conscience to the impossibility of "trac[ing] the line of separation between the rights of religion and the Civil authority with such distinctness as to avoid collisions & doubts on unessential points. The tendency to a usurpation on one side or the other, or to a corrupting coalition or alliance between them, will be best guarded agst. by an entire abstinance [sic] of the Gov't from interference in any way whatever." In other words, his absolutism bore a prudential dimension: it was better, he concluded, to err on the side of caution than to risk violating the right of conscience. What Madison did not contend was that the boundaries of freedom of conscience were absolute and self-evident in themselves. See *WJM*, 9:485.

20. "Memorial and Remonstrance," *PJM*, 8:299.

21. "A Bill for Establishing Religious Freedom," in Frohnen, *American Republic*, 331. For Madison's praise of the statute, see the "Detached Memorandum."

22. "Memorial and Remonstrance," *WJM*, 8:303. The reference to the Statute for Religious Freedom as having resulted from an appeal to the community is contained in "Detached Memorandum," 759–766.

23. Madison wrote of freedom of conscience in 1822: "And in a Gov't of opinion, like ours, the only effectual guard must be found in the soundness and stability of the general opinion on the subject." Madison to Edward Livingston, July 10, 1822, *WJM*, 9:98–103. Note the importance of stability, a theme also encountered in exploring Madison's views of constitutional interpretation: the meaning of the Constitution was ultimately to be determined by persistent and settled public understandings.

24. See Rutland, *Birth of the Bill of Rights*, 219.

25. See his *National Gazette* essay "Universal Peace." *PJM* 14:207–208.

26. "Memorial and Remonstrance," *PJM*, 8:303.

27. On the common-law standards, see Levy, *Legacy of Suppression*, 14–15. In the Virginia Report, Madison denied that the Sedition Act liberalized the common law. However, years earlier, commenting on Jefferson's draft constitution for Virginia, he had remarked favorably that its "exemption of the press from liability in every case for true facts is also an innovation." Ca. October 15, 1788, *PJM*, 11:285–293.

28. "Virginia Report of 1800," *PJM*, 17:336.

29. Ibid., *PJM*, 17:346.

30. Glendon, *Rights Talk*. On the communal setting in which rights were typically contemplated, see Shain, *Myth of American Individualism*.

31. Meiklejohn, *Political Freedom*, 21, emphasis in original.

32. Rutland, *Birth of the Bill of Rights*, 91.

33. The idea of having property in one's reputation was commonplace at the time. See, for example, Blackstone's *Commentaries:* "The right of personal security consists in a person's legal and uninterrupted enjoyment of his life, limbs, his body, his health, and his reputation" (1:129).

34. Hamburger, "Natural Rights," 950–951. As Hamburger explains, Americans did not claim that natural law specified the precise limits contained in civil law, only that it permitted them.

35. "Virginia Report," *PJM*, 17:335–347.

36. Ibid., 17:337. Jefferson, too, acknowledged the permissibility of restraints on the press. His Kentucky Resolutions complained that such determinations were the province of the state governments. In forming the Constitution, Jefferson claimed, the people or the states retained "to themselves the right of judging how far the licentiousness of speech and of the press may be abridged without lessening their useful freedom, and how far those abuses which cannot be separated from their use, should be tolerated rather than the use be destroyed." Frohnen, *American Republic*, 400.

37. "Virginia Report," *PJM*, 17:338. In a 1790s opposition essay, Madison similarly associated freedom of political expression with "the nature of republican government"—i.e., on his analysis, majority rule—in which "the censorial power is in the people over the government, and not in the government over the people." He did claim an individual right to property in one's "opinions," but as in the case of the equal rights of conscience, that entitlement was established in a social context: property "embraces every thing to which a man may attach a value and have a right; and *which leaves to every one else the like advantage.*" "Property," *PJM*, 14:266.

38. "Speech Introducing Bill of Rights," *PJM*, 12:201. Madison's draft also limits what became the First Amendment right of free assembly to "assembling and consulting *for their common good*"—as opposed to asserting an inherent right to assemble for any reason. Madison thus followed the form not only of the Virginia Bill of Rights but also of those of other states. North Carolina, for example, joined Virginia in calling the freedom of the press "one of the great bulwarks of liberty," while Massachusetts specified that "the liberty of the press is essential to the security of freedom." See Lutz, "State Constitutional Pedigree."

39. "Virginia Resolution," *PJM*, 17:189. Note that public discussion—that is, appeal to majorities, not the courts—is the only effective guardian for liberties.

40. "Virginia Report," *PJM*, 17:338.

41. As we have seen, Madison also argued that the freedom of speech, like the freedom of conscience, had been withheld from the government. However, he referred to the specific fact that the Constitution did not enumerate a congressional power over either religion or speech. In speaking of a compact in this context, he referred to the Constitution, not—as he had in "Memorial and Remonstrance"—to the social compact.

42. "Virginia Report," *PJM*, 17:332. Madison wrote in a separate context during his retirement that the more liberal standards of common law that he advocated for America involved "questions of *expediency & discretion,*" thus placing them inherently within the province of Congress—not, significantly, the courts. *WJM*, 9:200.

43. "Virginia Report," *PJM*, 17:335. Madison made a similar point with re-

spect to the general welfare clause in his 1816 veto of the Bonus Bill: an essentially unlimited view of the general welfare clause "would have the effect of excluding the judicial authority of the United States from its participation in guarding the boundary between the legislative powers of the General and the State Governments, inasmuch as questions relating to the general welfare, being questions of policy and expediency, are unsusceptible of judicial cognizance and decision." See *WJM*, 8:386–388.

44. On this point, see Adrienne Koch's and Harry Ammon's account of a petition Jefferson drafted in collaboration with Madison calling on the legislature to have jurors elected by the public rather than chosen by what they took to be politicized courts. "These jurors [Koch and Ammon write] would be able to hamstring the activities of Federalist dominated courts." See Koch and Ammon, "Virginia and Kentucky Resolutions," 154. On the role of judges, the impeachment of Justice Samuel Chase is illustrative. One of the charges against him stemmed from his allegedly biased conduct of James Callender's trial under the Sedition Act. He was accused of preventing Callender from obtaining a fair hearing, but no one suggested he ought to have overturned the underlying law itself. (Madison did not express himself on the Chase impeachment specifically.) See Lillich, "Chase Impeachment." Incidentally, Lillich also reports that one of the offenses Jefferson thought to be impeachable was Chase's seditious charge to a grand jury in Baltimore.

45. Frohnen, *American Republic*, 403.

46. Virginia Report, *PJM*, 17:348.

47. Ibid., *PJM*, 17:350.

48. Madison to Edward Everett, August 28, 1830, *WJM*, 9:383–402, emphasis in original. Madison's attempt here to confine the meaning of *interposition* to calling on the people to speak out against the Alien and Sedition Acts was arguably self-serving. The meaning of *interposition* was always nebulous, but it seems to have been understood in 1798 and 1799 to mean something more than merely speaking out or voting the Federalists out of office. Moreover, in a separate but contemporaneous letter, Madison said that the "necessary and proper" measures included "the control of the Legislatures and people of the States over the Congress." See footnote at *WJM*, 9:387. This reference to the "Legislatures" resurrects the possibility that he meant for the states to interpose in some official capacity. Madison's communications on this topic are obviously informed by his deep alarm at the nullification controversy, perhaps to the point of attempting to roll back his own meaning in 1798 and 1799. The best we can do is attempt to ascertain the general tendency of Madison's reflections, which do seem to have been that the Virginia Report and Resolutions were rhetorical appeals.

49. Frohnen, *American Republic*, 401. Jefferson sent Madison a draft of his more radical Kentucky Resolutions on November 17, 1798. Madison's Virginia Resolutions are dated in his papers on December 21, likely soon after he received Jefferson's draft. The Virginia Resolutions as initially introduced by John Taylor declared the Alien and Sedition Acts to be not merely unconstitutional but also "not law, utterly null, void and of no force or effect." Jefferson, who received

Madison's original draft from a mutual friend, had insisted on adding this phrase. See editor's note, *PJM*, 17:190. Madison later recalled approvingly that the Virginia Legislature deliberately struck the words declaring the Alien and Sedition Acts to be unconstitutional. See Madison to Edward Everett, August 28, 1830, *WJM*, 9:402.

50. Madison to Joseph C. Cabell, August 16, 1829, *PJM*, 341–345.

51. Madison disclosed this desire in an 1829 essay (see *WJM*, 9:352) in which he blamed much of the subsequent confusion over nullification on the omission of that single word from the Virginia Report and Resolutions.

52. Madison to Jefferson, December 29, 1798, *PJM*, 17:191–192.

53. Madison's 1829 "Outline," *WJM*, 9:352–353. Also significant for my analysis of temporal republicanism, Madison described the Alien and Sedition Acts as having been "crushed at once" by the public outcry—a process that actually took two years. See Madison to Spencer Roane, May 6, 1821, *WJM*, 9:57–58, emphasis added.

54. Madison also objected to the hypocrisy of the sunset provision in the law by which it expired after the next election, when it might be available for a Republican majority to use against its Federalist sponsors.

55. Warren, *Congress, the Constitution, and the Supreme Court*, 91, emphasis in original.

56. Madison in Congress, June 8, 1789, *PJM*, 12:206–207.

57. Epp, *Rights Revolution*, 27–28.

58. Madison to Jefferson, October 17, 1788, *PJM*, 11:295–300. For an account of Madison's conversion, see Finkelstein, "James Madison and the Bill of Rights."

59. Madison in Congress, June 8, 1789, *PJM*, 12:203.

60. Lutz, "State Constitutional Pedigree," 40.

61. Madison to John G. Jackson, December 27, 1821, *WJM*, 9:75.

62. Madison in Congress, August 14, 1789, *PJM*, 12:336.

63. Madison in Congress, August 13, 1789, *PJM*, 12:332.

64. Deneen, *Democratic Faith*, 21. The quoted passage pertains to the relationship between Madison and Jefferson: Madison "came to share Jefferson's greater confidence in the democratic capacities of the populace, reflected in part by his confidence in the role of the Bill of Rights."

65. See his references to the phrases "we the people" and "general welfare" in Madison to M. L. Hurlbert, May 1830, *WJM*, 9:370–375.

66. Madison in Congress, June 8, 1789, *PJM*, 12:197–209.

67. Ibid., *PJM*, 12:203.

68. Speech Introducing Bill of Rights, *PJM*, 12:204.

69. Ibid., 12:204.

70. Madison to Jefferson, October 17, 1788, *PJM*, 11:295–300. The passage after the ellipsis is numbered as the fourth reason Madison provides for why he did not believe a Bill of Rights to be important. The first three reiterated the concerns Hamilton expressed in Federalist 84. We see further evidence that the Bill of Rights was primarily intended to protect the people against the regime,

not minorities against majorities, in the amendments proposed by the state rat- ifying conventions. Madison indicated that he based his proposal on the com- mon denominators between these. Most of them were either rhetorical declara- tions or measures that would rein in the regime.

71. Madison in Congress, June 8, 1789, *PJM*, 12:204–205.

72. On the educative function of the Bill of Rights, see Lutz, "Political Par- ticipation."

73. Madison to Jefferson, October 17, 1788, *PJM*, 11:295–300.

74. We recall that in all these cases, Madison believed the rights themselves had to be defined by majorities. In his Bill of Rights speech, as in his other dis- cussions of rights, Madison recognized that individual liberties could not be— and therefore ought not be—absolute. His letter to Jefferson counseled against "*absolute* restrictions in cases that are doubtful." Similarly, Federalist 41 warned against attempting to impose restrictions that were bound to be violated in crises. In both writings, Madison's concern was that violations in emergencies would seem to legitimate further violations in calmer circumstances. Madison in Congress, June 8, 1789, *PJM*, 12:205–206.

75. *PJM* 12:206–207 (emphasis added).

76. Madison to Thomas Ritchie, December 18, 1825, *WJM*, 9:231–232. See also Madison to Martin Van Buren, September 20, 1826, *WJM*, 9:251–255: "In all these cases, it need not be remarked I am sure, that it is necessary to keep in mind, the distinction between a usurpation of power by Congress against the will, and an assumption of power with the approbation, of their constituents. When the former occurs, as in the enactment of the alien & sedition laws, the ap- peal to their Constituents sets everything to rights. In the latter case, the appeal can only be made to argument and conciliation, with an acquiescence, when not an extreme case, in an unsuccessful result."

77. *PJM*, 11:81–82. This view is compatible with Joseph Priestley's *Treatise on Government*, a copy of which Madison requested by correspondence in 1774 (*PJM*, 1:145). Priestley argued that because an unjust law could best be undone first by remonstrances to parliament and, failing that, by electing new represen- tatives, political liberty was the best safeguard for rights.

78. Jefferson to Madison, March 15, 1789, *PJM*, 12:13–16.

79. *PJM-PS*, 2:365–366.

80. Madison in Convention, August 27, 1787, *PJM*, 10:157–158. Ironically, one of the commentators to take notice of Madison's ambivalence about the role of the courts was Charles Beard; see his *Supreme Court*, 29–33.

81. This constitutional gradualism may also help to explain Madison's ten- dency to refer to the courts in the plural—as in "independent tribunals of jus- tice" in the Bill of Rights speech—rather than to the Supreme Court as a single institution.

82. *PJM*, 11:293.

83. Madison to Monroe, December 27, 1817, *WJM*, 8:403–407, emphasis in original.

84. See, for example, Madison to C. E. Haynes, February 25, 1831, *WJM*,

9:442–443, in which he responded to an article that accused him of opportunistically changing his mind on the bank: "I am far from regarding a change of opinions, under the lights of experience and the results of improved reflection, as exposed to censure; and still farther from the vanity of supposing myself less in need of that privilege than others. But I had indulged the belief that there were few, if any, of my contemporaries, through the long period and varied scenes of my political life, to whom a mutability of opinion was less applicable, on the great constitutional questions which have agitated the public mind." The fact that Madison contemporaneously vetoed the internal improvements bill on constitutional grounds even though he supported it on policy grounds may help to rehabilitate him from the accusation of inconsistency. (See his annual message to Congress, December 3, 1816, *WJM*, 8:375–385.) My concern is with the particular grounds of his explanation for his change of mind on the bank.

85. Message to Congress, January 30, 1815, *WJM*, 8:327–330. Madison vetoed the bank bill on this occasion because of a specific policy dispute, but he indicated that he was waiving his constitutional objections. If Madison is chargeable with opportunism, it lies less in this standard for constitutional interpretation—which is theoretically coherent and compatible with his majoritarian beliefs more generally—than with his application of it to this particular situation: the bank remained hotly disputed at the time and for many years afterward, including its constitutionality, as evidenced by the fact that Madison remained under criticism for the decision as late as 1830.

86. Federalist 49:261 ("great and extraordinary occasions") and 262 ("disturbing the public tranquillity").

87. 17 U.S. 316 (1819) and 19 U.S. 264 (1821).

88. Although O'Brien is accurate in many respects, we should not discount the fact that Madison saw the majority as the source of the Court's authority and a control on its behavior even in ordinary cases. See O'Brien, "Framers' Muse."

89. Hobson, *Great Chief Justice*, 210–211.

90. Madison to Roane, September 2, 1819, *WJM*, 8:447.

91. Ibid., *WJM*, 8:450.

92. Ibid., *WJM*, 8:447–448.

93. Madison to Roane, May 6, 1821, *WJM*, 9:55–63.

94. Madison to Roane, June 29, 1821, *WJM*, 9:66.

95. Madison to Roane, May 6, 1821, *WJM*, 9:58.

96. Madison to Roane, May 6, 1821, *WJM*, 9:61.

97. Madison to Joseph C. Cabell, March 22, 1827, *WJM*, 9:286–287.

98. Madison to M. L. Hurlbert, May 1830, *WJM*, 9:372. The fact that the Court's role was limited even in cases involving federalism is also suggested by Madison's own pessimism as to whether the judiciary would wield sufficient clout to prevent the states from encroaching on the national jurisdiction. Part of his case for the negative was that it would be easier for Congress to prevent the passage of a state law encroaching on the national sphere than it would be for the judiciary to overturn one that was already in operation. See Madison to Jefferson, October 24, 1787, *PJM*, 10:206–219.

99. Madison to M. L. Hurlbert, May 1830, *WJM*, 9:372–373.

100. Madison to John M. Patton, March 24, 1834, *WJM*, 9:534–536.

101. Federalist 47:249. As Carey, "Separation of Powers and the Madisonian Model: A Reply to the Critics," in *In Defense*, has shown, the system of separation of powers is intended to protect the people against exposure to arbitrary rule, not to prevent discrete acts of oppression committed by majorities against minorities. This is the most persuasive response to Burns. The effect of separation of powers described above—that is, forcing examination of the same issue from multiple perspectives—is an auxiliary benefit. Although I argue that the system does in fact serve this purpose, Madison did not explicitly say he intended for it to do so.

102. Burns, *Deadlock of Democracy*.

103. Madison to Charles J. Ingersoll, June 25, 1831, in Meyers, *Mind of the Founder*, 497, emphasis added.

104. Madison to Adams, May 22, 1817, *WJM*, 9:390–391.

105. This seems to me to be among the implications of Willmoore Kendall's analysis in "The Two Majorities," which explores the simultaneous operation in American politics of congressional and presidential majorities.

106. Madison to Henry Lee, January 4, 1825, *WJM*, 9:216–217.

107. On the temporal dimension of the separation of powers, see Scheuerman, *Liberal Democracy*, 27–44. My analysis largely corresponds with his.

108. Beard, *Economic Interpretation*, 162.

109. The more than five years Calvin Coolidge ("the business of America is business") spent in the White House during the intervening period belies any claim that national majorities persistently favored the kinds of economic reforms enacted by the New Deal.

110. *West Coast Hotel v. Parrish*, 300 U.S. 379 (1937).

111. Burns, *Deadlock of Democracy*, 3.

Chapter 5: Politics and Patience

1. For details of the case, see Smith, "President John Adams."

2. We should roughly expect this interval to be proportional to the gravity of the decision in question. It should not take longer than a biennial congressional election—recall here that Madison believed the House to be the naturally stronger branch of the legislature—for a majority to express itself on a routine policy dispute. At the opposite end of the spectrum, a dispute that involves fundamental constitutional questions, and therefore such mechanisms as presidential vetoes or judicial rulings, should take longer.

3. Johnson and Broder, *System*.

4. There are too many differences between the Alien and Sedition Acts, twentieth-century economic reforms, and the health care debate to draw direct comparisons, but one cannot help but notice that the one among these in which political institutions were most directly and rapidly engaged—the protest

against the Alien and Sedition Acts—was also the most rapidly and conclusively resolved.

5. "Memorial and Remonstrance," *WJM*, 8:303–304.

6. The tendency on the left to pursue rights claims in the courts is well known, but the fact that several Republican attorneys general reacted to the passage of health care reform in 2010 by filing suit the next morning indicates the bipartisan nature of this phenomenon.

7. I use this term in a different sense from Boyd, "Madisonian Paradox."

8. Rosenberg, *Hollow Hope*.

9. On the other hand, as Glendon (in *Rights Talk*) and others have argued, the collapse of discourse that has occurred around the surge in rights claims is not conducive to dignity either.

10. Scheuerman, *Liberal Democracy*.

11. "Majority Governments," 1833, *WJM*, 9:522.

12. "Public Opinion," ca. December 19, 1791, *PJM*, 14:170.

13. Consider two among ample illustrations: scarcely one year into the 111th Congress, Representative Charles Rangel's Web site was already boasting that he had sponsored "over 100 bills" (http://rangel.house.gov/cosponsored-legislation.html). On the other side of the aisle, a writer at the conservative journal *Human Events* complained that Democratic Representative Alan Grayson "has only sponsored 4 bills, of which only one has been made into law, placing him in the basement of congressional effectiveness." See Ross Kaminsky, "The Biggest Jerk in Congress," *Human Events*, February 3, 2010, http://www.human-events.com/article.php?id=35432.

14. Carey, "Future of Conservatism."

15. Jonathan Martin, "10 Decisions for Obama's Next 100 Days," *Politico*, April 29, 2009, http://www.politico.com/news/stories/0409/21852.html. Other news outlets followed. These developments suggest that the constant appetite for news also fuels a never-satisfied appetite for change for the simple reason that the media cannot cover inaction.

16. Madison to Benjamin F. Papoon, May 18, 1833, *WJM*, 9:518–519. Note Madison's description of political life as a lottery rather than as a rational system from which perfection can be expected.

17. *PJM*, 1:12.

Bibliography

Abrahamson, James L. *The American Home Front.* Washington, D.C.: National Defense University Press, 1983.

Adair, Douglass. *Fame and the Founding Fathers.* Indianapolis: Liberty Fund, 1998.

Aristotle. *Nicomachean Ethics.* Translated by Terence Irwin. Indianapolis: Hackett, 1999.

Arkin, Marc M. "'The Intractable Principle': David Hume, James Madison, Religion, and the Tenth Federalist." *American Journal of Legal History* 39, no. 2 (1995): 148–176.

Bailyn, Bernard. *The Origins of American Politics.* New York: Knopf, 1968.

Banning, Lance. *The Sacred Fire of Liberty: James Madison and the Founding of the Federal Republic.* Ithaca, N.Y.: Cornell University Press, 1995.

Beard, Charles Austin. *An Economic Interpretation of the Constitution of the United States.* New York: Free Press, 1986.

———. *The Supreme Court and the Constitution.* Union, N.J.: Lawbook Exchange, 1999.

Blackstone, William. *Commentaries on the Laws of England.* San Francisco: Bancroft-Whitney, 1915.

Boyd, Richard. "The Madisonian Paradox of Freedom of Association." *Social Philosophy and Policy* 25 (2008): 235–262.

Branson, Roy. "James Madison and the Scottish Enlightenment." *Journal of the History of Ideas* 40, no. 2 (1979): 235–250.

Brant, Irving. *The Fourth President: A Life of James Madison.* Indianapolis: Bobbs-Merrill, 1970.

Bryce, Lord James. *Modern Democracies.* New York: Macmillan, 1921.

Burke, Edmund. *Selected Works of Edmund Burke.* Edited by Francis Canavan. Indianapolis: Liberty Fund, 1999.

Burns, James MacGregor. *The Deadlock of Democracy: Four-Party Politics in America.* Englewood Cliffs, N.J.: Prentice-Hall, 1963.

Calhoun, John C. *Union and Liberty: The Political Philosophy of John C. Calhoun.* Edited by Ross M. Lence. Indianapolis: Liberty Fund, 1992.

Carey, George W. *In Defense of the Constitution.* Indianapolis: Liberty Fund, 1995.

Corwin, Edward S. "The Progress of Constitutional Theory between the Declaration of Independence and the Meeting of the Philadelphia Convention." *American Historical Review* 30, no. 3 (1925): 511–536.

Dahl, Robert Alan. *A Preface to Democratic Theory.* Chicago: University of Chicago Press, 2006.

Deneen, Patrick J. *Democratic Faith.* Princeton, N.J.: Princeton University Press, 2005.

Diamond, Martin. "Democracy and *The Federalist:* A Reconsideration of the Framers' Intent." *American Political Science Review* 53, no. 1 (1959): 52–68.

Dworkin, Ronald. *Taking Rights Seriously.* Cambridge, Mass.: Harvard University Press, 1977.

Einhorn, Robin L. "Patrick Henry's Case against the Constitution: The Structural Problem with Slavery." *Journal of the Early Republic* 22, no. 4 (2002): 549–573.

Elliot, Jonathan, and United States Constitutional Convention. *The Debates in the several State Conventions, on the Adoption of the Federal Constitution, as Recommended by the General Convention at Philadelphia, in 1787. Together with the Journal of the Federal Convention, Luther Martin's Letter, Yates' Minutes, Congressional Opinions, Virginia and Kentucky Resolutions of '98–'99, and Other Illustrations of the Constitution.* New York: Burt and Franklin, 1888.

Elliott, Edward. *American Government and Majority Rule: A Study in American Political Development.* Princeton, N.J.: Princeton University Press, 1916.

Epp, Charles R. *The Rights Revolution: Lawyers, Activists, and Supreme Courts in Comparative Perspective.* Chicago: University of Chicago Press, 1998.

Erler, Edward J. "The Problem of the Public Good in 'the Federalist.'" *Polity* 13, no. 4 (1981): 649–667.

Ferguson, Elmer. *The Power of the Purse: A History of American Public Finance, 1776–1790.* Chapel Hill: University of North Carolina Press, 1961.

Finkelstein, Paul. "James Madison and the Bill of Rights: A Reluctant Paternity." *Supreme Court Review* 1990 (1990): 301–347.

Fiske, John. *The Critical Period of American History, 1783–1789.* New York: Houghton Mifflin, 1916.

Ford, Lacy K., Jr. "Inventing the Concurrent Majority: Madison, Calhoun, and the Problem of Majoritarianism in American Political Thought." *Journal of Southern History* 60, no. 1 (1994): 19–58.

Frisch, Morton J., ed. Alexander Hamilton and James Madison. *The Pacificus–Helvidius Debates of 1793–1794: Toward the Completion of the American Founding.* Indianapolis: Liberty Fund, 2007.

Frohnen, Bruce, ed. *The American Republic: Primary Sources.* Indianapolis: Liberty Fund, 2002.

Gabrielson, Teena. "James Madison's Psychology of Public Opinion." *Political Research Quarterly* 62, no. 3 (2009): 431–444.

Gargarella, Roberto. *The Scepter of Reason.* Norwell: Kluwer Academic, 2000.

Gibson, Alan. *Understanding the Founding: The Crucial Questions.* Lawrence: University Press of Kansas, 2007.

———. "Veneration and Vigilance: James Madison and Public Opinion, 1785–1800." *Review of Politics* 67, no. 1 (2005): 5–35.

Glendon, Mary Ann. *Rights Talk: The Impoverishment of Political Discourse.* New York: Free Press, 1991.

Grubb, Farley. "The U.S. Constitution and Monetary Powers: An Analysis of the 1787 Constitutional Convention and the Constitutional Transformation of the U.S. Monetary System." *Financial History Review* 13, no. 1 (2006): 43–71.

Hamburger, Philip A. "Natural Rights, Natural Law and the American Constitutions." *Yale Law Journal* 102, no. 4 (1993): 907–960.

Hartz, Louis. *The Liberal Tradition in America: An Interpretation of American Political Thought since the Revolution.* New York: Harcourt, Brace, 1955.

Haworth, Peter. "Community and Federalism in the American Political Tradition." Ph.D. diss., Georgetown University, 2009.

Henderson, H. James. "Congressional Factionalism and the Attempt to Recall Benjamin Franklin." *William and Mary Quarterly* 27, no. 2 (1970): 246–267.

Henkin, Louis. *The Age of Rights.* New York: Columbia University Press, 1990.

Hobson, Charles F. *The Great Chief Justice: John Marshall and the Rule of Law.* Lawrence: University Press of Kansas, 2000.

Holton, Woody. *Unruly Americans and the Origins of the Constitution.* New York: Hill and Wang, 2007.

Hume, David. *Essays, Moral, Political, and Literary.* Edited by Eugene F. Miller. Indianapolis: Liberty Classics, 1987.

Jefferson, Thomas. *The Papers of Thomas Jefferson.* Vol. 33. Edited by Julian P. Boyd and Barbara Oberg. Princeton, N.J.: Princeton University Press, 2007.

Johnson, Haynes, and David Broder. *The System: The American Way of Politics at the Breaking Point.* Boston: Little, Brown, 1996.

Johnson, Samuel. *Johnson's Dictionary Improved by Todd.* Boston: Charles J. Hendee, 1836.

Kendall, Willmoore. *John Locke and the Doctrine of Majority-Rule.* Urbana: University of Illinois Press, 1959.

———. "The Two Majorities." *Midwest Journal of Political Science* 4, no. 4 (1960): 317–345.

Kendall, Willmoore, and George W. Carey. *The Basic Symbols of the American Political Tradition.* Washington, D.C.: Catholic University of America, 1995.

———. "The 'Intensity' Problem and Democratic Theory." *American Political Science Review* 6, no. 1 (1968): 5–24.

Kerner, Samuel. *James Madison: The Theory and Practice of Republican Government.* Palo Alto, Calif.: Stanford University Press, 2005.

Ketcham, Ralph Louis. *James Madison: A Biography.* Charlottesville: University Press of Virginia, 1990.

———. "James Madison and the Nature of Man." *Journal of the History of Ideas* 19, no. 1 (1958): 62–76.

Kloppenberg, James T. *The Virtues of Liberalism*. New York: Oxford University Press, 1998.

Kobylka, Joseph F., and Bradley Kent Carter. "Madison, 'the Federalist,' and the Constitutional Order: Human Nature and Institutional Structure." *Polity* 20, no. 2 (1987): 190–208.

Koch, Adrienne, and Harry Ammon. "The Virginia and Kentucky Resolutions: An Episode in Jefferson's and Madison's Defense of Civil Liberties." *William and Mary Quarterly*, 3rd ser., 5, no. 2 (1948): 145–176.

Kramer, Larry D. "Madison's Audience." *Harvard Law Review* 112, no. 3 (1999): 611–679.

Kramnick, Isaac. "The 'Great National Discussion': The Discourse of Politics in 1787." *William and Mary Quarterly* 45, no. 1 (1988): 3–32.

Lee, Emery G. "Representation, Virtue, and Political Jealousy in the Brutus–Publius Dialogue." *Journal of Politics* 59, no. 4 (1997): 1073–1095.

Levy, Leonard W. *Legacy of Suppression*. Cambridge, Mass.: Harvard University Press, 1960.

———. *Original Intent and the Framers' Constitution*. New York: Macmillan, 1988.

Liebman, James S., and Brandon L. Garrett. "Madisonian Equal Protection." *Columbia Law Review* 104, no. 4 (2004): 837–974.

Lillich, Richard B. "The Chase Impeachment." *American Journal of Legal History* 4, no. 1 (1960): 49–72.

Locke, John. *A Letter Concerning Toleration*. Edited by James Tully. Indianapolis: Hackett, 1983.

———. *Two Treatises of Government*. Supplement, Patriarcha, by Robert Filmer. Edited by Thomas I. Cook. New York: Hafner, 1947.

Lutz, Donald S. *Colonial Origins of the American Constitution*. Indianapolis: Liberty Fund, 1998.

———. "Political Participation in 18th Century America." In *Toward a Usable Past: Liberty under State Constitutions*, edited by Paul Finkelman and Stephen E. Gottlieb, 19–49. Athens: University of Georgia Press, 1991.

———. "The State Constitutional Pedigree of the U.S. Bill of Rights." *Publius* 22, no. 2 (1992): 19–45.

Madison, James. *Notes of Debates in the Federal Convention of 1787*. New York: Norton, 1987.

———. *Papers of James Madison*. 17 vols. Edited by William T. Hutchinson and William M. E. Rachal. Chicago: University of Chicago Press, 1962.

———. *The Papers of James Madison*. Presidential Series. 5 vols. Edited by Robert Allen Rutland et al. Charlottesville: University Press of Virginia, 1984.

———. *Papers of James Madison*. Secretary of State Series. 7 vols. Edited by Robert J. Brugger et al. Charlottesville: University Press of Virginia, 1986.

———. *Writings*. Edited by Jack N. Rakove. New York: Library of America, 1999.

———. *Writings of James Madison*. 9 vols. Edited by Gaillard Hunt. New York: Putnam's Sons, 1900.

Martin, Robert W. T. "James Madison and Popular Government: The Neglected Case of the 'Memorial.'" *Polity* 42, no. 2 (2010): 185–209.

Matthews, Richard K. *If Men Were Angels: James Madison and the Heartless Empire of Reason.* Lawrence: University Press of Kansas, 1995.

Mayo, H. B. *An Introduction to Democratic Theory.* New York: Oxford University Press, 1960.

McCoy, Drew R. *The Elusive Republic: Political Economy in Jeffersonian America.* Williamsburg, Va.: Institute of Early American History and Culture, 1980.

———. *The Last of the Fathers: James Madison and the Republican Legacy.* New York: Cambridge University Press, 1989.

McDonald, Forrest. *E Pluribus Unum: The Formation of the American Republic, 1776–1790.* Boston: Houghton Mifflin, 1979.

———. *Novus Ordo Seclorum: The Intellectual Origins of the Constitution.* Lawrence: University Press of Kansas, 1986.

McGinnis, John O. "The Once and Future Property-Based Vision of the First Amendment." *University of Chicago Law Review* 63, no. 1 (1996): 49–132.

McWilliams, Wilson Carey. "Democracy and the Citizen: Community, Dignity, and the Crisis of Contemporary Politics in America." In *Redeeming Democracy in America,* edited by Patrick J. Deneen and Susan McWilliams, 9–28. Lawrence: University Press of Kansas, 2011.

Meiklejohn, Alexander. *Political Freedom: The Constitutional Powers of the People.* New York: Harper & Brothers, 1960.

Meyers, Marvin. *The Mind of the Founder: Sources of the Political Thought of James Madison.* Indianapolis: Bobbs-Merrill, 1973.

Miller, Eugene. "What Publius Says about Interest." *Political Science Reviewer* 19, no. 1 (1990): 11–48.

Montaigne, Michel de. *The Complete Essays.* Translated by M. A. Screech. New York: Penguin Books, 1993.

Morgan, Edmund S. "Safety in Numbers: Madison, Hume, and the Tenth 'Federalist.'" *Huntington Library Quarterly* 49, no. 2 (1986): 95–112.

Munoz, Vincent. "James Madison's Principle of Religious Liberty." *American Political Science Review* 97, no. 1 (2003): 17–32.

O'Brien, David M. "The Framers' Muse on Republicanism, the Supreme Court, and Pragmatic Constitutional Interpretivism." *Review of Politics* 53, no. 2 (1991): 251–288.

Paine, Thomas. *Rights of Man.* New York: Penguin Viking Press, 1984.

Rakove, Jack N. *The Beginnings of National Politics: An Interpretive History of the Continental Congress.* New York: Knopf, 1979.

———. "The Madisonian Moment," *University of Chicago Law Review* 55, no. 2 (1988): 473–505.

Ratner, Sidney, James H. Soltow, and Richard Sylla. *The Evolution of the American Economy.* New York: Basic Books, 1979.

Read, James H. *Majority Rule Versus Consensus: The Political Thought of John C. Calhoun.* Lawrence: University Press of Kansas, 2009.

———. *Power Versus Liberty: Madison, Hamilton, Wilson, and Jefferson.* Charlottesville: University Press of Virginia, 2000.

Rives, William Cabell. *History of the Life and Times of James Madison.* Boston: Little, Brown, 1870.

Rogow, Arnold A. "The Federal Convention: Madison and Yates." *American Historical Review* 60, no. 2 (1955): 323–335.

Rosen, Gary. *American Compact: James Madison and the Problem of Founding.* Lawrence: University Press of Kansas, 1999.

Rosenberg, Gerald. *The Hollow Hope: Can Courts Bring about Social Change?* Chicago: University of Chicago Press, 2008.

Rossiter, Clinton. *1787: The Grand Convention.* New York: Macmillan, 1966.

Rutland, Robert A. *The Birth of the Bill of Rights, 1776–1791.* Boston: Northeastern University Press, 1983.

Scheuerman, William E. *Liberal Democracy and the Social Acceleration of Time.* Baltimore: Johns Hopkins University Press, 2004.

Schumpeter, Joseph. *Capitalism, Socialism, and Democracy.* New York: Routledge, 1994.

Shain, Barry Alan. *The Myth of American Individualism: The Protestant Origins of American Political Thought.* Princeton, N.J.: Princeton University Press, 1994.

Sheehan, Colleen A. *James Madison and the Spirit of Republican Self-Government.* Cambridge: Cambridge University Press, 2009.

Sheldon, Garrett Ward. *The Political Philosophy of James Madison.* Baltimore: Johns Hopkins University Press, 2001.

Siemers, David J. *Presidents and Political Thought.* Columbia: University of Missouri Press, 2009.

Smith, Adam. *The Theory of Moral Sentiments.* Indianapolis: Liberty Classics, 1982.

Smith, J. Allen. *The Spirit of American Government.* Cambridge: Belknap Press of Harvard University, 1965.

Smith, James Morton. "President John Adams, Thomas Cooper, and Sedition: A Case Study in Suppression." *Mississippi Valley Historical Review* 42, no. 3 (1955): 438–465.

Storing, Herbert J. *The Anti-Federalist: An Abridgment of the Complete Anti-Federalist.* Edited by Murray Dry. Chicago: University of Chicago Press, 1985.

Tocqueville, Alexis de. *Democracy in America.* Translated by Harvey C. Mansfield and Delba Winthrop. Chicago: University of Chicago Press, 2000.

Truman, David B. *The Governmental Process: Political Interests and Public Opinion.* New York: Knopf, 1971.

Tully, James. *A Discourse on Property: John Locke and His Adversaries.* New York: Cambridge University Press, 2006.

United States Congress, House. *Proceedings.* 3rd Congress. 2nd sess. In *Annals of Congress,* 747–748. Washington, D.C.: Gales and Seaton, 1849.

Veit, Helen E., Kenneth R. Bowling, and Charlene Bangs Bickford, eds. *Creating the Bill of Rights: The Documentary Record from the First Federal Congress.* Baltimore: Johns Hopkins University Press, 1991.

Wainwright, Nicholas B. *History of the Philadelphia National Bank: A Century and a Half of Philadelphia Banking, 1803–1953.* New York: Arno Press, 1976.

Warren, Charles S. *Congress, the Constitution, and the Supreme Court*. Buffalo, N.Y.: William S. Hein, 1930.

Werner, John M. "David Hume and America." *Journal of the History of Ideas* 33, no. 3 (1972): 439–456.

Will, George F. *Statecraft as Soulcraft: What Government Does*. New York: Simon & Schuster, 1984.

Wills, Garry. *Explaining America: The Federalist*. New York: Penguin Books, 1982.

———. *James Madison*. New York: Times Books, 2002.

Wolfe, Christopher. "On Understanding the Constitutional Convention of 1787." *Journal of Politics* 39, no. 1 (1977): 97–118.

Wood, Gordon S. *The Creation of the American Republic, 1776–1787*. Chapel Hill: University of North Carolina Press, 1998.

Zuckert, Michael P. "Federalism and the Founding: Toward a Reinterpretation of the Constitutional Convention." *Review of Politics* 48, no. 2 (1986): 166–210.

Zvesper, John. "The Madisonian Systems." *Western Political Quarterly* 37, no. 2 (1984): 236–256.

Index

Virginia Plan, 13, 14, 35, 49, 92, 154n68
voting eligibility, 27
constitutional interpretation
constitutionalism
  quantum, 132–135
  as self-restraint, 34, 52
constitutions, duration of, 59–60
  See also state constitutions
contemporary society
  health care reform, 134, 173n6
  speed, 8, 137–138
contracts, 70
Coolidge, Calvin, 172n109
Cooper, Thomas, 133
corporations, 77–78
Council of Revision, xi, 80, 119–120, 144n30
Council of Revision proposal, xi, 119–120
  criteria, 126
  gradualism, 124, 139, 156n111, 170n81
  by judiciary, 97, 108, 118, 120, 122–124, 136
  Madison on, 97, 118–126
  by majorities, 97, 118–119, 121, 123, 124
  by people of states, 109
  by political branches, 118–120
  temporal republicanism and, 121, 124–126
courts. *See* judiciary branch; Supreme Court
critical school, 1–2, 7, 50, 79
  See also Beard, Charles
currency. *See* paper money

Dahl, Robert, 61, 84
debts
  of Articles Congress, 9–10
  paper money and, 12, 73–74, 159n28
  securities, 158n10
  of states, 12
  transgenerational, 58–59, 60

delays
  constitutional mechanisms, 4, 130–131
  deliberation and, 3, 57
  in extended republic, 85
  national veto and, 95
  preventing hasty decisions, 44, 46–47, 48, 52–54, 88, 130
deliberation, 3, 51, 57, 136–137, 144–145n39
democracy. *See* majority rule
Deneen, Patrick J., 112–113
DeRetz, Jean François Paul de Gondi, 140
despotism, fear of, 35–37
"Detached Memorandum" (Madison), 77, 86
Diamond, Martin, 2, 33, 46, 62, 154n77
Dickinson, John, 35
Dworkin, Ronald, 96, 100, 164n2

ecclesiastical corporations, 77–78
economic equality, 77–78
economic factions, 47
  See also factions
economic issues, 80, 133–134, 160n36
  See also debts; paper money
Electoral College, 15
Eleventh Amendment, 110
elites
  fear of aristocracy, 17, 76–77, 87
  preventing wealth accumulation, 76–77
  as representatives, 46, 87
  seen as favoring monarchy, 37–38
  See also property
Epp, Charles, 111
equality
  economic, 77–78
  religious freedom and, 100
  See also rights
Europe
  aristocracies, 77
  Neutrality Proclamation and, 20, 104
  See also France; Great Britain

Senate
    direct election to, 154n76
    equal representation of states, 13–
        14, 66
    powers, 14–15, 19
    proposed election by House, 13
    role of, 48, 49–51, 57, 60, 154n73
    staggered terms, 50–51, 128
    temporal republicanism and, 48–51
    term length, 48–50, 57, 152n29
    treaty ratification, 19
    See also Congress
separation of powers
    intent, 80, 126–127, 172n101
    majority rule and, 127–129, 131
Shay's Rebellion, 10
Sheehan, Colleen, x, 2, 46
Siemers, David J., 21–22
slavery, 17, 30–31, 148n85
slave trade, 70, 159n16
Smith, Adam, 44
Smith, James Allen, 4, 90
Smith, Melancton, 17
social compact, 70, 101, 164n7
southern states
    Marshall Court and, 122
    nullification doctrine, 23–26, 30,
        123, 135, 146–147n69
    slavery, 17, 30–31, 148n85
    tariff opponents, 23, 48, 125
Spain, Mississippi River navigation
    rights, 50–51, 54, 155n91–92
speech, freedom of. See freedom of
    political expression
speed, 8, 137–139
"Spirit of Governments" (Madison),
    18
state constitutions
    bills of rights, 113, 167n38
    of Kentucky, 27, 28, 32, 59, 70,
        143n26
    majority rule, 110
    Virginia, 32, 49, 144n30
state of nature, 69–70, 75
states
    debts, 12
    disputes between, 163n103

equal representation in Senate, 13–
    14, 66
factious majorities, 32, 71, 90
federal judiciary and, 171n98
interposition by, 104–105, 109,
    168n48
laws, 71–72
legislative branches, 49, 71
majorities within, 9, 11–12, 18, 23–
    24
nullification doctrine, 23–26, 30,
    123, 135, 146–147n69
paper money issued by, 10, 12–13,
    50, 73–74
religious freedom violations, 78
small territories, 84, 86
See also national veto; southern
    states
supermajorities
    for constitutional amendments,
        33, 34, 149n104
    proposals for, 16, 144n30
Supreme Court
    decisions, 124
    judicial review, 6, 111, 122, 128
    opposition to New Deal, 128
    rights cases, 111, 135, 136
    See also judiciary branch

tacit consent, 60
tariff issue, 23, 48, 125–126
technological change, 137–138
temporal republicanism
    assessing regime success, 132–135,
        138–139
    Bill of Rights and, 96, 112–116,
        130–131
    change in, 51
    constitutional interpretation and,
        121, 124–126
    elements, 1
    freedom and, 52
    information gathered over time,
        57–58
    judiciary branch and, 96, 124–125
    law of compounding
        disappointment, 135